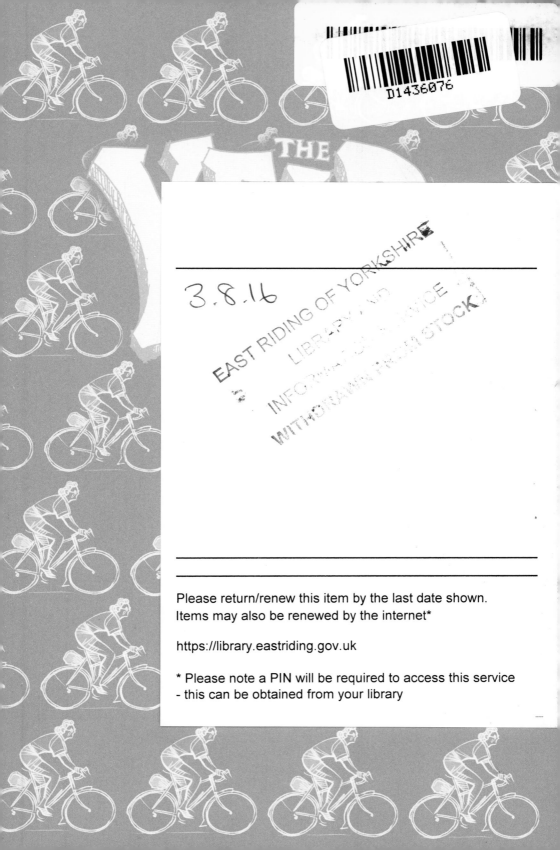

REAWAKENING THE LEGEND OF CYCLING'S HARDEST ENDURANCE RECORD

DAVE BARTER

Published by Vertebrate Publishing, Sheffield.
www.v-publishing.co.uk

The Year
Dave Barter

First published in 2015 by Vertebrate Publishing.

Vertebrate Publishing
Crescent House, 228 Psalter Lane, Sheffield S11 8UT.
www.v-publishing.co.uk

A CIP catalogue record for this book is available from the British Library.

ISBN: 978-1-910240-43-4 (Hardback)
ISBN: 978-1-910240-44-1 (Ebook)

10 9 8 7 6 5 4 3 2 1

Titling and jacket design by Nathan Ryder,
inside design and production by Jane Beagley Vertebrate Graphics Ltd.
www.v-graphics.co.uk

Vertebrate Publishing is committed to printing on paper from sustainable sources.

Printed and bound in the UK by T.J. International Ltd, Padstow, Cornwall.

Contents

This book is dedicated to
the memory of Billie Fleming.
13 April 1914 – 12 May 2014

*'You've got to want to do it, whatever the weather when you wake up
in the morning you've got to put your clothes on and get out on your bike
and it's not funny walking out in the pouring rain.'*

PROLOGUE

4 a.m. An alarm drones incessantly in the background, fading in and out of my dream state and eventually convincing me that it exists in the real world. I wrap warm bedclothes around myself, savouring the comfort they offer before wearily dragging myself to my feet. Every element of my nervous system attempts to convince me to return to bed. My head tells me that it's not quite ready to process information at this hour and my optic nerves refuse to deal with the light that falls upon them, presenting blurred surroundings instead. Every muscle fibre signals pain and protests against even the slightest movement. My mind is in conflict, thoughts of sleep fighting against a planned double-century cycle ride.

It's a close-fought battle, with curiosity gaining the victory. I've not done a continuous ride this big before and a small part of me forward-projects the feeling of accomplishment that's packaged with a 200-mile ride. This accomplishment comes with extra benefits: bragging rights that can be expended in forthcoming conversations, incremental changes to my physical form that will make future rides that bit easier, and a brief distraction from the electrical storm of a modern existence and its constant barrage of information.

I trawl through my fuzzy thought process to retrieve a checklist that I lodged there the night before. In the haze I find it and begin to work my way down a list of priorities.

Food. Breakfast is a chore at this hour as my digestive system is still dormant. I force porridge down tubes that feel full already, imploring a protesting stomach to accept this offering in order to stave off the spirits of future fatigue. Coffee follows for two purposes: a caffeine dose to kick-start mental processes, and as a liquid reminder to the digestive system that there are some things I'd like to leave behind.

Clothing. The weather forecaster refused to commit to any particular pattern the night before and scattered the map with question marks. I'm unable to decide on a single clothing strategy and I'm forced into layers and options. I have limited room in jersey pockets that must be efficiently shared between fuel, clothing and contingency. Do I leave an inner tube behind for the sake of some warmer gloves? Will I find a shop along the way, thus negating the need for two more energy bars? Every choice I make is hampered by a streak of disorganisation that's followed me from youth, and the items I decide upon need to be hunted from one of many potential resting places.

Equipment. This ride will start and finish in the dark. I disentangle a spider's web of charging cables from my lights and adorn the bike with enough LED power to fry an egg, should the need arise. I retrieve a GPS unit and check the previous night's route-planning has downloaded. Additional batteries are sought and placed in jersey pockets. I yearn for the age of photosynthesising bicycle accessories. A pre-printed laminated map is also retrieved; I've learnt the hard way – alone, 80 miles from home and shouting at a failed GPS while regretting the decision to leave my phone behind – that no single technology can be relied upon.

It's now close to 5 a.m., an hour since the alarm called reveille, and I still haven't left the house. There are creams that must be applied, tyre pressures to check and a search for loose change to fund a meal along the way. I know full well that an element of lag is gained from distraction therapy. A small part of me is working hard to delay the inevitable. Ultimately it loses. I wheel my bicycle to the side of the road and introduce posterior to saddle for a very long acquaintance.

My planned distance will take me into new territory, but I know the mantra of long bicycle rides. The first hour always feels sluggish. It takes my system over sixty minutes to acclimatise to the rhythm and rigours of pedalling. The early miles come hard and my mind insists on playing out a number of scenarios for disaster. What have I forgotten? Which parts of the route will be closed? Will I have the right gearing for the steep climb at the end? Have I properly planned my hydration? The thoughts are compounded by familiarity. I know these roads, these hedges and these dimly lit fields. There's not much in the dark to distract me and my focus locks on to my negativity, rather than anticipating the adventure of this extended ride.

After that first hour the devils of self-doubt dissipate and I begin to celebrate my lonely early-morning ownership of the open road. I find myself 'bipolarised', a twin-state machine of task and contemplation, half of me subconsciously moving myself and my machine forward, the other half travelling around my trove of stored thoughts and occasionally selecting one for analysis or decision. I've reached the plain of the long-distance rider. A state akin to the stasis entered by fictional space-travellers where time and length are compressed. I only become aware of this when I am surprised by my GPS unit informing me of forty miles travelled. In the same period the sun has risen and I've traversed into another county, mindlessly negotiating numerous junctions and roundabouts. It all seems to have happened so quickly, although my average speed of 16 miles per hour tells another story.

On most rides I'd now be nearing the end and looking forward to a shower. Today is different; forty miles is only twenty per cent. I pull out the mental calculation machine and start to punch in some numbers. A further 160 miles at this pace gives me ten hours of riding to go. But I need to factor in a decreasing average speed, food stops and the inevitable puncture. I settle on twelve to be on the safe side. It's close to 8 a.m. already. I loosely plan to make it home before the watershed.

I don't make it much further before water arrives, with its message of inconvenience and distress. The irony of rain is never lost upon me. In my bottles I carry water as a necessity for my survival and sustenance, yet when it falls from the sky I hate it with a vengeance. The rain clouds my sight, slowly turning my spectacles from vision aids to hindrances. Its persistence overcomes my waterproofs and water trickles uncomfortably down to my extremities, the discomfort in sharp contrast with the areas that have remained dry. The comfort of riding in dry clothing is long gone. Muck, liberated from the road, plasters my bike and my back. The picture painted by rain across an English country scene is rarely a masterpiece.

It takes an hour for the rain to properly subside and by then the damage is done. I want this to be over as quickly as possible. My electronic display creeps towards three figures. Normally I'd pass this mark, the boundary of a century ride, with a solitary celebration, an air punch or chocolate treat. Today, it's simply a halfway marker, a reminder that I have to do it all again even though the fatigue is beginning to tell.

The mileage ticks past 130 miles and I move into uncharted territory. This is a distance that I've never previously recorded. I now have 70 miles of riding left to cover that I have no evidence of being able to accomplish. I start to monitor myself ever more carefully. Hill efforts become more measured and the big ring is ignored more and more in favour of a higher cadence. I start to obsess about eating and hydration – little and often, little and often.

An hour later and muscular fatigue becomes apparent. A long uphill drag that would normally serve as a simple annoyance becomes a huge hurdle that requires sustained effort to surmount. This person riding my bike seems almost a stranger. I question his pondering cadence and slow ascent … I'm sure he used to be much better than this. Flatter terrain serves only to heighten the pain of ascent; everything feels normal until gravity sticks in its oar and reminds me of the true energy depletion in my legs. There are other issues as well. My hands are aching with the constant pressure of gripping the bars. My feet scream reminders of their imper-fections which press hard into unyielding sections of cycling shoes. All points of contact with the machine have suffered damage and are in need of repair. This ride is hurting and the light is beginning to fade.

Darkness gently arrests my speed. There are now only 30 miles left to ride, but I'm physically and mentally fatigued and well aware of the consequences of a single poor line choice – potholes shred tyres and unseat riders. The possibility of abandonment – and the subsequent requirement to start all over again – is unthinkable. I'm close enough to be nearly there but there are still over two hours of effort between me and my final goal. I concentrate on the small section of road visible in the arc of my lights and try to put aside the various bodily messages imploring me to stop and call my wife. At this stage each hill is interminable, every stop at a junction a gurning effort to get started again, and each passing car a reminder that there are easier ways to accomplish this journey. I'd stop and rest, but my wet clothing prevents it – I need a modicum of physical effort to generate warmth. Home is my only salvation, but it still seems so far away.

Familiarity is my salvation. The route has returned to my usual cycling territory and to roads that I ride as part of a weekly ritual. I hand myself back to the portion of my brain able to ride on autopilot and the last miles disappear from memory. They are no quicker than any others during the day, but I've lost myself to another consciousness, one that is guiding me home.

Then it arrives. The penultimate mile. No matter what, I'm home. I can carry the bike from here if needs be. The GPS tells me that I've cycled for 203 miles. This final mile is uphill and I leave the saddle to execute a triumphant sprint to the house, only to be quickly beckoned back down by a set of leg muscles shouting in unison – 'STOP!'

It's a huge effort to open the garage door and lock the bike inside. I want to abandon it on the drive as I did in my youth, leaving it for a responsible parent. It's an effort to remove shoes and gloves as rivulets of cramp threaten to escalate into huge volcanoes of muscular pain. It's even an effort to talk to an inquisitive family who are politely enquiring about the ride.

I made mistakes in that final quarter and have returned home dehydrated and not properly fed. This hadn't been apparent on the bike, due to other discomforts, but now I need to act. Food is greedily hoovered up between noisy slurps of juice and demands for cups of tea. Clothes are abandoned expectantly next to the washing machine as I shower for much longer than is really necessary – the kiss of warm water is hard to leave. I nap for an hour then struggle to rise and take the steps downstairs for a late-night meal. In the garage my bike needs oiling, its poorly indexed gears need attention and the tyres need a bit more air. My lights are still on the bike, needing a charge, and the GPS unit needs its batteries refreshed. The carefully packed food in my jersey pockets is now a mess of sticky, ripped wrappers and my drinking bottles are festooned with mud and detritus sprayed from the road.

Nothing about me or my equipment is ready to ride again tomorrow. I have no urge to rise at 4 a.m. and cycle another 200 miles. I'm too tired to do the planning, too tired to do the preparation and the weather has taken its toll, convincing me that a ride of this distance is not something I want to repeat any time soon. I know that if I tried to drag myself out of bed tomorrow for another attempt I would instead stay enveloped in the comfort of warm bedding, procrastinating until the fatigue had gone away. Then I'd defer again until the time could be found to tune my bicycle, prepare my food and carefully plan a route based upon the prevailing wind. It would probably be months before the pain of those 200 miles morphed into a happier memory of a hard distance accomplished.

That's me, a rider who can ride the distance given certain conditions. A rider content with occasional achievement, but equally keen to stay abreast of the comforts of an ordinary life. But there were others who were different; men and women who overcame discomfort on a daily basis as they put themselves to the road. Riders who managed the logistics necessary to ensure that, no matter what, they'd be able to ride day after day for a year or more. These were the year riders, the ones who could ride the most miles on a bicycle in a single calendar year. The achievements of these cyclists would have fed an army of statisticians for months as they hammered out miles in a valiant quest for their own place in history. But who were these people? Why did they do it? What hurdles did they overcome and why have their stories been lost to time?

These questions drifted around my mind that night as I began to lose consciousness. I knew now how those riders must have felt every day and I found it hard to contemplate the drive and motivation that pushed them for so long to seek the ultimate endurance record. I'd ridden 200 miles in one day. Tommy Godwin had averaged this distance for 500 days in a row in 1939 and 1940.

I needed to know more.

THE MILE-EATERS

E very night of the week a ritual is played out in public houses around
the United Kingdom. A group will gather under some vague
pretext in order to grasp a glass of ale and share a couple of hours'
worth of inane conversation. The pretext will vary wildly; some groups will
be societies, perhaps of climbers, divers, bird watchers or stamp collectors.
Others will have known each other from school, or met at college, or served
in the same regiment. Many will have simply turned up at the same pub
for years and, as regulars, melted into the fabric of the establishment.

Our pretext was juggling, or ex-juggling. We were former members of
the Swindon Juggling Club and had always met for a beer after throwing
some clubs about for an hour. The juggling had faded into the mists of
time, but the beer drinking had the stamina to live on and so we met every
Thursday for a discussion over a few pints, and that discussion often
veered into cycling.

It was during one of these Thursday sessions that I first heard about the
year record. In fact 'heard about' is a bit weak – the record was used to put
me firmly back in my place on the cycling achievement landscape. I'd been
casually bragging about the 'huge' amount of miles I'd managed to clock
up on my bike that year. I think it was somewhere in the region of 9,000
miles and I was tipsily placing myself upon some imaginary podium of
long-distance cyclists.

This was a foolish boast in the presence of Bill Potts. Bill is a Moulton-
riding fountain of cycling trivia. He has a house and garage stuffed full of
memorabilia and a mind loaded with two-wheeled facts, figures and physics.
Bill took a quiet sip of his Wadworth IPA and leaned gently forward.

'Of course, Tommy Godwin wouldn't be impressed by that mileage Dave.'

I saw the playful glint in Bill's eye and the cock of his head told me he
was about to follow this statement up with a fact that would relegate my

achievement to kindergarten status. I placed my glass on the rickety wooden table in front of me and looked at him quizzically. 'Come on Bill,' I thought, 'who the hell is Tommy Godwin? And what has he done that even comes close to my hard-fought 9,000 miles?'

Bill leaned back, folded his arms neatly and calmly delivered the *coup de grâce* to my lengthy bragging session.

'Tommy rode 75,000 miles in a single year in 1939. I think you'd have trouble competing with that.'

I was floored. There were three things in that single sentence that were beyond my fuddled comprehension:

75,000 miles.

A single year.

1939.

It would have taken me almost eight and a half years to ride 75,000 miles at my current pace, and I'd been training hard. Compressing such mileage into a single year was surely impossible. It was an average of over 200 miles a day, every day, without a break. The longest ride I'd done in my life was 127 miles and that nearly killed me. This guy would have done that before lunch.

Then I considered the year, 1939. This was the year that war was declared, the year that signposts were removed from the road network, the year that blackouts began and lights were banned from cars and bikes. Furthermore, bikes were basic, cycling apparel was limited to breeches and a mackintosh, and the roads were not the smooth tarmacked surfaces that we know and love today.

The conversation around me had moved on to cricket or football, or maybe to the difficulties of teaching primary school children. I was oblivious to it. Bill had catapulted me back to 1939 and I sat enthralled, picturing a cycling superman grinding his bike around the country as the war raged around him. I wanted to know more and the last thing I did that evening, before falling into a beer-addled slumber, was write the name 'Tommy Godwin' on a piece of paper beside my bed.

The next day, in a slightly hungover fit of work avoidance, I typed Godwin's name into an internet search engine. Details were scant. I found a few internet forum posts that briefly mentioned his record and I found his namesake, also a cyclist, who had won bronze for Great Britain in the 1948 Olympic Games. But I couldn't find any real details about the man himself, or his record year. I rested my chin in my hands and stared out of the window. Seventy-five thousand miles. Did he really do that? What did he eat? How did he cope with winter? Where did he ride? Did he do it alone or was he paced or helped in any way? Who helped him? How did he prove that he had ridden the mileage? My head filled with questions. The more I considered the mileage the more impossible it seemed. My car hadn't covered that sort of distance, yet it was definitely showing signs of wear. How on earth had Godwin coped physically? Had the record left him with any lasting damage?

My quest continued. I flicked through my library of cycling books, finding plenty of details of Tour de France riders, but nothing at all concerning Tommy. Then I remembered Dan.

Dan Joyce is the editor of CTC's *Cycle* magazine and is very well connected within the cycling world. He had published a few of my articles and even chucked the odd commission my way. Dan would know. I dropped him an email and tentatively asked whether he had heard of Tommy Godwin. As usual, Dan came up trumps. Not only had he heard of Tommy, he had been in touch with his family and was looking for a writer to research and write a small piece on his record – would I be interested?

I wasn't just interested in writing the article, I was desperate to do it. Luckily, single-word emails make it difficult to convey emotion – if they could, the 'Yes!' I sent Dan would have screamed at him from his computer screen. Yes, I was interested; yes, I wanted to meet Tommy's family; yes, I wanted to know more. The year record had grabbed my attention and I was well and truly hooked.

But researching and writing about Tommy Godwin raised as many questions as it answered. Why would any rider want to take on this record? Why had the bar been set so high? It became clear that Tommy's year was the end product of something that had a deeper history than I had realised. His was no one-off ride but one of many, the result of an obsession that had gripped riders around the world – a fixation with mileage that still pervades cycling today.

Further research led me all the way back to 1911 and a year-long competition run by the British magazine *Cycling*; a competition that appeared to have formalised a set of rules for recording mileage over a year. But where had this competition and these rules come from? How had it come about? Who had entered? Was this the pivotal moment when cycling decided that a year record was something it needed in its history books, the start of a chain of rides that led to Tommy's phenomenal record? It was tempting to think that it was, but the cycling world is never as simple as it first seems. While *Cycling* and the self-appointed British 'inventors' of the year record trumpeted their own successes, more research revealed that they had conveniently forgotten to mention a prior generation of riders in the USA, who had been quietly riding year-round before the British even had the idea.

I was convinced that the stories behind these year-rides would be full of incident and achievement, but my internet searches began to draw a blank. What little information existed appeared to be either hearsay or short articles with little detail. If I wanted more I'd need to leave the online world and dig into the varied archives of the cycling community. This still proved difficult, as the lives and details of these year-riders had been documented across a hugely fragmented set of media. Digging through early cycling magazines unearthed some real gems of information, but was time consuming, as their contents are not indexed and each magazine had to be read cover to cover for fear of missing the smallest titbit of information. Just tracking the magazines down was difficult enough; some collections were incomplete, while others were hard for the casual searcher to find. And once found, accessing them required travel, form-filling and adherence to rigid opening hours. The task was so time-consuming that my wife Helen slaved for nearly four months, diligently visiting archives and cataloguing information. Between us we probably read over a thousand magazines and could compete at an international level in skim reading.

However, the research began to reap dividends and within a few years I had put together a picture of all the major players in the history of the year record and begun to gain a personal knowledge of the riders themselves. Dan Joyce introduced me to Tommy Godwin's daughter, Barbara Ford. She gave me a deep insight into her father and his character, and described his later life, which clearly showed echoes of the rider who'd set the bar so high in 1939. Barbara gave me a thirst to hear from the families of other year-riders and, by chance, I read a newspaper clipping where former pro-cyclist Doug Petty talked of his experiences riding and laughing with Walter Greaves, who'd held the record in 1936. One meeting later and I was introduced to Walter's son Joe, who had taken great pains to keep his father's memory alive through fastidious collecting of memorabilia concerning his father's ride and through school projects completed by his own son.

Going back to the generation before Walter proved more difficult, until Barbara Ford introduced me to a genealogy site that she'd used to trace and complete her own family tree. My wife tentatively searched for the family of Marcel Planes, winner of *Cycling* magazine's 1911 competition, and eventually came up trumps, discovering living relatives and an email address. In 2014 we met the descendants of this pioneering rider and were not only fascinated by their memories of this unconventional man, but overwhelmed by the information the family had retained in his memory. Martin Planes showed us every single one of Marcel's mileage checking cards for his record year, perfectly preserved and ordered. These cards detailed Planes' rides and had been signed every day by witnesses Marcel met on the road. The family then glowed with pride as Martin pulled out the medal that *Cycling* had awarded to Marcel.

As I dug further still, I realised that the year record stood out from other cycling accolades. Until 2015, it had never been officially recognised by any cycling body. The record had been born in endurance cycling clubs and was later adopted by a cycling magazine and the rules and verification procedures had changed little as its validation has changed hands, mostly relying upon the honesty and integrity of the cyclists undertaking the ride.

I approached the British Road Records Association (RRA) and asked why it had never officially recognised the year record and whether it would consider retrospectively listing Tommy Godwin as holding it. The RRA was clear in its response: its charter requires unequivocal evidence that the route and distance has been ridden in a time independently verified by third-party witnesses. It does not believe that this is possible for the duration of a whole year record attempt, even with the advent of modern GPS-tracking technology. In order for the RRA to sanction an attempt, roadside observers would be required every day of the year and riders would need to give advanced notice of their routes and schedules to support this. The manpower and logistics required would clearly overwhelm the RRA and its volunteers in overseeing such an attempt.

The year record also stands apart in the mechanics of undertaking it. Beating the hour record requires an extraordinary degree of fitness, primarily the ability to hold a high level of power (over 400 watts) for an hour. Taking the Land's End to John o'Groats record requires fitness and also mental and physical stamina, but only a day's worth of luck to ensure that the weather and traffic conditions are conducive to the attempt. The year record requires not only fitness and stamina, but also 365 (or 366) days of good fortune. Riders are continually battling the weather, the logistics of keeping fed and watered, the need to keep their machines in the best possible condition (and thus limit delays due to mechanical failure or punctures), and must also try to keep themselves injury and malady free. It is not only a test of physical prowess; it stretches every facet of the human make-up for a period that is almost always greater than one per cent of the rider's total time on this earth.

It's also a lonely record that is followed only at a distance by the general public. Riders have a brief flirtation with fame and kudos at the starts and finishes of their attempts. In between they are mostly alone on the road and required to self-motivate. Their mileages and tribulations might be closely followed by those with a particular interest (or as closely as is possible through the limited press reporting), but the riders are usually unaware of this support, having no time to read and digest what is written about them. Of course, the internet and social networks are changing this, and one could argue that riders of today seeking to resurrect the record hold a significant advantage over previous generations as they receive virtual roadside cheers from the international online communities of Strava, Twitter or Facebook, where users proffer their support in real time.

History also shows us that the year record is not a route to fame and fortune. Many of the riders attempting it do so to raise their profile within cycling, but none has ever gone on to achieve the status of a Tour de France winner. In fact the record year has usually proved to be the zenith of the cycling careers of those who have undertaken it, most of whom subsequently fade from the riding limelight. Ossie Nicholson's racing career fell into disarray after his 1937 record ride, René Menzies curtailed his racing after failing to take the record the same year, and Arthur Humbles retreated back to the world of cycle touring following his brief flirtation with celebrity. The two who rode the furthest, Tommy Godwin and Bernard Bennett, were unlucky enough to put up their huge mileages just as World War II broke out – we will never know whether Godwin would have been elevated to cycling celebrity after his seemingly unassailable mileage was clocked up as war then intervened and he was whisked off into the Royal Air Force.

As I write these words, three men spread across three continents are making their own attempts upon the record. These riders have taken the brave decision to resurrect a challenge that has remained unconquered for over seventy-five years. All three are amateurs and all three have worked hard to put in place the support, funding and logistics required to enable their attempts. To date there has been no indication that a professional team will step up to the challenge, probably due to the complete lack of interest from professional riders who know full well that success in a higher-profile event will prove far more lucrative in a far shorter space of time. This underlines a further aspect of the challenge that differs wildly from other areas of cycling: not only must a rider have the endurance and will to see the year's ride through, they also need the tenacity to get the ride off the ground in the first place. This has become increasingly hard since the halcyon days of the 1930s when companies fully understood the commercial benefits of having a year-rider take the record while using the company's bicycle or apparel. The approach and support mechanisms of the three current riders provides the evidence: a British man relying upon a network of cyclists to host and feed him as he strays away from home, an American living semi-permanently in a camper van to reduce living costs while out on the road, and an Australian attempting to ride huge miles in between shifts at work.

Only one rider, Ossie Nicholson, ever received the permanent attention and support of a professional team. Every other rider before and after him relied upon the generosity and good nature of others to aid them through the year. As such the record belongs not only to those riders but to those who helped them on their way. It is another element that makes the year record unique: it is one of the few cycling disciplines where outside assistance is not only allowed, but is essential if the rider is to push the record on to a new level.

Following the daily updates of the three current year-riders allows me to live their attempts vicariously and reflect upon the journey I've taken since making my idle boast in the pub many years ago. The flippant comment I made back then led me to uncover a set of achievements that remain unparalleled within the cycling world we know today. The riders behind those achievements made personal and physical sacrifices in order to achieve a goal that came with little guarantee of financial reward. They knew full well that these rewards were secondary. It is clear that the year record is as much a personal journey for the rider as a route to better things. The characters of the men and women who attempted it show traits similar to the explorers of previous years. These were cyclists who primarily wanted to challenge themselves to see just how far they could go. But where did this will to 'explore' come from? What was it that ignited the race to ride the furthest possible distance in a single year and why did these riders give up so much when the rewards were seemingly so small? Where did the cycling year record begin?

The only way to find this out is to trace the evolution of competitive distance riding back to its roots.

THE GENESIS OF THE
CYCLING YEAR RECORD

In 1879, rear-wheel chain drive was introduced, along with pneumatic tyres, and the modern bicycle that we now know and love was born. This birth and, more importantly, the mass production of the bicycle in the last quarter of the nineteenth century, liberated working-class people from their home towns and allowed them to venture further afield in search of work and leisure. A bicycle was significantly cheaper than a horse, cost less to run and could be stored easily without the need for pasture or food.

Mass-produced cars did not become a common sight upon the roads until the early 1900s, giving our cycling pioneers relatively quiet and uninterrupted riding, compared to their modern-day peers. Quiet roads, relatively cheap transport and a lack of disposable income led a generation of cyclists to seek affordable pleasure upon the open road.

Road-mapping in the late nineteenth century was not well developed, and cartographers had yet to properly turn their attention to leisure cylists, who had to rely instead upon signage and the knowledge of others to find the best routes. This spawned organisations such as the Bicycle Touring Club – later renamed the Cyclists' Touring Club (CTC) – whose original role was to identify overnight stops and hostelries for cyclists, which it documented in a series of guidebooks. The growth in leisure cycling also gave rise to a number of supporting publications and, on 24 January 1891, the first issue of *Cycling* magazine was published.

The period between 1870 and 1910 also saw huge momentum in bicycle engineering innovation. Cyclists went from having to throw their legs over cumbersome penny farthings to riding 'safety bicycles', which truly opened cycling to the masses. The safety bicycle was designed by Harry John Lawson and had its pedals much lower down than a penny farthing, allowing the rider to stop easily and safely by placing their feet upon the ground.

With this convergence of engineering, organisation and information cyclists were able to spread their wings, with the whole of the road network open to their touring plans. Many used this new-found freedom to explore and visit places that were previously beyond their holiday budgets. A number of these riders began to document their exploits in diaries or travelogues that made their way back to the mainstream cycling press, which then fed its readers with these tales.

It's tempting to think that it was this period of development that led to the first high-mileage riders, but think again. As soon as the first bicycle was invented, riders had set out to push the limits. In 1881 a '100 miles' list was published by *The Cyclist* journal, which sought to document all rides carried out over 100 miles or more. These rides were completed using direct-pedal 'high' bicycles similar to the penny farthing, with 4½-inch cranks, solid tyres, 48- or 50-inch wheels and desperately uncomfortable hard saddles. The bikes themselves weighed in the region of 50 to 60 pounds, nearly three times the weight of a modern bicycle, which would have caused a mild degree of consternation going downhill as the bikes were originally made without brakes. In 1910 the cycling journalist Henry Sturmey made the following observation as he fondly recalled the compiling of that list:

Even today (1910) with light machines with high gears and pneumatic tyres 100 miles in the day is more than an average accomplishment for the average rider, although of course, it is nothing beyond the capabilities of the average enthusiast, who keeps reasonably fit. But in the days of the high bicycle it was an accomplishment worthy to be proud of. Today if a cyclist covers the century within 24 hours, no particular notice is taken of it, and it does not even get into the local paper. But in those early days of the pastime such a ride would be given quite a lot of publicity in many papers. It was indeed looked upon as quite a hall-mark of cycling quality, for there were few who had accomplished it.

The list straddled a period of seven years, from 1874 to 1881, and documented over 250 centuries – no mean feat considering the road conditions of the time and the nature of the bicycles. The first entry was Thomas Sparrow of the Surrey Bicycle Club, who rode from Bath to London in ten and a half hours on a 65-pound bike. Sparrow was a bike maker by trade and clearly undertook the ride as a marketing exercise to showcase his innovative leather tyres, which were designed to eliminate side slip.

Things gathered pace in 1876, when the first ever double century was recorded by Messrs E. Coston and F. Smyth, who rode from King's Lynn to Wisbech and back eight times in twenty-four hours. This was a remarkable achievement, even setting aside the fact that the route is entirely flat. Take a moment to consider the magnitude of their accomplishment. Riding a fixed-wheel bicycle such as a penny farthing is never easy. There is no freehub, which means that if the bike is moving forward the rider must pedal. And when not pedalling, trackstanding on a bike with such a high centre of gravity is an achievement in its own right, meaning the only way to pause would be to stop and dismount from the awkward machine. Consider too the roads of the time, which would not have been well surfaced. As bicycles of this era had solid tyres and no form of suspension, the two riders would have felt every bump directly through their undercarriages. The single advantage a penny farthing would have over a modern bicycle would be the rider's view, as the increased elevation would allow them to see over fences or hedges as they wobbled along. As this double-century ride spanned a twenty-four hour period a portion of it must have been ridden at night. Bicycle lights as we know them today would not have been available and the riders would have to have made do with candle lamps carried by hand which would have shed minimal light upon the road ahead.

The Coston-Smyth double century was the only 200-mile ride upon the list. Other riders came close, but nobody else managed to hit that magic figure. This was more than likely down to the terrain. Pedalling a heavy, high bike up any gradient is exceedingly difficult and these two riders had picked a pan-flat course specifically for this reason. The closest and arguably even harder ride, due to the hillier terrain, was completed by Stanley Thorpe of the Pickwick Club, who had ridden from London to York in 1875 and ended with a grand total of 197 miles on 5 June, despite crashing on his journey.

1876 also saw G.B. Cooper of Stroud ride 106 miles from Cainscross to Kensington. He was known as 'Inextinguishable Cooper' after his invention of a lamp which was carried inside the front wheel and suspended from the axle. This lamp became very popular and Mr Cooper subsequently joined Messrs Hillman and Herbert in the firm of Hillman, Herbert and Cooper, which afterwards became the Premier Cycle Co.

In 1878 the single-ride mileage record was pushed to 221 miles by W.S. Britten, who rode from Hyde Park Corner to Bath and back on 12 September in twenty and a half hours (23 hours 54 minutes total time) riding a 52-inch Stassen – one of the heaviest and most substantial bicycles ever built.

An additional thirty-seven centuries were added to the tally during the year, many by the owners of bicycle manufacturing companies. These men were often hardened road riders, determined to show off their machines in action. They also used the experiences they gained out on the road to influence their product engineering. Gaining publicity via a long-distance cycle ride was an ideal marketing mechanism and message to potential customers. What better way to show the mettle of a bicycle than having its rider drive it forwards over a seemingly impossible distance? What better way to inspire potential customers to take on their own challenges? This was to be a recurring theme throughout the history of the cycling year record. Manufacturers of bicycles, cycling components and accessories were exceedingly keen to have their equipment associated with record attempts.

This first list of centuries certainly provided the kindling for the fire that led to the formation of the year record, but the true origin of the record appears to come from the United States of America. In the late 1890s the USA was also going through a bicycle boom and the Americans had formed the Century Road Club of America, at least twenty years before the British incarnation.

The emergence of the Century Road Club of America was very much down to the efforts of Mr F.E. Spooner. In 1891 Spooner proposed that a club be formed for those – and only those – who had ridden 100 miles over a known cycling route between Chicago, Elgin and Aurora. This gave rise to the Century Club of Chicago, to which fourteen charter members were recruited. Sadly Spooner became seriously ill and the club's management was passed on to a Mr William Herrick, whose tenacity and full-time dedication saw club numbers rise to 650 by January 1898. During this period the scope of the club was widened beyond the Chicago area and so the Century Road Club of America was born. Herrick was subsequently given the fantastic title of 'chief centurian' within that club, whose constitution also saw the creation of roles such as 'state centurian' and the enigmatic 'traveling centurian'. The club created a detailed handbook which included a set of century 'bars' that dictated the time limits within which defined distances must be ridden:

Single century – 14 hours
Double century – 24 hours

Triple century – 36 hours
Quadruple century – 48 hours

Riders were able to gain century bars by completing each of these challenges. These bars were engraved and displayed below a member's century road club badge in a similar fashion to military insignia. But the rules for completing an accredited qualifying ride were strict and a formal application process was put in place to adjudicate:

The previously mentioned time limits must be adhered to.
The course upon which a century is ridden must be greater than 20 miles in length.
The entire distance must be covered either 'awheel' or 'afoot'.
Centuries ridden on tandems earn a bar for each member of the crew.
Riders should either be accompanied by a witness for their ride or the application must be attested by a notary public.

Members were also able to apply for a 'meritorious' ride medal for rides that demanded 'an unusual demonstration of the possibilities of cycling to attract general public attention'. Two notable awards were made in 1897, the first to L.H. Bannister for winning the Buffalo–Pittsburg road race of 242 miles in just under twenty-four hours (and it really was *just* under – 23 hours, 58 minutes and 30 seconds) on 29 September 1893, the longest race distance ever run. The second was to A.A. Hansen, who rode 21,053 miles in 1894 – the first benchmark for a cycling year record that I am able to find. At the time the club were awarding an annual prize for the highest mileage ridden each year, and that had already been awarded that year, to M.N. Keim of Philadelphia with a highly creditable 18,528 miles. Hansen applied for the record after Keim had already been awarded the honour and, as a result, a technicality was found to allow Keim to keep his medal while presenting Hansen with a special award recognising his extraordinary year.

As the 1890s progressed, high-mileage competitions became commonplace across many American states with regional clubs and Century Road Club chapters running their own localised competitions. A report in American paper *The Sun* in 1896 highlighted that mileage records had gained widespread interest across the country with riders thinking nothing of covering distances in excess of 16,000 miles in twelve months. The report went on to document a number of rides in the New York area that exceeded an annual figure of 14,000 miles, including that of Fredrick Allart, who took the Brooklyn Bicycle Club record with a final figure of 16,172 miles, ridden April to April. Fredrick, a sprightly twenty-four years of age at the start of his ride and described as 'short of stature yet stockily built', had apparently ridden through the night on a number of occasions to up his mileage and finished his year with a spin round Central Park.

The article went on to proclaim that none of these record attempts appeared to have had a detrimental effect upon the riders or their love of cycling. This was in contrast to the Manhattan Bicycle Club who had abandoned their contest that year due to the alleged ill effects that a few of their competitors had experienced in their struggles to gain the record. *The Sun* stated that these views were not shared by the majority of aspirants and went on to comment that some of the highest-mileage performances reported by the Century Road Club were being ridden by women, 'without other than healthful results'.

However, all of these rides were soon to be eclipsed by the incredible performance of Chicago-based rider E.N. Roth, with his highly controversial ride of 1896. His record was reported in *The Sun* with a compelling opening paragraph:

> Anti-bicyclists who regard the wheel as the father of ills moral, mental and physical, should consider the record of a Chicago wheelman from last year.

Roth had claimed a massive annual mileage of 34,380 miles over 340 days, averaging over a century every day – apparently the first person ever to achieve this feat. His ride had commenced on 25 January 1896 and ended on New Year's Eve, and he had ridden nearly 12,000 miles in excess of any other rider that year (A.A. Gracey came closest to him with 22,848). Roth's biggest month, October, totalled in excess of 4,000 miles and he claimed 146 distinct centuries, thirty-two double centuries and one triple during the year. His 300-mile ride had been accomplished in twenty-two hours at an average speed of over 13 miles per hour.

The details of Roth's record set the scene for all of the future attempts. Although his ride ended in terrible weather in a driving rainstorm on New Year's Eve, he had made a valiant attempt to keep conditions on his side by following good weather across twelve states, focusing his ride on the area around Texas, Illinois and Colorado. Roth rode an 'ordinary' single-wheeled bike (or penny farthing, as they are often nicknamed in the UK) with the wheel alone weighing 25 pounds and its tyre tipping the scales at an additional 5 pounds. During the year he wore out a tyre due to extended riding along railway tracks, presumably as they offered a better-maintained pathway than some of the early roads. This cannot have been a smooth ride and his record seems even more extraordinary given that he claimed only a single puncture throughout the year.

Roth claimed to have detailed evidence for his record and subsequently filed an application with the Century Road Club to be given the annual record, along with the 200-mile record (fourteen hours), the 300-mile record, and the Illinois State number-of-centuries record. *The Sun* was convinced of Roth's authenticity:

> In the light of this achievement, what have the non-cycling pessi-mistic scare-alls to say? Judging from the experience of Roth, some cyclists may keep on pedalling, undismayed, with the pros-pect of becoming fat and hearty, and perhaps of reaching the mag-netic goal of a world's record smashed.

But the Century Road Club of America was having none of it. Roth's application was rejected and the 1896 record handed to Gracey. The exact reasons for rejection are lost to time; maybe Roth had not properly verified the distances travelled with witnesses or records. Maybe he had earned the club's displeasure by seeking out good weather. The CRCA advised that Roth had not provided satisfactory proof. Roth subsequently issued a suit against the CRCA, but it appears that he did not win his case. If Roth's application had been accepted it would have set an exceptional early benchmark for the cycling mileage record and in addition set a figure for the single-wheeled bicycle that would still stand today.

These attempts clearly underlined an American interest in the cycling year record that led to the CRCA running its first ever structured mileage competition in 1897. This appears to be the first competition of its kind to have a formal set of rules and an overseeing body to adjudicate the mileages. Riders were required to carry a checking book for the recording and verification of their mileages, and to submit this book to the club monthly, along with a detailed report. In addition, the riders were required to seek signatures of 'reliable parties' who had seen the rider pass through their towns. These submissions were scrutinised and verified, and rider rankings published monthly. Interestingly, the cumulative mileages of riders were not shared, meaning that each had to rely upon self-motivation in order to push for the highest distance, rather than being driven on by the statistics of their competitors.

The rewards for the competition were simple. Each rider was presented with a certificate of meritorious riding and category winners received a medal. Such meagre pickings did nothing to deter Century Road Club members, with the top ten riders recording astonishing mileages for the age. The following table shows the top ten results from the competition:

Rider	State	Mileage	Record	Centuries	Doubles	Triples	Quads
John H. George	Philadelphia	32,479	American Record	226	19	3	
John M. Nobre	Philadelphia	28,718		258	17	1	1
Dr Milton N. Keim	Philadelphia	28,517		225			
Irving Harrison	Jersey City	26,252					
Chas Parkins	Jersey City	24,669		46	2		1
Frank R. Lang	Portland, Maine	21,259	New State Record	126	4	1	1
Mrs A.M.C. Allen	Worcester, Massachusetts	21,026	New State Record	108			
W.H. Kueck	Colorado Springs, Colorado	20,215	New State Record	158	1	1	1
John H. Hunter	Toledo, Ohio	19,460	New State Record	130			
Louis Rippetoe	Terre Haute, Indiana		New State Record	52			

The performance of the year was that of the winner of the competition, John H. George. His 32,479 miles showed an average of almost 89 miles every single day of the year and included 226 centuries, nineteen double centuries and three triples. By getting within 2,000 miles of Roth's 1896 claim, George's ride went some way towards proving that the claims made by Roth were achievable.

Equally notable was the 21,026-mile ride by Mrs A.M.C. Allen, a ride that seems to have been conveniently forgotten by the British press when Billie Dovey exceeded that distance in 1938. Mrs Allen's ride was all the more remarkable as it came at a time when women were actively por-trayed as the weaker sex in the cycling press. Her performance won her the Johnson Century medal and the Massachusetts State medal, and a photograph within the club handbook of 1898 shows a statuesque and determined lady resplendent in plus fours astride her drop-handlebarred and ladies-specific bicycle.

Slightly above Mrs Allen on the list was Irving Harrison. Irving lived and worked in Hackensack, New York, and used his bicycle to ferry himself around the city, where he worked as a street-light inspector. His standard inspection route was 45 miles and he was often required to cover it twice a day. Irving had originally used a horse and cart for his inspection round, but a bicycle allowed him to cover ground faster and did not need feeding. His work saw him cover 26,252 miles in the year, with only eight days off due to illness or bad weather – an average of just over 73 miles per day. At first glance Irving's daily average may seem modest, but think again. He would have often had to carry a ladder with him in order to ascend and check each of the lamps, and his ride must have differed significantly from that of all of the other year-record aspirants due to the staccato rhythm of his cycling. He would have been continuously stopping to alight from his bike and perform his duties and must subsequently have found it hard to build up the kind of pace or monotony usually associated with long-distance rides. The Century Road Club saw fit to investigate Irving's claims and subsequently advised that 'as far as posthumous evidence could be accepted' they seemed to be in order.

There were other impressive rides outside the top ten too. The oldest rider to complete a year was Mr W. Davis of Preoria, who recorded a creditable 10,518 miles in his seventieth year, while the youngest was Will Wittig of Terre Haute, who knocked off a credible 5,403 at the tender age of fourteen.

It is clear that the pioneering American distance-riders blazed the trail for the formal cycling year record under the scrutiny of the Century Road Club of America. The club's 1897 manual provides very interesting reading, highlighting the organisation's aim of forwarding the cause of cycling advocacy and in particular the promotion of the cycling mileage record. A subsection of club information reads:

A larger list of contestants in the 1898 mileage competition is desired. This competition is one of the many features of a membership in the Club and serves to create enthusiasm in every section. State centurions should induce as many members as possible to enter the competition.

The CRCA clearly saw that high mileages gained press column inches. These rides were inspiring to cyclists and non-cyclists alike and cemented the credibility of the CRCA as a national organisation for cycling advocacy and as the repository for distance and endurance records. The CRCA wanted to promote the year mileage record for the greater good of cycling itself and its constitution contains many other items to this effect.

Sadly, we have to remember that this was America in the late nineteenth century and the document also included a caveat: 'Any white cyclist may become a member of the Century Road club.' Racism was a common theme in early American cycling history, with many clubs featuring constitutions that excluded non-white cyclists. An article in the 1893 edition of the *Wheeling Daily Intelligencer* even stated that a number of members of the local cycling club were planning to form a new organisation as their local racing league 'admits the negro and the national assembly would not draw the colour line'.

The 1897 competition had caught the imagination of riders and a year later a new challenger arose. Edward S. Edwards, a New Yorker and British ex-pat, managed to convince Pope Manufacturing Co. (maker of the Columbia bicycle) to sponsor his attempt to ride a century every day of the year. This was more than a simple marketing exercise, it was a key battle in the fight between chain- and shaft-driven bicycles. Pope manufactured a bevel-gear-driven bike and was keen to prove its worth against the chain drive.

Edwards set out on 1 January 1898 under a great deal of scrutiny, having to get an hourly signature from a member of the public to verify his location. Edwards rode 258 centuries without a day off – a record for continuous hundred-mile rides that would stand for a long time – and completed a total of just over 25,800 miles before he succumbed to typhoid, with his year ending on 15 September 1898. His illness made waves within the cycling community, which believed that his typhoid was actually a form of 'fatigue fever' caused by riding for too long without a rest. For that reason the next challenger to step up decided to take Sundays as a rest day throughout his attempt, driven by a mixture of concern and public pressure that this should form a foundation of future attempts for safety reasons.

This flurry of high-mileage activity in 1890s America was starting to cause ripples abroad. Initially, sections of the British cycling press occupied a position of sneering cynicism at the high mileages being ridden on the other side of the pond. The fact that many of these had been ridden by women caused utter disbelief in a country yet to allow the female vote.

The British cycling press compared the American regional club century counts to that of their own and felt that the figures tallied, but then pointed out that the records coming out of the CRCA were 'extra-ordinary'. The British journalists complained that these mileages were clearly not ridden in the course of ordinary road riding, and went further, claiming that the verification of such records was suspicious. This claim came from the fact that the road network and associated cycle touring facilities in late nineteenth-century America were undeveloped. The British questioned how these riders could be accumulating such miles in the absence of these facilities. Even the idea of riding small circuits where the roads were good was discounted by a journalist from *Cycling*:

> We believe the monotony of such a course would, in one month, drag the heart of any man or woman.

However, the envy caused by the American performances was impossible to hide and as the writer was unable to overturn the credibility of these rides he began to attack from another angle:

> It is evident that what was a pleasant and interesting recreation for the average road-riding wheelman has now become the sport of the professional record maker. The latter by his apocryphal performances behind pacemaking wind shields, has made a farce of racing and racing records and road riding records are entirely at the mercy of these who can draw the longest bows.

The discredited record of E.N. Roth was used as a further weapon against American credibility, citing the 'ingenuity of this terrible traveller' in making his false claims. The British press was clearly rattled; the Americans were way ahead of the rest of the world in pioneering cycling mileage records and post-imperial Britain did not like this one bit. A final stab was made at discrediting the Americans:

> We cannot say that it is impossible for a man to ride an average of 58 miles a day, ill or well, winter and summer, for an entire year, but we can say that it puts a breaking strain on our powers of belief.

So, as the new century approached, it was time for the British to take action. Scorn could only be poured upon the Americans for so long and a rider was needed to prove that high mileages could be ridden on the east side of the Atlantic Ocean.

It was now that Teddy Hale stepped forward and set a benchmark on the British side of the pond. Edward 'Teddy' Hale had a huge cycling pedigree and the interesting distinction of being claimed as both an Irish and English rider. The Irish claimed that Hale was born in Templepatrick, Belfast in 1864, but the truth appears to be that he actually came into the world somewhere near London. Hale first threw a leg over a bicycle at the age of sixteen and rode a boneshaker around the streets of London for six months before trading it in for a Pioneer model and taking up cycle racing.

He rose quickly up the cycling ranks and two years later became the captain of Gainsborough Cycling Club after competing in numerous time trials and track races. His first real impact on the cycling world came when he took a 50-mile record on the Brighton road with a time of 3 hours 35 minutes, which, at the time (in 1885), was unprecedented. The next year, Hale started to set his sights on longer rides and took the 100-mile record with a time of 6 hours 39, returning eight years later to smash it further down to 5 hours, 12 minutes and 2 seconds. His greatest achievement, however, was undoubtedly winning the Madison Square Garden six-day race in New York in December 1896.

Six-day racing is another forgotten classic of the early cycling calendar. Possibly originating in Birmingham in 1875, the events were hugely popular in the formative years of cycling. The races would start on a Monday and culminate at the weekend, with riders racing for fourteen to eighteen hours a day until the finish. Six-dayers fizzled out at the end of the first quarter of the twentieth century but enjoyed a brief revival in the 1960s and 1970s, sponsored by Skol lager and named the 'Skol Six'. The races were usually held on indoor tracks, keeping the riders out of the weather, with the winner being he who could ride the longest distance. The 1878 race, at the Royal Agricultural Hall in Islington, saw the winner, Bill Cann, cover a staggering 1,060 miles on a single-wheeled ordinary. The crowds were kept engaged with regular updates concerning the riders' distances and apparently rose to their feet to cheer riders as they notched up successive centuries.

Hale was linked with the Simpson Chain, a type of bicycle chain formed by linked triangles, when Simpson was approached by the organisers of the American Madison Square Garden race, who wanted a set of riders to represent the constituent countries of the United Kingdom in their 1896 event. Tom Linton rode for Wales, E. Lumsdon for Scotland and C. Happle for England, and it was decided that Hale would represent Ireland. One presumes that it was this decision that led to Hale being mistakenly labelled as Irish in many subsequent articles about him. Hale recounts that he did not feel well-prepared for the race and that when the twenty-seven riders hared off at a furious pace after the starter's gun fired he was quickly dropped. It took Hale six hours to wind the leaders back in and gain the advantage. He continued to ride well but, when it became clear that he had a commanding lead, he was approached by other riders who asked him to throw the race. Hale refused and thus became subject to a campaign of dirty tricks to either run him off the track or interfere with his pace. Incredibly, Hale rode nearly continuously for three days before taking a nap, surviving on a mere seven hours' (total) sleep until the end. He crossed the line having ridden 1,910 miles, some 300 more than his nearest rival, and then he began to eat. In his own words:

'After the finish I dressed and drove to the Bartholdi Hotel and had a good feed, followed by a warm sponge bath and 4½ hours' sleep. Then I had another good meal and slept about 5 hours. I fed again and slept for four hours, ate again and had 1½ hours sleep, then rose for the fourth time, had a warm bath, put on fresh clothes, sat for my photograph, and went out for a walk. Beyond being chafed somewhat severely, I was quite fit and well.'

Hale went on to describe how his race had been punctuated by a cigar or cigarette each day to relieve the monotony of the riding.

After his success in New York, Hale gained sponsorship from the Acatène Company of Holborn Viaduct in London. Acatène manufactured a shaft-driven bicycle which had yet to attract the attention of the masses and hence it was keen to showcase its machine on a professional endurance ride. It was decided that Hale would set out to ride a century every day for a year, with the exclusion of Sundays as they were deemed his day of rest. Hale was to ride on working days only.

Hale set out from Bristol on 30 July 1899 on his shaft-driven bicycle which featured not one, but two sets of handlebars: an upper set for easy riding and a lower set that was dropped for riding at a pace. His front brake was a pad mounted upon a rod that simply pressed down upon the wheel to slow the bicycle. He sported a flat cap, jacket and smartly shorn beard.

His ride went terribly underreported, possibly due to the lack of support from the cycling press. The failure of Edwards in 1898 had not gone unnoticed by the British press and one would have imagined that the attempt by Hale would have been welcomed. However, 'The Magpie', writing in *Cycling*, reacted to news of Hale setting off with a certain degree of cynicism, commenting that:

> I have not myself the slightest faith in it being accomplished. I do not think that Hale will be able to persevere to the end, for it is impossible for any man to ensure perfect good health for a whole year.

This did nothing to discourage Hale, who apparently stuck to his task in methodical manner, diligently riding 100 miles a day Monday to Saturday and resting every Sunday. The records indicate that he took the opportunity to travel around the north and south of England and mentions were made of him appearing in Eastbourne, Land's End, York and Tunbridge Wells. Occasional mention was made of his perseverance in poor weather conditions; on one occasion he was almost forced to abandon due to terrible ice and snow near Penzance – which fortunately melted overnight. Yet Hale and his machine held up well. At the halfway mark it was reported that he had broken his bottom bracket axle twice in crashes and replaced the cups and cones of his wheels, but that everything else had survived. Fortunately his sponsor had furnished him with a spare machine while these repairs were carried out.

By April 1900 he had not wavered, with over 22,200 miles to his credit as he appeared at a track event, and, on 31 July 1900, The Magpie was forced to eat his words. When Hale completed his task, with a final mileage of 32,496 miles over 312 days of riding, The Magpie magnanimously gave credit to Hale's wife and his bicycle with fleeting recognition of the rider himself:

> It has been by the thoughtful preparation and the skilful attention for which Mrs Hale has been wholly responsible that Hale's task has been made possible.

He went on to describe how the shaft-drive remained intact while a chain-driven bicycle would have seen at least three chain replacements over the same distance.

Teddy Hale had successfully planted the mileage record flag on British soil. However, his feat was poorly acknowledged by the press and cycling community, and his professional status and summer start had their detractors. Hale's figures were somewhat marginalised and he faded from the cycling limelight. For a rider who had enjoyed a stupendous racing career prior to the record and had ridden solidly for the entire year, this was undeserved. Hale ultimately hung up his racing shoes and took up work in the motor industry. He remained a keen cyclist for the rest of his life, dying in 1911 at the age of forty-seven and leaving behind a wife and five children.

It took an amateur rider to really grab the attention of the British cycling press and accelerate the year record 'challenge' into a proper competition with a defined set of rules. This amateur, Harry Long, came to the attention of the British cycling media after the submission of two extraordinary mileage charts to *Cycling* in the years 1909 and 1910. Before I detail Harry's exploits, it's well worth delving into the history of these charts, as they played an incredibly important part in the creation of the 1911 century mileage competition that kick-started the rest of the rides described within this book.

The British cycling fixation with paper mileage charts has now waned, what with the advent of many software and internet technologies that allow riders to collate and share their ride statistics with others. But in the early years of the twentieth century many riders became fixated with the completion of their charts and the annual submission of each became an informal competition of rider endurance and consistency.

The first documented British mileage-recording device that I can find was a diary published by Chas. Letts & Co. in the late nineteenth century. It was a standard pocket diary with space for noting daily and weekly cycling mileages along with other information such as lighting up times, road and paths taken on the rides, railway rates paid and other information. It even came with a form allowing the rider to purchase cover against fatal cycling accidents to the tune of £100. However, the genesis of the mileage chart is a letter written to *Cycling* magazine by a single individual, H.E.S. of Sleaford (sadly his or her full name was never printed). In 1901 H.E.S. had recorded his or her mileages on a weekly basis for the period of a single year, and was clearly no slouch, covering a credible 292 miles over a six-day period in August (although the mileages shown fell a long way short of any of the previous American records). The figures appeared to be linked to an analysis of the wear of the tyres upon their bicycle. Rather than table these mileages as a set of numbers, H.E.S. had graphed them, thus clearly showing the monthly peaks and troughs. The Magpie commented in the magazine that:

> The chart is such an exceedingly interesting way of recording one's mileage ... the most graphic method that I have yet seen ... conveying at a glance an impression which a column of figures will never do.

The Magpie was so enamoured with the chart that it was printed in *Cycling* and the columnist wondered aloud whether a competition could be run on an annual basis with charts such as this used to illustrate the miles ridden. A question was posed alongside this rumination as to the sort of chart that would define what was 'best'. Would it be the highest mileage ridden? Or would it be the rider who had been the most consistent, riding maybe shorter distances but with a greater regularity? The Magpie left the matter open to debate and invited readers to submit any of their own charts that were in any way notable. This single article created a flood of responses from the readers of *Cycling* which was detailed in a January issue in 1902:

> We are accustomed, in *Cycling's* office, to the receipt of fairly extensive correspondence upon such subjects as warrant discussion, but the correspondence upon mileage records constitutes a record in itself.

So many readers replied to the article written by The Magpie that the magazine was unable to cope with the response. Readers sent in their own charts, along with letters commenting upon the article, and it was clear that H.E.S. had tapped a nerve within the cycling community. *Cycling* was keen to ride this wave of interest and extolled its readers to continue to record their mileage from 1 January and to wait for an announcement in the next issue.

On 25 January 1902, *Cycling* magazine published the first official annual cycling mileage recording chart. The format was very similar to that designed by H.E.S., with mileages to be recorded on a weekly basis throughout a calendar year and then used to create a graph. Along with the chart came a competition open to all readers of *Cycling*. The competition would reward both distance and consistency, but it was not made clear how these would be measured in detail. The onus of proof was clearly upon the rider, with no mechanism whatsoever presented for mileage verification. The rules simply stated:

> Prior to announcing the awards, we shall call upon the senders of the selected charts to furnish us with such proofs as are obtainable.

Charts were to be completed throughout the year of 1902 and submitted monthly to *Cycling*, with the final chart to be received no later than 7 January 1903. The magazine believed that outside of the competition the chart would provide a means for riders to create consistency within their cycling. A rider's lack of enthusiasm throughout the winter months would be rewarded by a chart that showed erratic peaks as the weather improved and the magazine believed that a truly consistent rider should see a chart that increased gradually and steadily from the damp and dreary months of January into the better weather of summer.

There were prizes on offer, and the description of them is worthy of a direct quote as it clearly exhibits the ethos behind the competition:

> And let us parenthetically state that these prizes are to be small in value, so that there shall be no inducement to exaggeration, though, for ourselves, we have sufficient confidence in our readers to leave this matter entirely to their honour.

This was not for the professionals, or for one who may exaggerate their distances in order to seek material reward. This was an amateur competition run in the spirit of 'Britishness' with consistency and 'cummulativity' being their own reward.

To say that the chart and competition was well received would be an understatement – the previous correspondence record was smashed in the weeks after launch and *Cycling* was inundated with further correspondence ranging from congratulatory texts thanking the magazine for the launch of the scheme to readers requesting additional copies of the chart for friends or other riders who had missed the printed issue. The magazine generously fulfilled all of these requests, printing and dispatching a large number of additional charts to those who had missed out. Other riders mourned the fact that they would not be able to enter as their distances would be too low. *Cycling* assured them that this should be no barrier as there was no fee for entry and its judging would err towards consistent riders rather than mile-eaters. A number of racing cyclists advised that they would be riding their year out on the track. *Cycling* saw this as an area where distance would be hard to measure and hence disallowed track miles – an assertion I find strange, as the distance of a racing track would have been far more accurately known than the mileage between towns. Readers also offered improvements to the charts themselves, such as distances free-wheeled, or distances on specific gears or specific bikes. *Cycling* politely brushed these aside as complicating its relatively simple chart. Other suggestions included number of days on which a cycle was ridden, the number of hours riding, mileage of the longest ride, mileage of the shortest ride, average mileage per day or per ride, average speed or weather for the week.

There was a large amount of debate as to what constituted a week and when it should end. *Cycling* magazine had defined a week as Sunday to Saturday inclusive; a number of readers preferred the notion of Sunday ending the week, but *Cycling* was not prepared to budge. One area of debate that did sway the rules was around the submission of charts on a monthly basis. 'R.I.' wrote in and suggested that a monthly letter would suffice instead and remove the need for the submission of a part-complete monthly chart. The magazine agreed and adopted this as a new rule immediately. Readers' letters would be kept on file throughout the year and cross-checked against the final mileage-chart submission. *Cycling* magazine would keep a chart in its offices on behalf of each entrant, which would be updated as the letters came in monthly.

Therefore, riders needed to get hold of three charts: one to send back to *Cycling* to be kept up to date, one to record their own mileages upon and keep for posterity, and a final chart to be returned to *Cycling* at the end of the year.

Many correspondents questioned the ultimate verification of mileages ridden, but *Cycling* was reluctant to publish a definitive rule as:

> In the magnitude of counsellors there is wisdom, and amongst so many striving to provide proofs, a good idea would be hit out.

It was clearly looking to see what ideas emerged from its readership before rushing to adopt a process that might form a lesser proof. In the meantime, it advised readers to purchase and fit a cyclometer to their bicycles and use this in tandem with a diary to record the mileage for each day.

Things then went quiet for the rest of the year as *Cycling* magazine got on with reporting other matters and its readers studiously piled on the miles while faithfully completing their charts and submitting them to the magazine. On 27 December 1902 *Cycling* reminded its readers to wrap up their riding and prepare to submit their returns for the year. The charts were to cover a period of exactly 52 seven-day weeks from 29 December 1901 to 27 December 1902.

A few weeks later *Cycling* began to publish the charts submitted by readers, printing a series of those it felt worthy of comment in a 'roll of honour'. Over one thousand charts had been applied for, six hundred of which made it back to the *Cycling* offices. The magazine pronounced this a huge success, with not a single dissident in all the correspondence it had received, and committed to providing the charts for at least another year. It quickly published a new design of chart for 1903. This followed the same format of the previous year, with a few additions: weekly, monthly and cumulative totals, and monthly cyclometer readings, although there was to be no competition associated with the chart in 1903.

The 1902 charts proved very interesting reading, with the average annual mileage of the submissions being between 6,000 and 7,000 miles, or a weekly average somewhere near 125 miles.

The first chart published was that of Harold Freeman of Malvern Wells, who had doubled the average with a figure of 14,800 miles. Freeman was apparently an accomplished tobogganer who spent three months of his year training in Davos Platz, Switzerland, which accounted for his lack of miles in January and February and the subsequent huge peak in May that saw his mileage figures leave the scale of the chart, which only allowed for a maximum of 500 miles in a single week. Freeman was already a hugely accomplished sportsman and it is no surprise that he'd risen to this challenge, even at the age of fifty-two. He was an old boy of Marlborough College (known as a Marlburian) and was famously one of the four of the committee that oversaw the inception of Rugby football at Oxford University. Freeman had played rugby for his country, gaining caps against Scotland in 1872, 1873 and 1874, and scoring winning drop goals in two of the matches. He'd taken to cycling upon an original boneshaker bicycle in 1869 and had been riding ever since, keeping a record of his own cycling from 1877 onwards and notching up an impressive 144,100 miles.

Freeman's mileages had been seriously eclipsed by those ridden by Chas Holman, who'd ended the year with 18,087 – the highest total recorded. Chas was a 'traveller' in the tyre trade and modestly advised that he should be discounted from the competition as his opportunities for riding were exceptional.

Cycling clearly had a habit of attracting those attending Marlborough College as another Marlburian was mentioned within *Cycling*'s roll of honour, T.W. Weeding of Kingston upon Thames. Weeding posted a year-end total of 14,091, the third-highest of the year, just behind his friend Harold Freeman and at a similar age of fifty-four. The two riders were well known to each other and had ridden together on a number of occasions.

Female riders were reasonably well represented in the returns and *Cycling* somewhat patronisingly 'candidly admitted their surprise' at finding Miss G. Lycett of Hampstead, London near the top of the distance pile with 7,006 miles to her credit.

When the prizes were announced it was revealed that they were to be originals of sketches that had appeared in the magazine previously, which the editors deemed to have value as 'no offers or displays of eloquence have ever induced us to part with them.'

After this competition mileage charts became a regular institution in *Cycling* magazine and a chart was designed and made available to readers each year, although in 1904 the chart was not provided with the magazine but had to be applied for via post with a stamped addressed envelope. After a failed attempt to stop producing them in 1905, *Cycling* began to charge money in 1906, with charts available for collection from its offices or by post for a fee of 1½d. The charging regime did not appear to deter the readers, who continued to submit them with, as always, a few notable characters and performances.

Miss Bentley of Leyton included a night run from London to Brighton in her 1903 annual total of 3,669 miles. H.J. Woods rode a hugely impressive 19,306 miles in his profession as a bicycle tyre tester in 1903 at the tender age of eighteen years old. Harold Freeman continued to rack up the distance and improved upon his earlier mileage with a 15,227 year in 1904, despite riding for only forty-one weeks. He had also achieved over 14,000 miles the previous year, and featured in every year's return including 1910 where he recorded a credible 9,691 miles at the age of sixty-one.

The charts inspired riders to spread their wings away from their home towns. Some returns talked of quests to visit as many counties as possible in the search for miles. Others described the fantastic scenery traversed or historic locations that had provided focal points for the rides. There was also a reasonable contingent of cyclists whose miles were down to utilitarian processes, such as the organ player who lived a long way from his church or the businessmen who used the bicycle to visit their clientele.

But it was the rides of the amateur rider Harry Long that led to the foundation of the formal cycling mileage year record via the *Cycling* magazine century competition. Long's contribution to the year record stems not just from his mileages but from the fact that he was the first rider to significantly increase his tally over consecutive years.

His mileages were documented via the *Cycling* magazine charts and he gained significant notoriety within the cycling community and press after his 1910 chart showed him finishing that year with 25,376 miles in the bank – no mean feat given that he had ridden 23,241 miles the previous year.

There was a reason for Long's mile-eating. His business as a Southport-based advertising consultant took him all over the UK and he used his bicycle to travel to and from his clients. Keen to provide for his family – wife Marian and daughter Hilda – Long used the bicycle as a hugely economical mechanism for covering his large annual mileage requirement.

Long was clearly a characterful man. He'd decided to eschew the use of a cape or any form of overall while riding, leaving him exposed to the elements. He was also a very accomplished cyclist who was venerated within the Yorkshire cycling community during his cycling career and was appointed club captain to the Yorkshire Road Club. He attempted and held a number of cycling records, including the 12-hour record of 183.5 miles in 1902 and numerous place-to-place records. The *Yorkshire Evening Post* commented that Long had so many medals and records that 'one scarcely knows where to begin writing about them.'

In 1909 Long had an impressive year, which included a ride around the entire coast of Great Britain, setting a record of 5,263 miles in fifty days. He rode from Land's End to John o'Groats twice and managed to cycle through every single county in Great Britain. A single week of his riding illustrates the breadth of his coverage: Saturday, Penzance to Plymouth, 91 miles; Sunday, Plymouth to Shaftesbury, 140.5 miles; Monday, Shaftesbury to Brighton, 105 miles; Tuesday, Brighton to London, 117.5 miles; Wednesday, London to Birmingham, 139 miles; Thursday, Birmingham to Southport, 120 miles. He did not take the direct routes, riding, for example, from Brighton to

London via Lewes, Tunbridge Wells and Maidstone to get in his mileage.

Long finished 1909 with 23,241 miles in the bag, but wasn't content with that. In 1910 he decided to go further.

As befits the British weather and winter, Long's 1910 totals were relatively modest during the months of January to March, requiring him to average over 2,500 miles a month for the rest of the year in order to beat his previous tally. He didn't even come close to this until June, when he logged 2,751 miles for the month, giving a cumulative total of 8,750 for the year. Set to end the year well below his previous annual total, one wonders whether it was this that spurred Long into action. He began to really bang out the miles in the later part of the year: 3,410 in July, 3,132 in August, just under 3,000 for September, and a whopping 3,501 in October. This gave a cumulative total of 21,753 miles with two months left on the calendar – but those two months had shorter hours of daylight and worsening weather. On he battled, eventually managing to better his previous best by 2,135 miles. His longest ride had been 221 miles in a single day and he rode 106 century-plus rides throughout the year.

A photo published in *Cycling* showed Long with his single-geared BSA 'Light Roadster' bike nearing the end of his 1910 year. The caption stated:

> Just as our photographer was preparing to 'snap' him on Saturday an aeroplane came into sight. Long immediately gave chase, and was first on the spot when the aviator alighted.

It's worth remembering that in 1910 aviation was in its infancy and so the sight and sound of a plane would have been an extraordinary occasion.

Cycling magazine was clearly enamoured with Harry Long and his status as an amateur. A glowing tribute to his ride appeared in the January 1911 issue under the heading 'A Marvellous Mileage':

> They [Long's mileage figures] furnish abundant evidence of the intense enthusiasm, persistence and power of the man who in purely amateur spirit cycled over 25,000 miles.

Cycling magazine clearly had its sympathies with the amateur rider. A previous article dismissed Hale's achievement against Long's as a 'professional performance' and therefore not meriting comparison. The magazine continued to praise Long and his mileages:

They are also noteworthy in that they reveal the immense possibilities of the bicycle.

It is probably safe to say that no other commercial traveller in the kingdom has covered anything approaching an equal mileage at such infinitely small cost. Never before has the bicycle been so completely vindicated as the ideal means of transit for the business man.

This second statement was definitely true of the British cycling scene, but conveniently forgot the higher mileage clocked up by the American Irving Harrison in his career as a New York lamp inspector.

Moreover, the health aspect of the pastime also gains, for the mere fact that a cyclist has ridden nearly 49,000 miles in two consecutive years, without missing a single day's cycling through illness, without even contracting a cold by sleeping out or by rigidly abstaining from the use of cape or overalls, is alone a splendid testimonial to the value of the pastime.

It adds something to our appreciation of the British bicycle to know that it can carry a heavy rider such an enormous distance in all kinds of weather without giving the slightest trouble.

Long's chart of 1910 would prove to be a significant catalyst to the birth of the British century competition and consequently, after a series of ever-increasing record year rides, for Tommy Godwin's phenomenal effort. Long's mileages and their subsequent publicity were a direct result of *Cycling* magazine's annual mileage charts, which had in turn been inspired – although it would not admit it – by the American mile-eaters and by the 'professional' Teddy Hale. The letter written by 'H.E.S.' to *Cycling* had been greeted with an enthusiasm by the magazine that was mirrored by its readers, and the subsequent rides of cyclists like Freeman, Holman and Lycett highlighted a real public zeal for mile-eating. When the accomplished and well-known amateur Long began to record his rides, the magazine was delighted. The editors of *Cycling*, enthusiastic as they were about riding, saw an opportunity to drive their readership figures upwards and, in 1911, they launched a competition challenging their readers to ride the most centuries in a year.

CYCLING MAGAZINE'S
CENTURY COMPETITION

ycling magazine had previously run a competition for readers that offered a gold medal to the first person who could complete a single century ride in under five hours without pacing. It had, however, recognised that this competition was severely limiting, with only 'half a dozen crack riders' able to compete for the medal. Harry Long's performance and the will to create a more inclusive competition saw *Cycling* announce on 14 December 1910 its intention to create the first ever British century riding competition. This was designed to be the antithesis of the previous contest, headlined in bold as: 'NOT A ROAD-RACING SCHEME.'

Cycling announced:

> Our Great Road-riding Competition for 1911, A Gold Medal for the Largest Number of Complete 'Centuries' Ridden During the Year. Bronze Medals and Certificates for Smaller Scores.

This was not a distance competition. It was designed to reward a cumulative number of centuries ridden rather than the total distance covered. Any ride that did not exceed 100 miles was to be discounted from the tally. It was allowable for a rider to ride on and score more than a single century in a day if they so wished, but *Cycling* warned that:

> Should he manage to squeeze 195 miles into one day and then continue to ride to 200 miles the next, he counts one century only.

A day was to be between midnight and midnight – rides that spanned multiple days did not count.

The competition was to commence on 1 January 1911 and continue until midnight on 31 December the same year. The exact detail of the competition rules were to be announced in a future issue, but *Cycling* made clear that the rules would preclude tandem riders or any form of assistance, such as holding on to a vehicle. Verification processes were also discussed and *Cycling* proposed to adopt a scheme already used by road clubs to check times for private time trials – the magazine would supply riders with a set of checking cards which were to be signed and witnessed at the start, middle and end of each ride. The number of witness statements would depend upon the nature of the route. An 'out and back' ride would simply require three signatures: start, turn point and end. However, a more circuitous ride would need more signatures as riders would only be credited with the *shortest* mileage between any two checks. Therefore it was in their interest to get as many signatures as possible to prevent the mileage being dictated by the shortest path rather than the route they had actually ridden. *Cycling* urged caution in the gaining of these checks and advised its readers that, were there to be the slightest doubt about the distance, they should ride a few miles further to prevent a presumptive century working out as 98 or 99 miles and hence being struck from their tally.

Cycling was very clear that the competition was open only to amateur riders and by design should promote and encourage enthusiastic, hard-riding year-rounders. It wanted riders to enjoy their cycling while partaking in the competition and not feeling that they were part of any race. Riders were welcome to ride alone or in company and the magazine went on to appeal to the sense of honour it felt its readers would have:

> Something has to be left to the honour of the competitor, and if the trust is abused and we find anyone trying to obtain an award by false representations, we shall not hesitate to adopt severe measures. Let us say, however, that we do not anticipate anything of this kind. We have an abiding faith in the good sportsmanship of the average cyclist, and we are content to rely to a great extent on his sense of honour.

The article ended with an invitation to readers to apply for their checking cards and a week later the magazine published the full set of rules, along with a large amount of correspondence it had received in response to its announcement:

I think that your road-riding competition is a splendid idea.

Your 100 miles competition for 1911 I consider one of the very best suggestions for the benefit of the ordinary cycle rider.

The scheme reflects great credit on its originator.

I hasten to express my appreciation of your road-riding competition.

I believe it will prove a strong incentive for real cyclists to venture further afield.

It should give a big fillip to the pastime.

Your enterprising scheme deserves the support of all hard riders, and should induce cyclists of the 'butterfly' type to interest themselves in the benefits of all-the-year-round riding.

The last comment, while providing a humorous analogy, also touched on a particular crusade of the magazine at the time. *Cycling* was on a long-term mission to promote cycling consistency throughout the year, just as it aimed to do with this competition.

Reader feedback was almost overwhelmingly positive. The competition had captured the imagination of cyclists who welcomed the new avenue that had been opened for cycling achievement, and the requirement for amateur status had clearly gelled with the readership.

However, the article had raised as many questions as it had answered. Many readers complained that a distinction needed to be made for those riders whose working lives meant that they only had time for cycling at the weekends. One, Bernard Slann, asked for those who rode for pleasure to be separated from 'business' cyclists; he had no hope of a medal but hoped to gain a certificate and planned to notch up his first century on 1 January. 'Liverpudlian' agreed, asking for discrimination in awarding the prizes between business and social riders. He suggested that the award should also consider the proportion of time available to the cyclist for riding. Cecil Cooke went further, requesting that only weekend rides should count, as otherwise the average cyclist would not stand a chance.

L.S. Davis, Chas Fletcher and W. Carpenter asked for multiple rides within a day to be totalled in order to count towards a century. Fletcher had hoped that long-distance club rides could be counted, as his club had recently ridden a distance of 200 miles to Southwold and back in a respectable twenty-seven hours. Carpenter noted that his working hours meant he could probably manage 60 miles in the morning, followed by another 40 in the evening. *Cycling* had already capitulated upon this point and replied that all mileage accomplished between midnight and midnight could be totalled for the purposes of the competition. Davis commented that: 'With what horribly swelled heads will we be able to swagger about announcing to all and sundry that we are "out for *Cycling's* Gold Medal".'

Sidney Vanheems raised the issue of mileage verification and asked that cyclometer measurements be submitted as part of a rider's proof. Strangely *Cycling* magazine declined this request, stating that the task of testing a cyclometer's accuracy was an impossible one for the magazine. Therefore only known place-to-place distances combined with witness signatures would be accepted as proof.

Some readers raised the issue of fraud. S.P. Taylor expressed concern that a rider could gain a century between London and Brighton by using the train, with signatures legitimately gained at each end of the journey. He suggested that intermediate checks would solve this problem. *Cycling* disagreed:

> We have already stated that much must be left to the rider's honour, and we do not wish to strangle the competition by imposing too many irksome obligations.

Whether this feedback was used to define the competition rules is only known to the editorial staff at the time. The full set was printed within the 21 December 1910 issue of *Cycling* magazine and is reproduced here:

> 1 The proprietors of CYCLING offer an 18-carat gold medal of the value of £5 to the rider who, during 1911, accomplishes the largest number of complete 100-mile rides in Great Britain and Ireland under the conditions specified in these rules; they also offer 12 silver and 30 bronze medals, struck from the same die, to the next in order of merit, providing they score at least 20 centuries, and handsome certificates to every competitor reaching that number and failing to obtain a medal.

2 Checking cards will be provided by CYCLING upon receipt of a penny stamp to cover postage, and a statement of the number required. One of these cards must be signed by the rider in the presence of a witness at the commencement of his journey, the witness adding the date, time, place and his own name and address in the spaces provided. A similar check must be taken at the end of the ride, and at least one near the middle, it being understood that a competitor is only entitled to claim the shortest mileage between any two checks.

3 Checking cards must be returned to the Editor of CYCLING, 7–15 Rosebery Avenue, London, E.C., within three days of the completion of each ride.

4 Each 100 miles must be completed in the day, i.e., between mid-night and midnight, any mileage covered after midnight counting to the next day's score.

5 Single bicycles or tricycles must be used, and riders must propel themselves, without any extraneous assistance whatever. Holding on to another vehicle will disqualify a rider from further participation in the competition.

6 Mileage covered in races or time trials for awards of any other kind will not be accepted for the purposes of this competition.

7 The competition is confined exclusively to amateurs, and no rider who is in receipt of direct or indirect financial aid from any individual, firm or company engaged in or connected with the cycle or allied trades may take part.

8 In all matters arising out of this competition, the final decision rests with the Editor of CYCLING, who reserves the right to alter or amend these rules as may be necessary.

A week later *Cycling* got properly stuck into reader feedback with a decent swipe at those who had raised the issue of leisure riders being at a disadvantage. *Cycling* curtly reminded its readers that certificates were available to all, with the only requirement being the completion of twenty century rides. There were also forty-two other medals to be had and as such 'no rider who enters the competition seriously can fail to obtain some guerdon.' *Cycling* also noted that the need to ride around work was a common complaint amongst readers and as such one which they would all suffer equally, thus levelling the playing field. Finally, the magazine issued a veiled challenge:

> In our experience we have found that those who work the hardest also play the hardest, and the man who is free only on Sundays and one other afternoon in the week is the keenest cyclist.

The magazine expressed some frustration with the interpretation of the rules by its readers and reminded them that while they were there to state what must be done and what must not be done, it was clearly impossible to catalogue a set of regulations covering what 'may' be done. Prime examples of these sort of queries were:

> Can I ride the same 100-mile course twice?
> Will Sunday rides count?
> Will relatives or club mates be accepted as checkers?

Cycling patiently replied yes to each of these and repeated the competition rules once more in an attempt to steer readers away from any continuing detailed analysis of them.

Other correspondence revealed that Harry Long was in a number of readers' thoughts, with one querying whether Long would be allowed to compete as there were surely few riders able to match his huge mileages. Long subsequently visited the magazine in person and advised that he wasn't going to ride as his attention had been diverted by motorcycling and a new quest to notch up the longest distance covered on a motorbike. He believed that a rider in the competition could potentially eclipse his record mileage of 1910 and suggested that a figure of 32,000 miles was within the reach of the committed cyclist. Long threw his support behind the competition, stating that were his record to be beaten he'd be back a year later to have another go. Clearly the motorbike stole his heart as Long never did return to breaking records in distance cycling, instead setting a motorcycling record of 40,000 miles in forty-four weeks during 1911.

One reader raised an issue that was beyond the powers of *Cycling* magazine to correct. The letter entitled 'A Wail from Wales' and its subsequent reply speak for themselves:

> I see you ask readers what they think of your road-riding competition. I do not know what my fellow Welsh riders think about it, but I do not think you give your Welsh readers a chance, considering the up and down dale with which we have to contend.
> E. Lewis

Cycling missed a golden opportunity to bring many other hilly areas of the country, such as Yorkshire or Scotland, into the debate, or perhaps limit all riding to the Norfolk area. Instead it curtly replied:

> We cannot accept any responsibility for the Welsh mountains. Does our correspondent think we ought to have them rolled out?

Cycling was also caught out by one area of the competition's definitions, that of entries from females. The rules had not explicitly stated whether or not ladies were allowed to enter and much of the language used to discuss the rules had been littered with the masculine: 'his ride', 'he should', 'men who'. A female reader wrote to the magazine in order to seek clarification and *Cycling* scrabbled to rectify the situation, quickly replying that it hoped to see a large number of female entrants.

The magazine then promised to issue weekly updates concerning rider performance throughout the year and hundreds of riders began to file their applications for checking cards – so many that *Cycling* was forced to change its procedure and issue a maximum number of twenty in the first instance in order to cope with demand.

And so, in late 1910, the scene was set. The competition had created a huge groundswell of interest across the British cycling spectrum, with many riders committing to heading out for their first century on New Year's Day. The focus of the cycling year record had crossed the Atlantic, ready to shine upon a set of British riders attempting feats that had become commonplace in the USA. And so, at the last stroke of midnight, the competition began, with the editorial staff of *Cycling* blissfully unaware of the future performances that this competition would inspire.

MARCEL PLANES –
THE ENGLISH FRENCHMAN

The first day of the 1911 Century Competition was steeped in typical Britishness as it rained continuously over the vast majority of the country. But the riders were undeterred. The first double century of the competition was recorded upon that first day and S. Vanheems of West Ealing surely won the award for the keenest of entrants after he set out not long after midnight and gained his first witness signature at 3.15 a.m. He went on to complete his century in 9 hours and 10 minutes, more than likely finishing before his fellow competitors had eaten breakfast.

By 18 January 1911, over 10,000 checking cards had been sent out to competing readers. At twenty cards per entrant this meant that over 500 riders were planning to enter, and the flow of applications had not abated, suggesting that the figure was destined to grow further. The competition had certainly captured the imagination of a nation, with one reader from Lincolnshire reporting that over a hundred spectators had lined the road to witness his checking card being signed by a local policeman, regardless of the fact that it was pouring with rain.

The mid-January results showed a clear leader for the first two weeks of riding: William (Billy) Robert Wells, a Salisbury-based cyclist, who had ridden his first century on the very first day of the competition and had now notched up an impressive total of nine. This was four more than his nearest competitor, J. Thomson of Battersea, who had completed five. Wells was no stranger to high-mileage riding. He was a member of the Bath Road Club and had owned his bike for six years prior to 1911, covering over 60,000 miles upon it during this period. He worked in the printing industry and used his bicycle for an extended commute to work every day – cycling formed an important part of his life. Wells was fifty years old at the beginning of the year, although this clearly had little or no bearing upon his performances in the competition as he was to continue to feature in the leaderboards right up until New Year's Eve 1911.

Wells' bicycle provides an insight into the machines that were being ridden by these riders in 1911. He set out upon a fixed-wheel road racing Premier bicycle. This had a single gear driven by Renold chains, with the wheels consisting of Constrictor tyres upon wooden rims, and, due to the fixed rear wheel, the bike had a single front brake. After 7,500 miles of riding Wells split his rear rim and had it replaced, at the same time adding a coaster hub that allowed him the luxury of being able to freewheel downhill. Wells reported at the end of his ride that he had used five tyres and three chains over a 30,000-mile period.

Such a machine would have provided an extremely uncomfortable ride when compared to modern standards. Most of Wells' mileage was notched up between Salisbury and Christchurch upon a road surface that was rough and prone to flints, increasing the likelihood of punctures. The wooden rims and Constrictor tyres would have by necessity been solid and weighty with little shock-absorbing ability. Wells would have felt every single bump in the road being transmitted through these wheels.

There are also very few flat roads between Salisbury and Christchurch. The total weight of Wells' bicycle would have been heavy by modern standards, coming in at over 30 pounds with the addition of a heavy front lamp and steel mudguards. He would have found the hills a decent challenge upon his weighty bike with its single fixed gear of 75 inches. (Simplistically, 'gear inches' is a measure of the gear ratio used, calculated by dividing the size of the chainring by the sprocket and then multiplying this by the size of the wheel. It allows the gearing of bicycles with varying wheel sizes to be compared by giving a figure expressed as the 'effective' diameter of the rear wheel. The larger the number, the harder the gear. Lower numbers represent smaller gears and are hence easier to pedal uphill. Wells' 75 inches was a relatively mid-range gear.)

However, Wells was not alone, as geared bicycles were a rarity at this point in cycling's development and the vast majority of century-competition riders would have been riding singlespeed or fixed. Those that did have the luxury of gears were not much better off as the coaster hubs of the time, such as the Sunbeam, only provided one additional gear with a range between 69 and 92 inches.

Braking was typically provided by a single front brake matched with a back pedal coaster brake on the rear hub. Many riders dispensed with the front brake and relied upon the rear hub and pedals alone to stop the bike.

Behind Wells, the century competition had got off to a good start. By 18 January, 187 centuries had been logged with *Cycling*. However, the competition was still having certain teething problems. A number of riders had clearly not paid enough attention to the rules. F. Holden of Accrington had sent in eight checking cards and as such should have been able to claim second place on the leaderboard. Sadly, he had forgotten rule 3, which stated that all checking cards must be returned within three days of the ride. As he'd sent his in a single batch, *Cycling* solemnly deleted five of his centuries. But *Cycling* had become aware of a greater transgression and took several column inches to remind its readers that the competition was purely for those of amateur status. It appears that a number of readers had approached businesses within the cycling industry to seek sponsorship for their rides. *Cycling* was having none of it; its view was that the industry would benefit directly as a corollary of their competition and as such should have no need to further promote goods via rider sponsorship. *Cycling* appealed directly to the manufacturers to turn away such 'sham-ateurs' and stamp out this 'threatened evil'. No punches were pulled:

> We shall not dwell on the canons of fairplay that have been violated by those who have sought this extraneous and forbidden assistance – it would be a mere waste of words – but we would point out to those offenders that had they carried through successfully that which they attempted, and secured an award from this journal, they would have rendered themselves liable to prosecution.

A week later, *Cycling* magazine was crowing about the success of the competition. The winter riders had totalled over 312 centuries, underlining the 'vitality' of the sport. *Cycling* lambasted the 'Jeremiahs of the press' who bewailed the decline of winter riding – there was now evidence to show that, despite the poor weather conditions, British riders were out there tackling the elements and riding impressive distances. This was all the more special in the eyes of *Cycling* as the fiscal rewards of its competition were so small; here were hundreds of riders content to ride in all weathers simply for honour. *Cycling* began to question whether Harry Long's seemingly unas-sailable total would be exceeded, cautiously pondering Wells' performance through the winter and extrapolating this to the fine summer months.

Around this period some serious competition began to arrive at the door of Billy Wells. In the figures published in mid-January, a certain Marcel

Planes of London sat forlornly towards the bottom of the list, with only two centuries against his name. This situation was soon to change. Towards the end of the month, the published figures showed Planes and T.J. Broome closing in on double figures – Broome with nine centuries and Planes with eight. (Broome would end the year on fifty-three centuries, gaining a bronze medal.) Planes' improvement was impressive given his total of two on the previous week's list. His checking cards showed that he rode one century on 10 January, to Brighton and back; five centuries back to back around London and Bedford between 15 and 19 January; and then twenty-six centuries consecutively from 21 January to 15 February.

Like Wells, Planes was no stranger to cycling, having amassed over 50,000 miles in the previous six years on his Mead Flyer 'Modèle Superbe' bicycle. Given his first name, Marcel, and the French naming of his steed it would be tempting to assume that Planes was a lone Frenchman adrift in a British competition. This was not the case.

Albert and Charlotte Planes were both descended from wealthy French families, from Toulouse and Paris respectively. They married in France but, much to the chagrin of their families, decided to leave their motherland and relocate to London in search of new opportunities. This was seen as a near-traitorous move and the family decided that, were the move to proceed, Albert and Charlotte would be cut off. Undeterred, the couple moved to London, settling in 75 Berwick Street, where Marcel was born on 6 August 1890. Life was not easy for the family as Marcel and his sister Graziella grew up. Albert Planes was a tailor by trade but the family, now living at 5 Little Pulteney Street, were forced to take lodgers in order to make ends meet. Young Marcel was in work at the age of fourteen, leaving home and signing as an apprentice to the Century Bicycle Company where he worked for six years in their Liverpool factory before leaving to return to London shortly before the start of the competition.

Planes was always conscious of his French roots, yet proudly British and was quick to correct any that assumed he was French. He was often mis-labelled by riders and cyclists alike as French and continued to remind them that he was British by birth. He also served in the British Army during the 1914–1918 Great War, fighting in France, and had an incredible war record.

By the beginning of February Planes had caught and passed Wells on the competition leaderboard. Both riders had ridden twenty centuries and thus qualified for competition certificates; Planes having ridden twenty-two and Wells lagging behind on twenty-one. The two men had drawn clearly away from third-placed Broome, who was seven behind with fourteen centuries. There were still forty-seven weeks of competition remaining.

Broome was listed as a rider from Ynysybwl in Wales so may have had the excuse of 'large hills' upon his side. There was a noticeable lack of riders from hillier regions. In its first report of the year, *Cycling* had listed every single century ridden, along with the locations of the riders. Although the northernmost century was recorded in Larkhall near Glasgow there was clearly a southern bias, with London being the clear centre. Forty-three of the 187 centuries ridden by that point were in London. This bias continued in the early February results and it appeared that the Scots were either disdainful of the competition or in the throes of terrible weather as very few Scotsmen featured within this list, which showed A. Mathieson of Irvine on nine centuries, D. Gibb of Larkhall (near Glasgow) on six centuries and J. Miller of Larkhall on five centuries. Hugh Hanna of Belfast represented Ireland with two centuries. Perhaps E. Lewis, in his 1910 'Wail from Wales' to *Cycling*, had a point about 'the up and down dale with which we have to contend.'

By the time *Cycling* published its 22 February list Planes had a commanding lead. The magazine attributed him with thirty-two centuries, Wells with twenty-five and Broome, a distant third, with seventeen. As February ended, the competitors' mileages were significantly reduced by bad weather and high winds. The rain had taken its toll upon many untarmacked road surfaces with one rider complaining that he'd had to abandon the popular Bath road and seek cycling elsewhere. *Cycling* spun this as a good thing for the competition in general as it set back the 'less determined' cyclists and allowed those who were likely to go the whole way through to come to the fore.

Some riders were meanwhile encountering more unique difficulties. Mr E.A. Wilson had been out riding a century that ended in the dark and had stopped at a fountain to add water to his acetylene lamp. (These lamps were commonplace on bicycles prior to advances in battery technology. Carbide was placed in a lower chamber and water dripped upon it from an upper chamber controlled by a valve. The reaction between carbide and water liberated acetylene gas which was then burned to create light.) A policeman approached Wilson and intimated that he was up to no good as he was taking water from a fountain for purposes other than drinking;

the implication being that he was attempting to poison the fountain. Wilson convinced him otherwise but this led to an additional line of questioning regarding his business at this time of the night. Wilson replied 'for a cycle ride' and was immediately subjected to a sustained interrogation as to why on earth any cyclist would be out in the dark. Wilson parried with his century checking card, which the policeman took a long time to study before accepting the excuse and subsequently refused to sign as he was now down a crime for that evening.

Similar stories would come out after the competition closed, underlining the tenacity and endurance of these pioneering cyclists. Unlike Planes, the majority of competitors were working men who had to be at their desks at 8 a.m. and who could not leave until 7 p.m. One told of his need to eat biscuits in the office in order to keep himself awake during the working day. Another had his progress hampered when encountering a menagerie upon the road and being hemmed in for a while between an elephant and a dromedary. Meanwhile, W. Little had attempted a double century one Sunday night and stopped for a short kip on Maidenhead Thicket. As he slept the temperature dropped and froze the roads and he had to abandon his ride as a result. Other riders had had problems getting their checking cards signed, with requests turned down by those who could not write, by a man who was stone deaf and by those who were terrified of these strange cyclists requesting signatures. Planes had himself been physically threatened by a Brighton man armed with a stick.

But the riders ignored their troubles and *Cycling* magazine cracked before its readers did. The results page on 22 February had been littered with multiple centurions and *Cycling* decided to stop listing those with only one to their name, of whom there were ninety-two. In the same issue the magazine announced that the processing of checking cards within the week of going to press had become impossible. Clearly it had not been prepared for such huge interest in the competition and glossed over this fact as it told its readers that a weekly summary would now be prepared each Thursday rather than every Monday, as it had done previously. This would allow weekend centuries to be included, as riders had three days in which to submit their cards. One cannot blame *Cycling* for this move; 14,000 checking cards had been issued to 731 riders and the process of checking and tallying the centuries was entirely manual and handled by *Cycling's* staff alone. While the figures for January had been encouraging, *Cycling* was anticipating a huge influx of cards as the spring weather approached.

By the end of the first week in March Planes had increased his total to thirty-seven. Wells was biting at his heels again, four behind on thirty-three and some twelve centuries ahead of the Welshman Broome in third place. Over 200 cyclists had now registered centuries with the magazine, which continued to rebuff suggestions that the wider industry should become involved:

> It has not been instituted for the benefit of the trade ... This competition is being run entirely by ourselves for our readers ... a glance at the list of centuries will show how little the competition is in need of outside support.

The totals continued to accumulate throughout March and *Cycling* began to look at the magical total of over one million miles for the year, which was in fact deemed to be a very modest estimate as the magazine readers were knocking out in excess of 10,000 miles per week and it was still winter. By 22 March 1911, Planes had forty-seven centuries to his name, with Wells close behind on forty-one. It was increasingly looking like a two-horse race as Broome had added no centuries to his total, which was just over half that of Wells.

On 22 March *Cycling* continued its subtle disparagement of the American riders with a short article decrying the results of the previous year's American competition. This had been won by T. La Rossa with 128 centuries, fewer than half the number ridden by John Nobre in 1897. The *Cycling* article was littered with the word 'only' when listing the rider's performances and ended with the patronising statement that:

> It is of course not possible to compare this with our own century competition, as the American riders all belong to one club.

In the same issue *Cycling* upped the hypocrisy a level by proposing their own idea for a club:

> An organisation of century riders – a scheme to enable hundred-milers to become acquainted with each other, and to participate in organised rides in various centres.

This was the genesis of the Century Road Club (UK), which still remains in operation today. *Cycling* put the proposal to its readers and invited feedback, suggesting a national network of organisations set up around metropolitan areas with cities such as London potentially being further subdivided. The aim was to create rider solidarity, support in the picking of hundred-mile routes and an easing of the process of gaining checking signatures as large groups of riders could potentially self-verify. *Cycling* suggested the name 'Century Road Club' and offered to fund the preliminary costs of such an organisation. This proposal was reaffirmed within a strong editorial implying that an 'enormous majority' of competitors desired such an organisation. Reader feedback was plentiful and in the main supportive, with many hoping that such a club would help weaker riders complete their centuries in company whereas riding alone they would fail. Only A. Lusty dissented, worried that such a club would remove the essences of freedom from the current competition that allowed competitors to go where they liked, when they liked. However, Lusty's voice was ignored and momentum began to gather. Organisers were found for Manchester, Birmingham, Bristol, Brighton and three London districts. *Cycling* clearly wanted this initiative to succeed as it would keep the centuries rolling in and heap further relevance upon its own competition.

By 12 April 1911, a degree of formality had been achieved and rider applications received for the initial regional chapters. By June the project was effectively complete, with sixteen regional chapters in place and accepting members, including Scottish and Irish chapters. The Century Road Club would go on to become the home for riders who could 'satisfy the committee of their ability to ride 100 miles in ten hours,' which remains a requirement of the club to this date.

As Easter came and went the checking cards continued to pile through the letterbox of *Cycling* magazine. Planes and Wells were now a long way clear of the pack, with Planes five centuries ahead on seventy-three. Their lead was looking unassailable. The Welshman Broome had been beaten back into eighth place, apparently due to family illness. But our two leaders had not deterred new entrants, with *Cycling* reporting that new registrations continued to arrive at its door, with an additional seventy arriving over the Easter week alone. The task of receiving and cataloguing the checking cards must have been monumental.

Each checking card contained four columns: date and time of checking point, the place of the signature, the rider's signature and the witness's signature. The card then had to be signed at the bottom by the rider, and their address provided. Fortunately for us, Marcel Planes was something of a collector and his cards remain in existence today, providing a fascinating insight into his year on the bicycle.

Each of Planes' cards is neatly completed and signed with his elegant copperplate signature; in fact a number of blank cards are present that bear Planes' signature, suggesting that he methodically pre-completed them in batches before heading out on the road. They show that his first century was ridden on 10 January, when he set out from London at 8 a.m. and arrived in Brighton at 12.15 p.m., where a B. Jenkins of 8 Ashford Road, Brighton, witnessed his card. Planes then turned around and rode home, where his card was witnessed by A. Moreau at 1 Little Crown Court in Soho. Little Crown Court would have been a logical place for Planes to travel to and from, being a popular area with French residents (the address disappeared after the area was redeveloped). Planes was lucky to have Moreau as a friend – Moreau, a cycle dealer and mechanic, signed Marcel's cards a remarkable 707 times, often at very unsociable hours.

The rear of each card carried the following set of rules:

The rider must first sign his name in the space provided.

The witness, who must actually see him sign, must then add the date, time and place, together with his own signature and postal address.

In stating name of place, full details must be given so that the exact point at which the card is signed can be located.

Checking cards should be returned within three days of completion of the ride.

It is clear from Planes' cards that these rules were not always rigidly applied. A number of the locations written upon his cards are vague, simply giving town names, and many of his signatures are so consistent and well-written that they were clearly signed after the fact. In a document published after his year Planes mitigates this with a further checking action that was carried out by *Cycling*. He states that the main roads traversed by competitors were patrolled by *Cycling's* 'private scouts', on the lookout for riders wearing cycling competition badges. These scouts would report the rider's name, location, date and time back to headquarters for tallying with any subsequent cards submitted. *Cycling* itself made no reference to this procedure, although in October of 1911 they alluded to a certain amount of surveillance after having to disqualify a number of riders who had submitted cards with bogus signatures. *Cycling* also randomly wrote to the addresses of those witnessing the rides to seek additional confirmation. An Irish rider was found out after one of these letters was returned to *Cycling* via the Post Office's dead letter office, an instrument designed to deal with non-existent addresses. When challenged he had shrugged his shoulders and stated that this was the address written by the witness on his card, so what could he do? *Cycling* replied that he could sign an affidavit before a commissioner of oaths. The Irish fellow deflected this with the somewhat immaterial fact that each ride cost him in the region of ten to fifteen shillings and he was able to prove this, but that *Cycling* should remove his name from the competition regardless, which it happily did.

Cycling felt that continually riding the same routes, as many competitors were doing, would become monotonous and it would be better to add variety by picking alternative routes. Planes disagreed and his cards show that he was, in the main, a creature of habit with the vast majority of his centuries sharing the same roads. His cards evidence the fact that he rode every single one of his centuries from home, and he subsequently claimed that this strategy was part of his will to play an honest game – an out and back ride meant there could be no advantage from prevailing winds. He frequently rode from London to a number of well-known destinations, with Brighton, Harpenden, Guildford and Bedford all featuring regularly, and would often ride the same route twice in a day, repeating his London-Harpenden-London route on a number of occasions to notch up his century.

Planes' first double century was ridden in his usual out and back style on 6 June, when, with less than six hours' sleep after the previous day's century, he awoke Moreau at five past midnight for a signature and set off to Girtford Bridge, arriving at 4.30 a.m. His ride continued along the Great North Road where he hit his first century at 10.20 a.m. at Meadow Lane in Nottingham. He then turned round and rode home along the same route, arriving at 10.45 p.m. after nearly twenty-two hours on the bicycle. Planes was clearly a fan of the Great North Road – in October he annotated one of his cards with: 'A rather windy day as usual did not care to push on to Bath, country is too open. Good old North Road cannot be equalled.'

However, even with Planes' constant habits, frustration could boil over, as it did on 20 December 1911 when his card recorded the curt: 'I am entirely disgusted with the weather', after an abandoned ride that totalled a mere 50 miles.

A short period of very poor weather in June dampened a few competitors' spirits somewhat and there was a brief decline in centuries, apart from the reader who wrote requesting more of the pink mileage cards: 'Kindly send one packet of your famous pink pills for pale people, as I find they are most suitable for my health.' However, 1911 is notable in British history as it was a coronation year. On 22 June 1911, King George V formally ascended the throne after his coronation at Westminster Abbey, having become king after the death of his father Edward VII the previous year. The resultant holidays saw a resurgence in centuries ridden and Planes saw his chance to push the gap to Wells further, riding two double centuries and increasing his lead to eight. Wells managed to complete 100 consecutive centuries by riding every day from 1 April to 10 July 1911, but things were about to get worse for him as his business activities began to interfere with his cycling. He'd been in correspondence with the magazine and advised that he'd have to limit himself to a mere four centuries per week as a result.

Through August and September the gap between Planes and Wells began to grow further as Wells' business activities took their toll. Planes was able to ride during working hours while Wells and many other competitors were forced to wake early, knock out 30 miles before work and complete the additional 70 after a full day's toil. *Cycling* noted that many of its readers were leaving north London at 4 a.m. and riding up to Welwyn, returning before 8 a.m. to begin work. The evening would be spent with a trip out past Welwyn to Hitchin.

Planes claimed difficulties of his own, stating that he faced additional hazards as a London-based rider due to many miles of traffic-riding and the additional worry of tram lines. He never fully explained how he was able to fund his riding activity, although he did state that he was able to subsist on less than a shilling a day and that some days his riding cost him nothing whatsoever. At the end of the year *Cycling* saluted his ability to exist entirely self-funded and get by upon 'microscopic' expenses.

While working as an apprentice with the Century Bicycle Company prior to 1911, he must have seen the competition as a way to boost his profile within the industry and hopefully lead him to better things. In the meantime, he presumably used either savings or assets to sustain himself throughout the year, or relied upon the kindness of friends and family.

Throughout his year, Planes had ridden his Mead Cycles 'Modèle Superbe'. It was a bike from the lower end of the market and would have cost him the princely sum of £2.15s. It was designed primarily for the utilitarian cyclist and was by no means a lightweight machine, weighing in the region of 45 pounds when fully loaded. Yet Planes remained loyal to it and, at the end of his ride, leveraged this fact extensively, publishing letters he had written to Mead themselves extolling the virtues of the bike and ending with: 'I firmly believe that there is not another cycle made that would have stood the terrible gruelling which my Mead has undergone.' Was this Planes hankering for a better job as a sponsored rider? Did he see winning the century competition as the ultimate act of personal PR? Only Planes will ever know, as little other evidence exists to reveal how he sustained himself throughout that year.

As the end of September approached Planes' lead was a commanding twenty-eight over Wells, but the latter had not given up and he abandoned his work-imposed four-century limit as he continued to give chase. And, at last, the ladies were beginning to make themselves known. Mrs Olive Elliot was the first woman on the leaderboard, having completed forty-three centuries by 21 September. Elliot went on to complete sixty centuries during the year and won the female category of the competition, setting the female year-mileage benchmark at 18,000 for British riders, a figure that stood until 1938.

Wednesday 11 October was a pivotal date for Planes; he recorded his 254th century, officially totalling 25,400 miles and thus eclipsing the British record held by Harry Long. He had probably passed the mark earlier than this, but as *Cycling* simply recorded his cumulative centuries rather than his total actual mileage – despite Planes recording his actual distances for all of his rides – we have no way of knowing when. Planes appeared to be blissfully unaware of this fact as he rode from home to Tempsford and back. His mileage card noted a ride of 102 miles but made no mention of this remarkable feat. Later that month *Cycling* published the certificate that was to be awarded to each competitor scoring twenty or more centuries in the year.

Poor weather during October and November did nothing to dent enthusiasm. On 24 October Wells joined Planes in eclipsing Long's record, but the real excitement built when *Cycling* realised that if Planes continued as he was, he would be on track to exceed the professional record of 313 centuries set by Hale in 1900. This prompted the readers of *Cycling* to make Planes a rather unusual offer.

Planes' Mead Cycles Modèle Superbe had served him well but was beginning to show its age. He refused to abandon it, despite a catastrophic failure of the seat stays; instead he simply tied the stays with string and cycled on. Readers' concerns began to mount as other components started to break – the forks cracked and the coaster brake began to fail. This culminated with a suggestion from readers that they would club together in order to fund a new machine. Planes was having none of it. He'd ridden this machine for well over 60,000 miles before 1911 and was determined to see the year out on it. He brushed aside the component failures as wear and tear while noting that many locomotives built in the 1860s were still in service.

Despite the reliable locomotives and the huge mileages being ridden, a humorous aside highlights the early twentieth century could be rather eccentric and that Planes was not alone in his approach to repairs. In an era devoid of health and safety regulations *Cycling* featured a picture of four uniformed men who had fixed a broken car's front wheel by strapping a bicycle to the front axle and having a rider steer it for two miles to get the car home. It was noted that the car suffered no injury. One wonders if the same was true of the rider.

Planes obliged his supporters by overtaking Hale's total and claiming the year record in the name of the amateurs on 10 December 1911, equalling the professional's record in a torrential downpour and marking his mileage card accordingly. The next day he rode the same route to Tempsford and back to also bring the record for total centuries ridden into the realm of the amateur rider. Planes had ridden 230 consecutive centuries in 225 days, with some doubles along the way for good measure. His run only ended when he wrecked a tyre after 40 miles at Hatfield on 7 December 1911.

Planes was not alone in suffering from damaged tyres. As the year came to a close, another competitor had nineteen centuries to his name. He needed one more in order to gain the coveted certificate, but work commitments meant that he only had a single day in which to complete it. After 60 miles he too blew a tyre. It looked as though he would have to forfeit the century, but the will to gain an award won over and he rode the remaining 40 miles upon the rim alone.

Wells called it a day on 12 December with a final tally of 287 centuries and a total of 30,638 miles for the year. *Cycling*, ignoring as usual the Americans who had gone before, hailed Wells as one of only three to have ever exceeded the 30,000-mile mark. Planes, meanwhile, continued to the bitter end, as did many other riders, and the newly formed Century Road Club organised a final run of the year from Girtford Bridge, which had become a popular meeting point for century cyclists. Planes joined the ride and through it completed his 332nd century at 10.15 p.m. on New Year's Eve. His cumulative mileage for 1911 was recorded as 34,366 miles – an amateur record that unequivocally brought the cycling mileage record back to British shores.

Somewhere in London an Irish cyclist named Murphy was celebrating. Planes told of a mysterious Hibernian wheelman who had taken serious interest in his ride in the early months. 'Paddy', as Planes nicknamed him, would enthusiastically hammer upon Planes' door at 4 a.m. and drag him out for a century ride. Planes attempted to deter Paddy by pulling off one of his 200-milers, but the Irishman would return early the next day as usual. Paddy's behaviour continued for months until Planes' lead was seemingly beyond reach, when Paddy disappeared. After he'd won the competition, Planes received a letter from Paddy stating that he'd managed to get 'long odds' from a bookie on Planes during the early period of the competition when he and Wells were close. Paddy had decided to become his daily escort as the stake placed was substantial and he continued until he was assured that Planes was well ahead of the rest.

January 1912 saw *Cycling* magazine proudly beating its chest at the reflected glory of the century riders. It pronounced 1911 a 'red letter year' and pompously suggested that such a competition had never been run before (with utter disregard for the American contests of previous years) and would probably never be repeated. The million-mile mark had not been reached, but the receipt of 8,500 checking cards was still a huge achievement for the magazine and its readers. Ultimately 650 cyclists had taken part and of these 162 had achieved the figure of twenty or more centuries in order to gain a certificate.

Cycling postulated that Planes' record would stand 'uneclipsed' for all of time (little did it know what was to come). He'd ridden one and a half times around the world while living a spartan existence to fund his rides. At the tender age of twenty-one, Planes was deemed to have smashed Hale's record on two fronts: firstly by riding an additional 1,870 miles, but more importantly by being entirely self-supported and by riding a six-year-old machine that was constantly in need of attention. The record of Edward Hale was brushed aside as that of a polished professional rider who had received significant financial support.

The magazine paid equal tribute to Wells, who had come a gallant second while still managing to run a business. The fifty-one-year-old rider was awarded a combined gold and silver medal in recognition of this fact, and *Cycling* crowed about him becoming the first rider in the world to knock out 100 consecutive centuries. A few weeks later a reader wrote in to correct the magazine and remind them of the previous performance of the Liverpudlian Edwards in 1898. *Cycling* initially declined to comment but, when pressed by other readers, stated that his ride had not been independently checked and as such could not be recorded.

Planes took possession of the coveted gold medal and his family still have it to this day. It's fashioned of eighteen-carat gold and bears the emblem of a winged cycle wheel with Father Time sat astride it holding his scythe. Planes treasured this above all of his possessions and stated directly in his will that it should never leave his family. His grandchildren resolutely guard this request and the medal remains in pristine condition to this day.

The medal and an accompanying certificate were Planes' only reward from *Cycling* magazine. He ended the competition tired and glad that the year of 'demnition grind is over'. Prior to the record Planes had been a keen racer, but felt that as a result of the long days his speed was gone. His bike had mostly survived but he'd had to replace his forks, four rear tyres, three front tyres, a chain, the bottom bracket and the front wheel bearings. This still provides remarkable testament to the bikes of the early twentieth century as one would be hard pressed to ride a modern machine over such distances with a similar level of repair. The ride had also cost him three pairs of knickers and two sets of shoes.

However, Planes' performance was not universally lauded. A journalist wrote that his feat was entirely unremarkable and easily repeatable by any rider who had the time to complete a century a day. He went on to state that at an average speed of 10 miles per hour a figure of 87,840 miles ought to be achievable within a leap year. The journalist was an eminent motorist and appeared to be subtly decrying the achievements of cyclists. Other cyclists immediately leapt to Planes' defence with recollections of riding with him in desperately poor weather while he maintained his cheery demeanour and the will to get out and ride the next day. The journalist was encouraged have a go himself, maybe replicating the feats of other working competitors who had completed their centuries overnight before riding on to work. Maybe he would then consider rewriting his article? The embers of a car against bicycle conflict were starting to become flames, a theme that would continue to expand as more motors took to the roads.

Having taken first place, Planes was now able to be approached by the cycling industry and began to appear in adverts for the Liverpool-based firm Mead Cycles. He was presented with a new bike by Mead, who saw Planes as excellent collateral to raise the profile of its mid-market brand. Planes also returned to racing, announcing in March 1912 his intention to ride as a middle-distance tandem-paced racer. He was accordingly selected to ride in the Herne Hill six-hour event in June of that year and went on to gain a French racing licence in order to race in international events under the membership of the Century Road Club (CRC). But trouble was brewing. Members of CRC began to question his amateur status; Planes' appearance in advertisements for Mead Cycles clashed with an 'anti-advertising' clause in their articles of membership. A long and drawn-out argument ensued, resulting in Planes' expulsion from the club and a ban from any of their amateur events. The Century Road Club went further and altered their records to show W.R. Wells as the winner of the 1911 competition – a status that remains unaltered to this day. It still maintains that: 'Although Marcel Planes did record the greater mileage, he was deemed to be a *professional* and disqualified from the *Cycling* competition as it was for amateurs only.'

Planes shrugged this off, riding for the Highgate Club instead and continuing to race and break records. He fought for the British in World War I and it's possible that his language skills were in demand and resulted in his partaking in a number of perilous missions close to the front line, where he was seriously traumatised. His medical record states: 'Rheumatism, Neurasthenia, Myalgia'. Neurasthenia is a psychological disorder characterised by chronic fatigue and weakness, loss of memory, and generalised aches and pains, formerly thought to result from exhaustion of the nervous system.

Despite this, in 1923 he set a benchmark of 1,000 miles ridden in a single week and continued to work in the cycle industry, running the cycle departments of Barkers Kensington Emporium and Selfridges department store.

He was a regular fixture at the Ripley Road rallies during the late 1950s, an event organised by the Southern Veteran Cycle Club that saw riders mount older machines and ride out from Ripley Green. Planes would be astride a 1913 BSA Light Roadster. He was on the entry list for the 1960 event but wrote to advise that ill health would prevent him attending. A few months later, Marcel passed away at home aged sixty-nine after a heart attack.

His family remember a 'can-do', slightly eccentric and loving grand-father who kept his enthusiasm for riding right up until his death on 10 August 1960, and who was present at the start and finish of many of the future year-record attempts. This remarkable man had opened the door to amateur mileage records upon the British roads and his performance continued to inspire riders for many years.

After the 1911 competition, *Cycling* magazine collapsed into an exhausted heap of checking cards, tallies and leaderboards. The competition had been a huge success for the magazine, but the time and effort required to police it had taken its toll. The magazine continued to feature its mileage charts in future years but quietly parked the century competition, which was never to be repeated. It had served its purpose as far as the magazine was concerned. The distance record flag was firmly planted upon British soil, while the magazine itself was now the self-appointed custodian of distance-record verifications. At the same time, the Century Road Club had grown and become self-managing, removing the need for the magazine to act as the catalogue of century rides.

After the explosion in distance-cycling records between the 1890s and Planes' record in 1911, it seems strange that no new contenders were forthcoming in the subsequent years. The instability in Europe leading up to the Great War of 1914–1918 was an influencing factor and the war itself curtailed the ambitions of many young British men who may have had their sights set upon bettering the 34,366 ridden by Planes. Across the Atlantic, the Century Road Club of America continued to tick over but either ignored or missed news of Planes' record and no attempt was made to drag the record back to their shores.

As post-war depression enveloped Britain, Planes' achievement began to slip from memory. In fact, the cycling year mileage record might have faded into time were it not for a plucky young Londoner who blew on its embers and ignited an era that would see distance riding pushed beyond any of the boundaries imagined in 1911.

ARTHUR HUMBLES –
THE 'ORDINARY CLUBMAN'

While no attempts upon the year record were made immediately following Planes' success, the continued interest
in the mileage charts submitted to *Cycling* magazine
showed that mile-eating remained at the forefront of the cycling public's
mind. Large annual mileages continued to be racked up by the readers,
although none came close to those produced by the 1911 competition.
The magazine continued to encourage annual submissions and continued
to report enthusiastically upon its readers' endeavours, but was probably
mindful of the huge administrative burden of the 1911 competition and
hence made no attempt to solicit a repeat performance. Yet the mileage
charts were probably directly responsible for the resurrection of the record
– along with an element of sibling rivalry.

When Albert Arthur Humbles announced that he would take on the
distance record set by Marcel Planes, he did not realise the magnitude of
his intention. It would trigger a cycling equivalent of the Ashes that would
run for a decade and drive a future set of cyclists to put themselves through
all sorts of extremes in order to take the record.

Humbles was born in 1910 in London and early records show that he,
like Planes, had a difficult childhood, with his family classed as having
pauper status. His father, William Humbles, was a wood carver and
struggled to make ends meet and support his family of eight children.
Albert, known as Arthur, and four of his siblings were consigned to a children's home, apparently at the request of their mother who was fed up
with her heavily drinking husband who was unable to earn more than
50 shillings a week working from home. She claimed that he was 'not right
in the head' and that this was causing her concern as she was expecting
another child at the time and had been moving from place to place,

'not living anywhere for more than a few months.' These early years clearly bred a vein of tenacity within the young Arthur Humbles and his brother Sydney George.

This tenacity would stand them in good stead when the two brothers developed a love of cycling, likely due to a will to escape the misery of life at home combined with the obvious health benefits. They were active within the London club cycling scene, apparently riding for pleasure with the occasional foray into racing. Initially, it was Sydney Humbles who came to the attention of the cycling press. He racked up an impressive 12,744 miles in 1931; a year proudly announced in *Cycling* amongst the pick of the noteworthy 1931 mileage charts submitted by readers as his best ever. (Sydney's mileage breakdown provides interesting reading: he states that touring made up 10,111 of these miles, 574 of which were pottering round in the Home Counties, with the remainder leading the Ingleside Cycling Club riders around Essex and Hertfordshire. Another 733 miles were given over to racing, and 1,900 miles to 'business' riding, probably his commute to work.)

Arthur had not submitted his own mileage chart to *Cycling*, leading me to wonder whether an element of brotherly rivalry had led him to look for his own challenge. Maybe Sydney's bragging had pushed him over the edge, or maybe it was his brother's excellent performance that inspired Arthur to carry on the family tradition of mile-eating. Whatever it was, on 8 January 1932, Albert Arthur Humbles stepped forward from the ranks of the Ingleside CC to attack the year record.

The press at the time spoke of an 'ordinary clubman' attempting the record upon a standard touring bicycle. To a certain extent this was true and Humbles himself wanted to show that an ordinary man and an ordinary bicycle could do extraordinary things, but Arthur had been doing his groundwork and set off with the backing of Hercules Cycles and Dunlop tyres. It must have taken some tenacity and persuasion to gain the backing of two major players in the cycling world. Arthur either had an excellent cycling pedigree or sales pitch – or both.

His attempt was the start of a new set of campaigns from companies seeking to use the performances of these riders as marketing collateral. Exceptional mileages completed on a company's steed provided significant advertising capital, with marketing messages at the time speaking of 'reliability' and 'solid engineering' – important considerations for a cycling public devoid of the disposable income thrown around today. That said, Arthur's messages were a little mixed throughout his ride as the *Gloucester Citizen* presented him as promoting leisure travel rather than bicycle reliability:

> He is out to prove, by breaking this record, that cycling is a more convenient way of seeing the country than hiking, and that it is far more economical and far healthier than motoring.

Despite his backing, Arthur's send-off was relatively low-key. A few spectators were present to see Humbles set off and *Cycling* reported that:

> A small band of cyclists gathered at Marble Arch to see A.A. Humbles of the Ingleside CC start upon his attempt to beat the unofficial record put up by Marcel Planes.

The phrase 'unofficial' clearly caused a flurry of letters to the editor as a week later *Cycling* published the following clarification:

> A number of readers have inquired why the year record of Marcel Planes was recently described in these columns as unofficial. Of course, none of the recognised cycling bodies takes note of rides at such a distance, and although that in question was accomplished in the Century Competition, being checked by *Cycling*, and can, therefore, be taken as authentic, it is, nevertheless, not an official record in the true sense of the word.

Official or not, Planes turned up on the start line to wish Arthur 'every success'. A photo of the meeting shows Planes and Humbles shaking hands. Planes looks dapper in shiny leather shoes, a woollen jacket, white neck scarf and bowler hat. A small medal is pinned to his left breast and I wonder whether this is the gold medal awarded to him by *Cycling* in 1911. Humbles looks more ordinary in a drab plus four suit, cycling wear typical of the working class rider. His only ornaments are two pins upon his jacket, probably the club badges of Ingleside CC.

Humbles' face is telling. He looks pensive, almost unsure as to whether he is capable of achieving his goal. His attire and bicycle certainly adhere to his 'ordinary' image and it's worth remembering that Arthur, like Planes in 1911, began his attempt upon a bike with only one gear (although Humbles was to later add gears part way through his year). Arthur had initially become a cyclist in order to improve his health and escape his predicament at home. Now here he was, about to take on a world record.

Planes was the first signatory in Arthur's mileage record log book, which was to form the basis of his record verification. Then, having completed formalities, Humbles set off from Marble Arch intending to ride to Cambridge and back that day – a distance of approximately 128 miles by road. His bike sported a lamp, suggesting that he was not bound to finish before dark.

Humbles had started his year late. He'd already missed seven days' riding (although this was effectively reduced to six by the fact that 1932 was a leap year and as such would have given him an extra day). He had 359 days left in front of him and a target mileage of 34,366 to beat. Ninety-six miles per day would gain him the record.

Humbles was not setting off unprepared. Just as he had arranged bicycle and tyre support, so too he'd thought through the logistics of his year and in particular the manner in which he was going to fund it. He had a plan. His idea was to use his unemployed status as a catalyst to increase his sponsorship and support throughout the year. He planned to use the publicity gained as an advert for the British cycle industry and thus endear himself further to potential sponsors. He knew that he'd need more than just miles to attract attention and thus sought to gain the support of his local members of parliament. This in turn required credibility and so Humbles rode quickly to a total of 10,000 miles before making a formal approach. The miles had the desired effect and from May 1933 Humbles was carrying with him a message from the four members of parliament for Islington. This message was to be passed to the mayors of Chelmsford, Colchester, Ilford and Southend, all of whom he intended to visit throughout his year. The message read:

The bearer, Mr A.A. Humbles an Islington lad, comes to you in the course of his progress to beat the existing world's record by completing within 12 months an average of 100 miles a day on his bicycle. When he called upon us at the House of Commons he had already left his first ten thousand miles behind him and we now commend him to your interest for two reasons. Last year, when young Humbles like so many thousands of our young men, found himself unemployed, he had the enterprise to hit upon this method of supporting himself, and at the same time demonstrating to all men the supremacy of the British bicycle and its equipment on which he is well on the way to achieving a world record.

Nobody would be foolish enough to suggest that our present grave state of unemployment is the result of the lack of enterprise of the unemployed themselves, yet we do feel that the sportsman-like challenge of this young man will be an inspiration to thousands of others eager to do something, yet almost desponding upon the very brink of effort.

In carrying out his plan he is helping in no small degree to maintain the position which the British bicycle industry has won for itself home and abroad.

Alfred William Goodman, MP North Islington

Tom Forest Howard, MP South Islington

Thelma Cazelet, MP East Islington

Patrick William Donnor, MP West Islington

Arthur wasn't just riding for the record. He was riding for his livelihood as well.

The early months of Humbles' year appeared to pass without huge incident. He was following a similar protocol to Planes in verifying his mileages with signed checking cards that he sent to *Cycling* magazine on a daily basis for their independent verification. However, Humbles differed wildly from Planes in his approach to gathering the miles. Planes had ridden almost exclusively from home. Humbles was required by his plan to spread his net much wider and thus rode all over the country.

Humbles probably enjoyed his approach of varied rides. He was fastidious in documenting his riding year, possibly explained by a love of photography which saw him frequently stopping to take pictures of his surroundings. Humbles' subsequent album must have been fascinating. Sadly, despite huge efforts, I've been unable to trace its location but live in hope that it is treasured within a family collection somewhere.

His mileages grew steadily through January to May and by 19 May he had amassed 13,515 miles. One of his excursions had taken him into the Lake District and the strain of grinding up the long hills and steep gradients on his single gear must have taken its toll on his legs, as after this visit Humble fitted a Sturmey-Archer three-speed hub to his bike to give him some more options when the hills intervened.

Humbles was clearly playing the steady game. By 4 June 1911 Planes had ridden his first double century, while Humbles' longest ride had been

151 miles. But his strategy to beat the record was to ride a consistent 100 miles per day for the whole of the year. Humbles set off inexplicably late, on 8 January, and thus calculated that given 1932 was a leap year he would have 359 days left available to him. A steady century every day would see him gain at least 1,500 miles on the previous record. By 23 June Humbles' steady-eddy strategy had proved its worth and he had a massive advantage over Planes' running total with a figure of 17,322 to Planes' 14,562. Humbles' average to this point was 103 miles a day – he'd stuck to his guns and maintained his consistency.

Although he was sponsored, Humbles was entirely self-supported on his ride. He carried all of his overnight equipment in a saddle bag and was attired in plus fours and a cycling 'suit'. He had, however, gained some valuable press for his sponsors in many of the localities that he'd visited. At the same time his sponsor, Hercules Cycles, was running adverts in the national press with Humbles extolling the virtues of his 'Empire Club Racer' as a 'quality cycle at the world's most popular price'. The bicycle was advertised for the princely sum of £5 11s. 6d. – I'm sure that a lower price would have been more popular. Humbles was depicted in the previously mentioned cycling suit, an open-necked shirt and with a well-groomed hairstyle more befitting of the commuter cyclist than one who had ridden over 17,000 miles. The adverts clearly had an impact in some quarters as a month later *Cycling* had nicknamed him A.A. 'Hercules' Humbles.

Unlike Planes, Humbles did not avoid the hillier regions of the country. By July 1932 he had ridden from London up the east coast of England to Newcastle, then on to the Lake District, Yorkshire, the Cotswolds, North Wales and then Devon, all areas notorious for their steep and long hills and difficult terrain. Humbles was following in the tyre marks of Harry Long, not only mechanistically grinding out the miles but venturing into areas of the country he had not previously visited. Humbles and Hercules were shrewd in managing their PR and used to advise the local press in advance of Humbles' arrival in an attempt to see him welcomed and gain further coverage.

Humbles' image as an ordinary man on an ordinary bicycle doing extraordinary things began to gain traction. In July he ventured further south and delivered his message by hand to the mayors of Hastings, Brighton, Eastbourne, Chichester, Lewes and Worthing. In August, *Cycling* magazine sat up and took notice. Humbles had 21,000 miles in the bag and it was clear that his consistency was going to allow him to take the record. *Cycling* sent 'Nimrod', a staff writer, to spend a day riding with Humbles and get into the head of a year-record rider. The article commenced with an observation that it would be any cyclist's dream to spend an entire year doing the one thing that they loved, but went on to slowly unravel this myth, highlighting some of the issues a year-rider would face.

Firstly, no time could be wasted off the bike. A puncture or mechanical failure meant that the day's mileage would be curtailed and a longer day required further down the line in order to catch up. Then there was the danger of theft. Humbles was especially cautious when stopping for food as the theft of his unattended bike would have disastrous consequences with days lost while obtaining a replacement model. Humbles, like Planes, displayed a huge affection for the bike that had carried him for so many miles and was willing it on to complete the year – as, undoubtedly, were his sponsors.

Next, nutrition. Humbles had to carefully manage the logistics of finding food along his routes and ensuring that he ate well enough to sustain himself upon his rides. Nimrod wrote that Humbles rode at a steady 16 miles per hour, much faster than the 12 to 14 of Planes, and had to ensure a 'wholesome' diet to maintain this pace. Humbles was not exclusively a vegetarian, but existed on a mostly meat-free diet for much of his year.

Humbles also had to deal with the logistics of getting his checking cards signed. This often came with a delay as any uninformed signatory would want full details of what exactly Humbles was up to and why he was undertaking this ride.

As the day's distance increased the ride began to take its toll upon Nimrod. A long section of the Holyhead road after Fenny Stratford drove home the grim reality of these distance rides. The author moaned that this section was meant for 'progress rather than enjoyment' and he began to appreciate just how hard and tedious the endless days of riding could become. Nimrod had to decamp to a pub to recover, eat and drink, and then grovel back to Harpenden Common at a pace of 10 miles per hour while silently praising the fortitude and strength of Humbles who, undeterred, was heading north at his consistent 16-miles-per-hour pace. Nimrod wrote his article in the middle of a thunderstorm in which Humbles was out riding, leading Nimrod into his final observation that Humbles was living proof that no day is too bad for the 'real' cyclist and the reliable modern bicycle.

It appears that Humbles kept his rides closer to home as he drew nearer to breaking the record. At the end of September he was escorted to Croydon by a meeting of cyclists from Purley railway station. Clearly, the cycling community were now fully engaged in his task and willing him on to the record. A few weeks later his confidence reigned as he announced that his ride would end on New Year's Eve at the National Cyclists' Union annual dance, which was to be held at the Horticultural Hall in Westminster. He had by now covered 27,446 miles and had just under three months to ride 6,920 miles – no mean feat given that winter was now approaching.

The braggers were circling. A number of riders began to decry Humbles' performance and one publicly stated that he would take on his record and beat it by thousands of miles. This may have been Ossie Nicholson, who was already planning an attempt for the next year; we cannot be sure. Humbles became defensive and felt forced to remind the public that his mission had never been to display a 'freak performance', but to show that breaking the record was within the capabilities of an ordinary clubman upon an ordinary machine. This also underlined the requirements of his sponsors, who were increasingly keen to point out that their components were affordable and within reach of the ordinary cyclist, yet also hugely durable. Humbles signed off in a somewhat frustrated manner: 'As for anyone going one better next year, let him get on with it and good luck to him.'

Humbles kept up his riding until it was clear that he'd pass Planes' record on 11 December 1932. Humbles and his sponsors planned his route so that he would pass this milestone at Hyde Park Corner and announced that he'd like to meet as many cyclists as possible there, so that they could accompany him as he rode the magic 34,367th mile. *Cycling* paid a special tribute to Humbles prior to the event. It had been the magazine's view that the mileage set by Planes in 1911 would never be repeated without the re-running of the competition, yet Humbles had proved them wrong, taken on the challenge and, in doing so, 'thrown a girdle about the earth', a reference to the fact that he had effectively circumnavigated it on a bicycle.

Humbles and *Cycling* could not have conceived of the reaction to his record-breaking ride. An estimated 3,000 cyclists made their way to Hyde Park Corner to accompany Humbles over the line. Riders travelled from all over London, as far west as Dorset and down from the Midlands to congratulate him, regardless of the bitterly cold wind and grey skies of the day. The ride began at 9.30 a.m. from Buckingham Palace and was led by Humbles along Constitution Hill to Hyde Park Corner, where photographers were waiting to capture the historic event. Apparently the crowd roared its approval and the police in attendance stopped traffic to allow the cycling throng to ride twelve abreast along the Carriage Road and on to Marble Arch, where Humbles' year had begun. The cyclists all rang their bells to serenade Humbles back to his starting point.

On arrival, Humbles was carried shoulder high to be presented with a trophy by Sir Malcolm Campbell, the holder of the land speed record, and with a laurel wreath by Ted Crane, one of the directors of Hercules Cycles. Campbell gave a short speech:

'Your great effort reflects very good credit upon the grit and determination of a young man who, finding himself unemployed, thought out this means of doing good, both for himself and the British cycling industry.'

Two policemen were required to part the crowd and escort Humbles to a reception held in his honour at the Dorchester Hotel. Humbles had cemented himself firmly within the hearts of ordinary cyclists. His record-breaking ride had captured their imaginations, particularly as it was done outside the confines of a competition and purely in the name of self-improvement and the promotion of cycling. A whole spectrum of the cycling community had turned out to see him break the record; not just ordinary club cyclists, but famous racers and household names. The centre of London was brought to a halt by the celebrations, a scene that could not be contemplated in modern-day cycling.

Humbles could have finished on that day but decided to soldier on. With twenty more riding days available he continued to pedal around the London area and finished 1932 with a cumulative total of 36,007 miles, 1,641 miles ahead of Marcel Planes and absolutely consistent with his quest to average approximately 100 miles every single day. The magnanimous Marcel Planes presented 'Hercules' Humbles with a silver cigarette case at the National Cyclists' Union dance at the end of his ride. There were no hard feelings on losing his record, only admiration for the young rider with whom he clearly identified. Humbles had ridden to the dance from Essex and arrived somewhere near 9 p.m. on a bicycle covered in mud. The dancing crowds parted and formed a human avenue to allow Humbles to ride into the Horticultural Hall and through a paper clock that had been erected at the far end.

Planes handed over the case and, ever the ordinary man, Humbles expressed his huge relief at finishing the ride in the company of other cyclists. The dancing then recommenced and continued into the early hours.

The tributes to Humbles did not end at the NCU dance on New Year's Eve. In 1932, *Cycling* magazine created *The Golden Book of Cycling*, designed to record outstanding rides and accomplishments. The introduction reads as follows:

The Golden Book of Cycling

In the pages of this book, dedicated to future generations of cyclists, are inscribed descriptions of great deeds done in the cycling world, and against each record appears the signature of the performer.

These entries tell of meritorious rides or series of rides in competition or against the clock on road or path; of performances in the touring world, of wheels that, by their prowess, example or universal utility, were deemed worthy of permanent record. There are inscribed, too, the achievements of men and women who, by their legislative ability or trade ingenuity or as a result of untiring and unselfish effort in general, have proved themselves benefactors to the sport and pastime.

The Golden Book of golden deeds is the gift of *Cycling* to cycling. It was opened to receive the first signature on the occasion of *Cycling's* second 'All-rounder' Concert at the Royal Albert Hall, London on Saturday January 30th, 1932.

The first rider in the book was Frank Southall, winner of the Best British All-Rounder competition in 1932. Albert Arthur Humbles became the fourth entry in 1933, in recognition of his year. He signed his page on 18 January 1933 at the tender age of twenty-two.

Humbles' fame was short-lived. In 1933 he was present at a number of cycling functions and continued to feature in the adverts of his sponsors. But then the record moved on and so did Albert Arthur Humbles. No details of any future cycling exploits were ever published and it is not clear whether Humbles' passion for riding and touring remained after his record year. He left his birth town of London and opened a shop in Bridge Street in Whitby. Humbles' shop is remembered by many of the locals, as is the man himself, who was a keen sea fisherman and member of the Whitby Sea Anglers Association – who still present a trophy in his name today. The exact date and circumstances of Humbles' death are unclear, although we do know that he left behind a daughter, the result of his failed marriage to Zota Scarr, which broke down in 1952.

A few days after he had finished his year, Humbles reflected upon his ride in *Cycling* magazine. He had, he said, been fortunate and dodged illness for the entire year, but, after spending every day of the year worrying about the things that could go wrong, was relieved to unshackle himself from the mental tension that the ride and its logistics had created.

It appears that his longest and shortest rides were 172 and 35 miles respectively, while his worst ride had been north to Newcastle in the cold and driving rain. But this had led him to York where he'd found supper, bed and breakfast for a bargain 4 shillings. The worst roads were between Sheffield and Leeds, and full of potholes and setts.

Most days Humbles had started riding at 8 a.m. and finished some-where between 6 and 10 p.m. – on average at least twelve hours per day. He claimed to have had no problems with his bike at all, although it must be remembered that he was a sponsored rider and it would have not been in his interest to publicly state any issues with his bike. His puncture tally was five, an average of one every 7,000 miles – a figure any modern cyclist would aspire to. Humbles continued to brush aside the assumption that his feat was, as his nickname, Herculean and continued to maintain that a 20,000-mile year was well within the capabilities of one who could commit to a 400-mile week, but said that this would require the renouncing of social activities and the embracing of the great outdoors. Bad weather was overcome by getting used to it and fitness was gained by 'cycling, more cycling and still more cycling.' The one tip Humbles did offer was to abandon underwear and replace it with a woollen combination from neck to knee (or a 'onesie' as it would be called today). This apparently prevented your vest climbing up your back and leaving a cold spot.

Humbles was clearly comfortable with his achievement, but pragmatic enough to know that now another would equal or better his ride. He stated on record that, 'if tempted', he'd get on the bike and have another go. Clearly, the temptation was never high enough as Humbles never did make another attempt at the record. He was a satisfied man with a satisfied set of sponsors, all of whom had achieved what they'd set out to do that year.

Little did they know that Humbles' mileage of 36,007 was to be dwarfed in subsequent years, and that, as Humbles travelled home to his bed on New Year's Eve, a wily Australian was preparing to mount his bike for his own record attempt.

OSSIE NICHOLSON –
THE PROFESSIONAL

rthur Humbles' ride of 1932 had been the first time a year record was reported in the wider press. Humbles was welcomed in many of the towns he visited and newspapers were used to spreading the word of his mission. Mention was also made in the national and international press which sparked the interest of the wider cycling community and, on 1 January 1933, five riders set out on the road to attempt to better Humbles' distance.

In Italy a veteran cyclist named Mario Gaioni set out to become the first Italian to take the year-mileage record. He would end the year on a loosely reported figure of around 37,500 miles that, while greater than Humbles' total, appeared to lack proper verification. Gaioni claimed to have beaten Humbles' record within 287 days, but there is little evidence to support this fact.

Over in the USA Leslie Seaward, a fireman from Savannah in Georgia, also took to the road. He would claim an even higher total mileage, of 42,900 miles. Seaward was a well-known and prolific racing cyclist active in the 1930s who held a number of distance and endurance records. These included the Century Road Club of America's annual mileage award for four years on the trot between 1930 and 1933, with a highest mileage of 33,000 in 1931 and a cumulative total of 90,082. A reference to Seaward in a 1934 edition of the Australian *Sydney Referee*, credited Seaward with 37,010 miles in 1932. This figure would have eclipsed the record of Humbles in the same year but appears to have been a mistake, as there are no reports in the American press to add verification.

The husband and wife team of Mr and Mrs Murray also set out, from Brighton, riding a tandem with the intention of cycling 48,000 miles in the year. Sadly, Mrs Murray died during the attempt after a short illness, after which Mr L.G. Murray rode on with other male partners until July, after which he rode solo despite an appeal via the *Surrey Mirror* newspaper where he invited local cyclists to get in touch if they wanted to ride with him. Interestingly, Murray's first wife had also died while riding with him through Europe. Murray ended the year claiming to have notched up 52,108 miles, but had done nothing to verify this claim and it was therefore ignored. It's hard to fathom whether or not Murray's claim was genuine, but it is clear that he had led a chequered life, serving as a French legionnaire, a member of the international brigade in Spain and receiving medals in France for 'distinguished cycling service'. It was even claimed that Murray had advertised for his second wife in the press and selected her from the applications received. Murray's assertions of his high mileages continued well into 1938 during which he 'apparently' sneaked out to beat Nicholson's record of the previous year despite forgetting to tell the cycling press. He popped up in the *Nottingham Evening Post* in February 1939 with a total of 5,590 miles for one month, but was never heard of subsequently.

The Dutch were also inspired to have a go, with P. Spruyt Blokker taking to the road. He rode for 146 continuous days before an injury hospitalised him. He got back on his bike, but it appears that he did not complete a full year as his name disappeared from the press after June 1933.

The fifth rider would have more luck. Humbles' ride had tickled the fancy of the professional cycling community, no doubt down to the fact that he had promoted himself as an ordinary clubman and made great pains to distance his achievement from those of the racing cyclists. An Australian bicycle company owner, Bruce Small of Malvern Star, heard of Humbles' ride and saw the potential for an antipodean publicity coup that would put his company properly on the map. He ran round his network of profess-ional riders looking for a candidate to take on the challenge and bring the record over to Australia. One of these was Hubert Opperman, or 'Oppy', as he was fondly known by the cycling community. Opperman was an Australian cycling legend known internationally for his racing prowess and record breaking. He was riding for the Malvern Star racing team at the time but chose to turn down Small's approach – probably wisely, due to the impact it would have had upon his illustrious racing career.

Small then turned to a young professional named Oserick 'Ossie' Bernard Nicholson, who also rode for the team and had competed and collaborated with Opperman in equal measure. Nicholson was a more willing candidate and decided to accept the challenge, possibly as he was in danger of being hidden in the shadow of Opperman, who was then the team's star rider. Like Small, Nicholson saw the year as a great PR opportunity and decided to throw himself at the challenge.

Nicholson had a formidable cycling pedigree. Born in New Norfolk in Tasmania, he'd moved to Victoria as a teenager and joined the Prahran Amateur Cycling Club, where he had learned his trade riding on various cycle tours. It appears that Nicholson had a precocious talent for racing and was encouraged by club members to enter a number of events, eventually winning the club's 25-mile event and going on to become a professional cyclist in 1928. He had come to the attention of Malvern Star in 1929 after beating Opperman in an incident-filled race. Malvern Star had decided to sponsor the Wangaratta to Melbourne road race in anticipation of its star rider winning and taking glory at a lavish presentation ceremony that they had organised in the Capitol Theatre in Melbourne. Unfortunately Opperman crashed early in the race and damaged his forks, rendering his bike useless. Nicholson and the rest of the field continued, but came to grief as a flock of sheep tangled with the riders on a poor section of road. Nicholson crashed, but was saved from real damage when he landed on one of the sheep, which cushioned his fall. Despite damage to his water bottles and a puncture Nicholson rode on and dominated the sprint at the end of the race to take victory. Malvern Star duly handed over the prize at the ceremony while also convincing Nicholson to jump ship and join its team in time for the start of the track season. Malvern Star immediately set Nicholson up with a record attempt, riding behind a motorcycle on the track to have a go at a motor-paced speed record. Nicholson failed at this first attempt, but returned in 1930 to have another go, eventually recording an Australian record of 90 kilometres per hour.

There was clear rivalry between Nicholson and Opperman. They had a finish-line dispute after the Warrnambool to Melbourne Classic, which Opperman had won only to be disqualified after Nicholson disputed his tactics in the final sprint. The argument continued after the race and Opperman successfully appealed, seeing him retrospectively take the win with Nicholson relegated to third place. This rivalry continued now the two men were on the same team. Opperman narrowly took the honours in a motor-paced track race between the two with huge crowds in attendance. Nicholson won the club road race championship in 1930, but lost out to Opperman in the Goulburn to Sydney road race.

The year was not without controversy for Nicholson, who served a suspension for petulantly switching pacers during a motor-paced track event. He'd also argued with race organisers concerning his allotted start position in a time trial event, successfully claiming that his status as an elite rider was not being properly recognised.

Regardless, 1930 was a stellar year for the twenty-four-year-old rider, who was well-placed in many prestigious Australian road races and, after marrying Annie Hawley the previous year, saw the birth of his first son, Oserick William. The following year, Malvern Star set Nicholson up for what should have been a pinnacle of his career. Along with Opperman, Richard 'Fatty' Lamb and Frankie Thomas, he was chosen to represent the team and Australia in the Tour de France. This was no mean undertaking as it was before the advent of the jet engine and the team were required to endure a month-long journey by sea. A confined journey such as this would have had a disastrous impact upon their cycling fitness, so the riders trained using rollers set up on the deck. Many of the passengers found this activity extremely puzzling and one lady eventually cracked, approaching the crew and enquiring as to what exactly was going on. She was told that the riders were producing the electricity to power the ship.

The team eventually reached France and began the race, where a lack of communication technology meant that reports of their progress were slow to reach Australia. The press responded to this setback by producing cartoons and articles speculating on the progress of the team. The reality for Nicholson was more distressing. He broke a crank on the third stage and was forced to walk 11 miles to find a replacement, only to finish the stage outside the time limit and be disqualified. Illness forced Frankie Thomas out of the race, leaving only Opperman and Lamb to arrive at the finish, which they did, in the positions of twelfth and last accordingly.

1932 was likely another frustrating year for Nicholson as a racing cyclist. He competed in numerous track and road events, but recorded few wins, and Bruce Small's timely year-record suggestion must have played upon Nicholson's frustrations. There is no doubt that Small would have presented Opperman's unwillingness to take up the challenge as an incentive, knowing full well that this would fuel Nicholson's competitive nature. Small was an extremely shrewd businessman who oversaw the growth of Malvern Star from a small Melbourne bicycle shop to a national Australian brand name. He knew the value of one of his riders taking a world record and would have used every trick in the book to convince the impressionable

Nicholson to give it his best shot. The final catalyst was probably the breakdown of Nicholson's marriage. He'd left his wife and son and moved out of the family home, so was now unencumbered by family life.

Plans were laid in late 1932 for Nicholson to make his attempt the following year. Humbles' figure of 36,007 miles could be bettered by a daily ride of 110 miles, which Nicholson felt was well within his reach. In fact he believed that at this mileage he could also continue his activities as a professional racer, a statement that showed his confidence but was perhaps a little over-optimistic for one who had never taken on such a challenge.

Malvern Star equipped Nicholson with one of its own-brand cycles adapted to use a three-speed gear mechanism recently introduced in Australia by Cyclo, a manufacturer of bicycle gearing systems. Nicholson was also provided with a coach, a local police constable named Guy whose job it was to provide massage and 'encouragement' at the end of each day's riding. Replete with all the support he had become accustomed to as a professional rider, Nicholson began his attempt from the Elizabeth Street General Post Office in Melbourne, just after dawn on 1 January 1933, deep in the heart of the Australian summer.

Melbourne lies in the southernmost region of Australia and its summer months can be stiflingly hot, with average temperatures of around 26 °C. Nicholson may not have properly factored this into his riding plans as he reported early on in his attempt that he was finding the task of riding 100 miles a day near-impossible in the summer heat. In fact, he found that rain was a welcome relief – a cold comfort for one who spent most of his day outside and sought out streams to dive into for a brief respite from the dust and sun.

Nicholson began to suffer badly. The road system surrounding Melbourne was devoid of interest and, crucially, of cycling companions. Nicholson bemoaned his lonely task and the utter absence of other riders with whom he could share his daily burden. This was a man used to riding in a peloton of riders and who now spent the majority of each day alone.

It wasn't just company that other riders would have brought Nicholson. They would also have been able to protect him from the wind and, without that protection from other riders, the open nature of the surrounding landscape meant that headwinds took their toll as Nicholson struggled up and down the Point Nepean road.

Nicholson's struggles were perhaps compounded by the fact that he had done no special training prior to taking on this ride. He had spent the months prior to the record riding track meets where explosive power is almost always required in preference to serious endurance and, as a racer, he would have been used to riding consistently at a fast pace. Perhaps this training and racing pedigree prevented him from taking things easy out on the road. He was reported to have been riding at a daily average of 17 miles per hour, while Humbles' figure had been lower, in the region of 16. A 17-miles-per-hour century ride is quite an achievement for a solo cyclist, who by definition heads out alone without the protection of cyclists to offer him or her shelter from the wind.

Nicholson quickly found that a night's rest was not enough to shake off the rigours of the day. This was compounded by the fact that his rest periods were often curtailed by the demands of his sponsors. Malvern Star required him to represent it at numerous public functions where he would give a presentation concerning his ride along with a demonstration of riding upon static rollers. He was paraded as a star exhibit at carnivals, bicycle club events and even rode all the way to Sydney in order to lead a procession of cyclists. It's clear that while Nicholson enjoyed the support of a professional team on the road, he was also somewhat hindered by the subsequent responsibilities when he ought to have been resting. In an early interview he noted that after 25 miles of riding he began to suffer 'a terrible weakness' that often forced him to stop or walk the bike for short periods. Nicholson clearly managed to ride through this weakness as the year went on, as it was never mentioned again.

Despite all his troubles, Nicholson continued to ride, and ride strongly. His constant presence on the roads around Melbourne and his semi-celebrity status made him a highly recognisable figure. Nicholson subsequently gained a few fans who turned out daily to watch him pedal by and he enjoyed a lot of support from the local population, who would supply him with food and drink to sustain him through his day. One of his most notable fans was an old lady in Carrum who, despite being confined to a bath chair, managed to wheel it daily to her front porch in order to offer Nicholson a cheery wave.

This support must have bolstered the young Nicholson, who began to make good progress through the Australian summer. By 18 March 1933 he had ridden 8,854 miles; an average of 115 miles per day and well ahead of Humbles' total at this point.

The autumn weather of April spurred Nicholson on to a total of 14,007 miles, maintaining his average of 115 to 116 miles per day. But then winter arrived and began to have an adverse effect upon Nicholson. The rider who had suffered so much from the heat in January now suffered badly from the cold and from crashes upon the wet and icy roads. A kind donation of cough medicine for a bout of influenza had the opposite effect when drowsiness caused him to fall asleep while awheel and he only narrowly avoided a serious crash. Even so, his average daily mileage was up slightly, to 118, and still well ahead of his desired figure of 110.

In August, Perth's *Daily News* reported that Nicholson was well on track to take the record from Humbles. His cumulative mileage to the end of the month was 28,712 and he had a real chance of achieving 'what will be the greatest cycling endurance test the world has known.' The paper went on to report that Nicholson had 'retained his weight in a wonderful manner', losing only 6½ pounds during the ride, having started out at a svelte 10 stone 12 pounds. His bike had remained mostly intact, with his drivetrain and gears requiring replacement at just under 22,000 miles midway through the year. Cyclo took great pleasure in advertising this fact, which provided them with excellent marketing capital.

On the morning of 30 October 1933 Nicholson set out towards Sorrento and returned to Bruce Small's shop in Elizabeth Street as the new world mileage record holder. Hubert Opperman turned up to meet him and Bruce Small had erected a paper banner for him to ride through. The inscription upon it read:

Australian Cyclist Ossie Nicholson Smashes Englishman Humbles Worlds 12 Month Record.

Nicholson was presented with a sash and victory cup by Ralph Small, brother of Bruce and partner in the bicycle shop. His mileage verification adjudicators were also present. Like the English riders before him, Nicholson's mileages were verified by signatories upon a route card. Nicholson's rides had been overseen by a well-known Australian cyclist G.R. Broadbent and a cycling official named H. Dungey, who was the secretary of the League of Victorian Wheelmen. These two had ensured that Nicholson's cyclometer readings tallied with the signature cards that had been signed and witnessed at every town he passed through.

Having completed his checking card formalities, Nicholson announced that his ride would continue. He was clearly determined to put the record beyond reach and intended to ride at least a century a day for the rest of the year. With the worst of the Australian winter behind him he could look forward to the onset of spring weather, which would have further improved his morale. He had sixty-two days left of 1933 to pile up as many miles as he could and in which to increase his tally of consecutive centuries, which stood at 302 on the day of the year record.

Things went well until 12 December when Nicholson was hospitalised after colliding with a car. It looked like his record would stop, yet Nicholson apparently discharged himself and went back to riding. If, after that, anything else were needed to underline Nicholson's determination to put the record beyond all reach, the last day of 1933 did so. 1933 was not a leap year and it had been suggested that Nicholson's consecutive-centuries record could be taken by someone riding a century every day in 1936. Nicholson was having none of that and so, on 31 December 1933, rode out to Bendigo in the early hours and returned to Melbourne some 250 miles later, recording a double century to push his year-end total to 366 centuries.

Nicholson's year ended with a final tally of 43,996 miles as he rode into Mordialloc, a suburb of Melbourne, and was greeted by a huge crowd of 20,000 well-wishers who had gathered to see him end his ride. Yet again a paper banner was erected for him to ride through, this time bearing the flags of Great Britain and Australia, along with the statistics of his year's ride and a welcome message.

Nicholson finished his ride at night and the scene was lit with thousands of arc lights to aid those with movie cameras who'd come to record the momentous occasion. The crowds were packed so tight that a team of police had to force a passage through them to get Nicholson to the podium for his presentation. The police resorted to carrying him shoulder high as the crowds continued to push forward. Speeches were given and Nicholson was presented with a number of gifts, trophies and bouquets. He then made a speech paying tribute to his sponsors and trainer, but also recognising the contribution made by those at the roadside who had willed him along when the riding had become hard. Apparently his modesty shone through and the crowds kept him late into the night, keen to meet and greet a popular, yet unassuming, hero. His rival Hubert Opperman was absent from the ceremony, apparently beset with flu.

After the celebrations Nicholson was examined by a doctor and deemed to be the perfect picture of athletic health, his vital signs consistent with those of a perfectly trained athlete. He was advised to taper down with short rides of 30 miles a day for the next couple of months.

Nicholson had done it. He had the record and a total of 366 centuries in a single year. He'd achieved huge prominence within the Malvern Star team and delivered the international recognition and exposure that his sponsors and Bruce Small wanted. Apparently his own personal rewards were meagre. There was no doubt in his celebrity status within the cycling community, but the financial reward was a silver cup from Cyclo, a small cheque and gold wristwatch from Dunlop, and a continuing contract with Malvern Star.

He continued to race into 1934 but never quite managed to retain the limelight that his record year had achieved. His race results dropped off and his career and fame began to dip. In contrast, his rival Opperman travelled to Britain, where he smashed the Land's End to John o'Groats record and went on to set a number of other highly prestigious records, including a 461.75-mile 24-hour ride.

But Nicholson was not finished. The tenacious young Australian would return with another attempt at the year record, inspired by a most unlikely rival – a one-armed, vegetarian Yorkshireman.

WALTER GREAVES –
THE ONE-ARMED COMMUNIST

There is one man whose character, without doubt, best underlines the ethos of the cycling mileage year record. A man who overcame adversity on a daily basis before he'd even swung a leg over a bicycle frame. A man whose eclectic background shaped his social and political views firmly against the establishment and instilled within him a heartfelt determination to follow his own cause, no matter what obstacles might lie in his way. This man was Walter Greaves, a tough, outspoken and slightly eccentric Yorkshireman who, in 1936, grabbed the cycling establishment by the lapel and shook it hard.

Greaves decided that the cycling mileage world record was going to return to the UK, and that he was the man who would bring it back. This decision was taken despite a missing left arm and despite the fact that Greaves was currently only riding as an amateur. He had no professional support to back his attempt and only a mild pedigree for eating up the miles. However, it is clear from his background that he was a man unlikely to allow barriers to curtail his ambition.

Walter Greaves was one of seven children born to Albert and Martha Greaves on 30 March 1907, sharing a small Bradford house with his siblings Doris, Winnie, Tommy, Albert, Betty and Gladys. The eldest child, Walter was quickly swept up into the alternative world of the travelling salesman. His grandfather, also named Walter, was a renowned herbalist who claimed to be one of the most successful in the country, offering cures for cancer, epilepsy, nervous exhaustion, lost manhood, indigestion, dyspepsia and consumption, amongst others. He founded the Yorkshire Strong Men's Herbal Remedy Company and toured the country selling his tonics, which he backed up with his own feats of strength. Greaves senior was often pitching his wares to communities of miners or textile workers and as such it was critical that he could back up his potions' claims via his own abilities. One of his feats was to leap over a blacksmith's anvil while carrying a second one in his arms, after which he would immediately proclaim that this ability was down to the ingestion of his tonic.

Albert Greaves followed in his father's footsteps and acted as lead salesman for the tonics, working in tandem with his father's feats of strength. Albert had inherited the Greaves physique and an element of his father's banter, and continued the wild claims as to the effectiveness of the Yorkshire Strong Men's Herbal Remedy. As they toured the factory communities of the heavily industrialised north, Albert was affected by the inequality of the wealth distribution and became very grateful for his independence and lack of reliance upon the factory bosses. There was a strong flame of socialism within the family, which Albert made no secret of and would weave into his travelling sales pitch.

Albert proved to be a huge influence on his eldest son, taking him out on the road as soon as he was old enough to aid him in scratching out a living from the sales of the mythical tonic. As time moved on this task became harder – education improved and the public wised up to the claims of 'miracle' tonics. Albert found it harder and harder to practise his quackery, which may have led to his habit of excessive drinking, although, given the depression sweeping through the country in the later 1920s, there may have been many other factors.

Looking at this upbringing, it is clear to see how the character of Walter Greaves junior was formed. A heavy drinking father pushed him into teetotalism, and he never touched a drop throughout his adult life. His family's herbalist heritage formed Walter's views on diet and health and he became a committed vegetarian, never losing the herbalist beliefs preached by his elders. His socialist views, inherited and honed by his travels, saw Walter enrol in the British Communist Party in his twenties and he became no stranger to public debate as he sought to recruit others into the fold.

The bedstone of Walter's determination, however, appears to have come from an indelible mark Albert left upon his son. Walter had the lower portion of his left arm amputated after an accident at the age of fourteen and, although we will never know for sure, it seems that Albert may have been responsible for this loss. Over the years a number of versions of the accident have been told: an arm dangled out of a speeding train window, an incident involving a door and an inebriated father, a collision with a speeding tram. It appears that the most likely cause was Albert's habit of

drinking excessively and then driving home. The car would travel errati-
cally at speed and Walter could never quite feel safe stuck in the passenger
seat. Walter's son Joe believes that his father had a habit of travelling standing on the running boards of the car so that he could jump free were Albert
to crash the car. Joe goes on to tell:

'I remember Dad telling us that his dad was driving his Model T Ford in
a drunken state. Dad was resting his arm on the window sill (the window
was open), Grandad lost control on a corner and crashed into a lamp post.
In the crash the car roof, which was made of canvas over a collapsible
scissor-type metal frame, collapsed crushing and trapping Dad's arm.
He was taken to hospital but they were unable to save the arm and it had
to be amputated.'

Walter was patched up and sent back to school missing a large portion
of his left arm. This caused him immediate grief as before the accident
he'd won a fight against one of his schoolmates. The aggrieved boy saw
his opportunity and meted out a sound thrashing to the disadvantaged
Greaves on his return to school. A weak character may have sought to
avoid conflict from that point on and hide within his disability. Walter saw
it differently. This and other incidents formed a will within the young
Greaves to fight back regardless of his disadvantages. He did not need
the help of others to survive and was determined to forge his way in the
world independently, unafraid to make plain his own personal views.

This forthrightness, his views and his disability were to cause Greaves
considerable disadvantage. The 1930s job market was slow and even
slower for a belligerent one-armed communist vegetarian. Greaves had
left school and been unable to secure an apprenticeship, but had achieved
a national certificate in engineering from the Bradford Technical College.
The qualification did him no good as his disability was seen as a deal-
breaker for a career in a metal shop or other engineering discipline.
Greaves struggled to earn money throughout the depression of the 1920s
and 1930s and stints as a vacuum salesman and as a part-time mechanic
provided much-needed coinage.

Like many men at that time Greaves owned a bicycle and used it as his
primary means of transport in search of work and leisure. Every cyclist
reading this will empathise with the fact that Greaves yearned for a better
and faster machine. Cycling clubs were extremely popular and active at
this time and the time trialling scene was well supported, with decent
prizes on offer for those able to win. Greaves' huge break came with the

placing of a bet on a horse after a tip had been passed to him by Joe Partington of the Yorkshire Walking Club. Apparently 'Dorrigen' came in at odds of 25/1 at Lincoln. Greaves had borrowed 2 shillings from a friend and come away with a grand total of 50 shillings. This was used as a deposit upon his first decent bicycle, a 20-inch Sun 'Wasp'.

It also led Walter to his first cycling club run, which was to Ribblehead with the West Bradford Cycling Club, a distance of 110 miles. Greaves was unsure at first but found himself untroubled by the mileage and equally untroubled by the village sign sprints and summit chases. He sat near the front of the group and listened intently to talk of an upcoming time trial. He decided to enter, his confidence clearly bolstered by his ability to hold his own in this group, and duly put in a creditable time of 1 hour 12 minutes for the 25 miles.

It was within this club that Greaves learnt his cycling craft, but he caused his fellow members discomfort with his forthright political and vegetarian views, both of which were extremely unpopular in 1930s Britain. Most people were desperate to keep the jobs they had and extremely cautious of rocking the establishment boat with talk of improving the lot of the workers. Others took umbrage at Greaves' proclamation that meat was simply 'second-hand vegetables' as he stood munching a cabbage and looking disdainfully at their ham sandwiches.

Greaves appeared to be gainfully employed during the period of 1931 to 1934, putting in many hours of overtime but equally keeping up his attendance at cycling time trials and club runs. He improved both his fitness and his equipment and recorded a decent 194 miles in a 12-hour time trial. However, things took a turn for the worse in 1935 after Greaves lost his job and was forced back on to the dole. A staccato period of short work-placements and part-time jobs followed. Greaves was finding it hard to hold down a full-time job, more than likely down to his bolshie nature – Greaves apparently lost one job after 'gesticulating' at a Rolls Royce that had passed him while he was training. The owner of the car was also the owner of the engineering works that employed him. A few days later Greaves was sacked for an apparent stores error. Probably no coincidence.

Greaves had also parted company with the West Bradford Cycling Club, becoming instead a member of the Vegetarian Cycling and Athletic Club. His cycling ambitions remained unabated and in 1935 he took part in his first 24-hour time trial, an incredibly demanding event. Unbeknown to Greaves, a heated committee meeting had almost prevented him entering, as there was a huge degree of nervousness concerning the safety of the one-armed cyclist during the event. The committee eventually acquiesced in the name of fair play. Greaves went on to finish with 327.5 miles in the bag despite a stomach upset along the way.

It was clear to his fellow club members that Greaves had some pedigree. In a previous club he had been asked his views on the year record and came back with the immediate retort that he saw himself as capable of beating it. While fixing a car for fellow VC&AC member Norie Ward, the question came up again. Greaves had no full-time job, more spare time than others and also a clear will to prove himself against the more able-bodied.

'How many miles could you do Walter?' Ward asked.

'47,000' was the answer. The seed had been sown.

Coincidently, Ward was working for another high-achieving cyclist, T.P. Fox, who had set his sights on the Land's End to John o'Groats record. Fox was running a publicity agency and the two men saw the commercial possibilities that could arise from two record attempts occurring simultaneously. They met with Greaves and a plan was formed to seek sponsorship and a salary for the three men to make their attempts: Greaves and Fox riding the bikes, Ward as the higher-paid manager. Greaves started training while Fox and Ward set out on a long and difficult path in search of sponsorship.

Many letters were sent to cycling manufacturers and companies. Almost all were returned in the negative, and some were not returned at all, as Ward and Fox were not the only people seeking support. Possibly inspired by Arthur Humbles, a large number of unemployed riders were seeking similar sponsorship, with one dealer receiving in excess of six applications a week. A visit to the London Cycle Show to seek sponsors proved fruitless and it looked like Greaves' attempt was doomed to failure before he'd even started. However, a chance meeting with Alec Shuttleworth, a cycle dealer and inventor of the TriVelox gear – a derailleur-based bicycle gearing system – offered a glimmer of hope. Shuttleworth owned a cycle shop in Keighley and suggested that the trio contact Coventry Bicycles Limited, which manufactured his gear system. Ward dashed off a letter and Greaves waited in hopeful expectation of a reply.

The days passed and Greaves became frustrated with the lack of communication, especially given that the start of the new year was fast approaching. On 23 December 1935 Greaves took matters into his own hand, mounted his bicycle and set off for Coventry himself, for some reason choosing to ride overnight. He pointed himself south at 10 p.m. and set off into a snow storm that had been brought in on a north wind. It took him six hours to cover the 40 miles to Sheffield, fighting through the snow and ice with only one hand on the handlebars. Many more hours of riding and a couple of lifts from sympathetic motorists saw him arrive, somewhat bedraggled, in Coventry the next day. Greaves' first stop was a tailor's shop, where he pleaded with the owner to fix a hole in his plus four trousers that had been burnt on a heater in a cafe stop.

Finally Greaves arrived at the offices of Coventry Bicycles and sought an audience with Mr Downes. Greaves was clutching a drawing of a bicycle he had designed himself that he'd hoped Coventry would manufacture for his ride. This crucially included a twist-grip gear shifter to make it easier for a one-armed rider to change gear without having to move his hand from the bars. Downes brushed the drawing aside, but told Greaves that Coventry was going to sponsor his ride and that a letter was already in the post. However, he'd have to do it upon one of its standard bicycles.

Greaves decamped to a cafe and prepared himself for the long ride home, which was probably equally as epic as the ride down as weather conditions had not improved. On visiting the offices of Ward and Fox he was greeted with a chorus of 'Where have you been?' The letter had arrived, postmarked 4.30 p.m., 24 December 1935.

Greaves' ride had clearly sealed the deal; Downes had not posted the letter until Greaves had left his offices. The pluck of the wily Yorkshireman in dealing with the distance and inclement weather had convinced Downes that in Greaves he had a real contender. And Greaves had the sponsor he needed.

Coventry Bicycles' models were not ideal. Its heavy machines were a far cry from the racing bike Greaves desired. Greaves was to be provided with a model from its Three Spires range, which he could adapt to his particular needs, but progress stagnated as the promised machine failed to arrive. The planned start date was pushed back to 6 January 1936 and Greaves waved goodbye to his leap-year advantage. When the machine finally arrived a flurry of activity saw Greaves adding a specially adapted single handlebar with a twist-grip gear shifter mechanism and a single brake lever that would allow him to operate both cantilever brakes simultaneously. The gears were tested on the bench and appeared to work as intended, but there was still work needed on the brakes. The real test would have to be when Greaves set off as, with all of the other modifications that needed to be made, time was running out for proper road testing.

Greaves was still training in the intervening period, riding on his own machine in early January. Tragically, these miles were lost to his record attempt as his sponsor had advised *Cycling* that his official start was to be 6 January. The magazine's editor, H.H. England, refused to recognise the attempt if it crossed calendar years and rigidly enforced the advertised start date.

Greaves was not alone in his ambitions. Another rider, Bob Walsh, had set off from Manchester on New Year's Day 1936 and ridden over 600 miles before 6 January. This was despite the tragic death of his daughter three days into the attempt. He'd ridden well over 100 miles each day, leaving Greaves with a deficit of 610.3 miles before he had even begun.

Unfortunately for Walsh, he suffered a serious accident a short while later, being hit by a lorry while out riding. While terribly unfortunate for the poor man – who had already suffered bereavement – this should have been a mild blessing for Greaves and possibly given him a small boost to his morale, as he was the now sole British representative for the record in 1936.

An Australian named Alexander Crawford had also set out to take the record. He'd started from Darwin in August the previous year and ridden through Alice Springs, Perth, Adelaide and Melbourne. His attempt clearly ignored the strict convention that the record was to be ridden in a single calendar year and would thus likely have been dismissed by the British press. Crawford was mentioned in the Australian press in June 1936 but no further record of his ride or mileage achieved exists. He presumably abandoned before finishing.

Like many of his British counterparts, Greaves had a relatively low-key start to his riding when he set off from Bradford Town Hall on Monday 6 January 1936, although, given that the start was on a working day and that Greaves' plans had suffered setbacks and were thus probably not well-advertised, it is not surprising. The lord mayor read a speech and gave Greaves a letter to be delivered to the lord mayor of York. Greaves was then waved off by the mayor and his alderman, and one hopes that Ward and Fox were also present to see him off.

Greaves' route for the day saw him ride to Bradford, Leeds, Seacroft, Tadcaster and then York, where the letter was delivered to the mayor in the presence of Greaves' sponsors and a few speeches were given. This all appeared to go to plan and Greaves had his checking card signed at a post office in York. He then returned via Easingwold, giving him a starting mileage of 115 miles for the day. Greaves continued to ride around the north of the country for three days, eventually ending up in Newcastle.

The weather now turned for the worse and Greaves found himself engaged in a daily battle against the elements in order to hit his own personal target of 130 miles per day. On his fourth day he decided to head south, with the intention of going a lot further than the previous days' average of 115 miles, but with the weather deteriorating, Greaves found himself riding into a steadily increasing headwind that became a full-on gale as he arrived in Wetherby. As it was raining, Greaves was forced to wear a cape, which acted as a sail and caused him no end of trouble. But he still had hours to spare before the day was over and so the enterprising Greaves simply turned around and headed north with the gale on his back. Dodging falling haystacks and branches blown into the road, he sped north and, in his own words, 'sailed merrily into Thirsk at speeds close to 40 miles per hour.' Greaves made light of the fact that he'd had to steer his bike at speed through the debris of a wooden hut that had been blown into the road and survived gusts that had been recorded at 100 miles per hour that day.

Bedding down in a cafe, Greaves reviewed a week of sleepless nights and less than ideal mileages. To top things off, his finances were already suffering. His sponsors had promised a weekly wage of £3 to cover his expenses, but the payments were falling short.

A few days later he had committed to a guest appearance in London at a dinner hosted by the Vegetarian Cycling and Athletic Club and had a long ride ahead of him to get there. The weather forced Greaves to use the train for part of his journey, before riding into London from Newark, via Grantham and an overnight stay. The dinner proved to be a blessing in disguise for Greaves, as his agent Fox laid out the hardships Greaves was suffering and asked the room full of athletes for support. Many sympathised and Greaves was offered free bed and lodgings whenever he ventured close to their homes.

However, London was not all roses for Greaves, who was knocked off his bike by a bus. He remained unfazed and remarked to the journalist A.W. Brumell that he'd enjoyed riding in the capital as the traffic provided a welcome contrast to the monotony of the countryside. How times have changed!

Bradford called Greaves north once more, where his sponsors had arranged for him to cross the 1,000-mile marker in the presence of the mayor.

Greaves then decided to continue north up the A1 for a change of scenery. He rode as far as Catterick Bridge, but was soon to regret his decision as the poorly surfaced road was heavily used by lorries with little tolerance for cyclists. Greaves was continually forced into the gutter by impatient drivers and so retreated south to continue his riding in the Leeds and Bradford area.

By 17 January Greaves had notched up approximately 1,389 miles, putting him some 629 miles behind Nicholson's record pace of 1933. The pressure was already building and, to make matters worse, the weather turned again, with three inches of snow appearing on the ground overnight. Greaves had a lucky escape in Leeds when, after successfully negotiating a myriad of frozen tram tracks, he finally came to grief and fell badly across a set of tracks, his vision temporarily restricted by the steam emitted from a steam wagon. As he desperately fought to get himself and his bike off the tracks a tram approached. The driver must have looked on in horror and hit the brakes hard as his engine loomed towards the stranded Greaves, finally coming to a halt with the fender touching the prone bicycle.

This particular crash had been part of a ride that was being filmed for the Pathé newsreel. The crew were waiting at Beverley, where Greaves put on a great show for the camera by falling again, into snow. His pain continued on the icy roads with many more falls on his journey home. Greaves responded by resolving to ride faster in order to avoid the numerous spills that occurred when one rode gingerly over the ice. He reckoned that momentum reduced the frequency of these crashes and that the price of less-frequent but harder crashes was worth paying.

Greaves noted that these crashes taught him a sage lesson: when falling it was important to get clear from the bike as the most damage was done when the rider fell upon its awkward metal shape. His tumbles must also have reminded him and his sponsors of the plight of poor Bob Walsh as it was decided that Greaves would ride over to Manchester and pay him a visit in hospital as a mark of solidarity. This plan was almost thwarted by an over-zealous nurse who initially refused the wet, tramp-like cyclist entry to the ward. Greaves was eventually granted admittance and spent some time with Ward who was in a sorry state due to his injuries. The day ended with a trip home through the now-frozen snow and a hard-won 115 miles punctuated by further crashes.

There was no let-up in the weather during January 1936, yet Greaves continued regardless and began to exceed his 130-mile-per-day target on a number of occasions. His tribulations began to lessen and became almost surreal on occasion. Accepting the kind offer of a bed for the night from a cyclist who'd been following him in the news, Greaves arrived to find a young lad named Bill Woods who lived in a tiny house and had not really thought through the sleeping arrangements. The two men were forced to share a single bed and subsequently became lifelong friends – no wonder after such a close encounter.

Most of Greaves' January cycling had been spent in the Leeds and Bradford area, but as the weather began to improve in February his rides took him further afield and his daily mileages began to climb accordingly. Greaves was starting to get into his stride and began to appreciate the real issues facing one determined to take on such a record. He resolved to ride at a steady pace and simply maximise his riding hours. Stops were kept to an absolute minimum, which could cause a tinge of frustration when he'd pull into a cafe for food. Often the owners were aware of his attempt and welcomed the opportunity to have a genial chat and spend time in his company. Greaves had the opposite view; his objective was to get fed as quickly as possible and be on his way, although all encouragement was gratefully received.

Greaves' vegetarian diet and pickiness were also causing issue. He was not a fan of eggs or cheese and as a result drank huge amounts of milk to take on the protein he required. This was carried in a large feeding bottle attached to his bike, nicknamed his 'cow' by the journalist A.W. Brumell. Greaves averaged five pints of milk each day, until he drank some bought near Brighton that had come from cows fed on fish meal. The fishy aftertaste added to his pickiness and he reduced his milk intake to a mere three pints a day, making the rest of his liquid intake up in ginger beer. This left him somewhat lacking in protein, and he started to suffer from depression, which was thought to be due to this deficit.

In order to topple Nicholson, Greaves had to average over 121 miles per day. After fifty-five days of riding he'd totalled 6,625 miles giving him an average of 120.5 miles, but he still had a deficit of over 600 miles due to his late start. Greaves could have relocated to flatter parts of the country to replicate the conditions under which Nicholson had ridden his mileage, but this sturdy Yorkshireman was made of strong stuff. He'd proclaimed to a Yorkshire Cycling Federation dinner that he saw part of his role as being to show those Londoners that there were 'some *riders* in the

Yorkshire area.' He was clearly determined to ride his share of hills over the course of the record and relocated to Hereford in early March 1936 in order to travel around Wales, a portion of the country where flat roads last only momentarily. It was reported that he rode his 8,000th mile in the Brecon area on 9 March and was now in front of Nicholson.

Further barriers were raised in front of Greaves as he broke his handlebars – repeatedly – losing half a day on one occasion while waiting for them to be repaired at a cycle dealer. His one-armed riding and braking requirements were putting extra strain upon this area of the bike.

Consider also that Greaves' lack of a left forearm would have magnified the difficulty of roadside repairs, specifically punctures, which required the removal and subsequent replacement of the wheel and tyre. Greaves countered this by frequently changing his tyres between rides in order to ensure that they never became overly worn and susceptible to punctures.

With the first three months of the year behind him, Greaves had over 10,000 miles on the clock and cranked up his daily target in earnest, to 135 miles. April passed without major incident and as the end of May approached Greaves had virtually doubled his tally – in two-thirds of the time. He'd apparently suffered more fatigue than he had anticipated during this period and, after discussions with vegetarian colleagues decided to up his milk intake again, to an astonishing gallon a day. This worked immediately and he began to ride further and harder, visiting Chester, Blackpool, Lancaster, Chorley and Birkenhead, with many days exceeding 160 miles. In June Greaves hit his longest day for the year with a 220-mile ride from Chester to Croydon, after which he headed west to Bristol for a lap of honour at a local cycling event. By the middle of the month he was some 2,000 miles up on schedule. His form continued into July as he ground out a daily average of 132 miles.

Things were looking good for Greaves. His profile was now significantly raised, and he was picking up some famous signatories on his mileage cards. Arthur Humbles, who clearly understood just what Greaves was going through, signed a card, as did England football star Dixie Dean, on a meeting at the Mersey tunnel. *The Bicycle* magazine reported Greaves as being 'tanned and weather beaten, a picture of fitness.' He had discarded long johns in favour of shorts and the magazine celebrated his progress to date as:

A monumental example of the triumph of courage and determination over great obstacles.

Greaves told the magazine that he was now enjoying the adventure immensely and was confident of beating Nicholson's mileage by October. Unbeknown to him, things were soon to take a turn for the worse.

In late July Greaves was following a lorry that swerved to avoid a pole in the road. Greaves didn't manage to avoid this pole and hit it hard, injuring his right leg. He continued to ride on the damaged leg, possibly causing an abscess which got worse and worse until it required a surgical procedure to remove it. The impact of the accident and operation kept Greaves off the bike for a fortnight, during which time he effectively bled 2,000 miles of riding. Once again the record appeared to be slipping away from his grasp, but once more Greaves proved he was no ordinary man and, on 18 August 1936, he threw leg over bike once again and recommenced his attempt with a 101-mile ride.

Greaves rode to *Cycling*'s offices in London a few days later, presumably to have his cyclometer inspected, and reported to the assembled journalists that while he was feeling an element of stiffness within his leg, he was confident that his 130-mile days would shortly resume. He was good to his word, clocking a total of 29,420 miles by the end of August. But with four months remaining and some 20,000 miles still to ride, Greaves had his work cut out. He reacted accordingly by increasing his riding, waking at 5 a.m. in order to get out on the road early and attempting to ride over 150 miles most days.

Things were clearly back in order on 9 September when Greaves was met by a large crowd in Barnsley and demonstrated his fitness by leading a throng of club riders on an ascent of a steep local climb. Greaves also indirectly led some minors astray as a magazine reported that a ten-year-old Irish lad, clearly inspired by the mile-eater's endeavours, had extended a 10-mile cycle to school by some 42 miles in an attempt to ride 105 miles to Belfast. Fortunately he was stopped in his tracks after seven hours and escorted home.

As October approached the press realised that Greaves' mileage was coming close to that of the previous British record holder Arthur Humbles. Greaves had by now relocated to the house of a cycle dealer, Jack Johnson, and the flatter roads of Lincolnshire. His mileage average had improved significantly. He averaged some 180 miles per day over a nineteen-day period and it was anticipated that he would take the record from Humbles on 19 October. He didn't need that long – on 8 October 1936 Greaves rode out from Lincoln to Birmingham, where he was interviewed by *Cycling* magazine before turning back towards Lincoln and taking the British record just north of Newark. A crowd of Lincolnshire cyclists was waiting to see him ride his 36,008th mile and provided an escort for the remaining 16 miles into Lincoln, where he was welcomed by the mayor at 11 p.m. A photo shows a clearly fatigued Greaves weighed down by a huge wreath of flowers with the smiling, moustached mayor in the background.

Greaves now had the British record, but still needed another 7,973 miles to take the world record from Nicholson. He had been riding over 160 miles per day for five weeks in an effort to catch up and now, with eighty-four days remaining, only needed to ride an average of 95 miles a day. Greaves was seriously back on track.

As winter began to encroach once more, Greaves remained in the Lincoln and London areas but reduced his daily average, probably to conserve himself and ensure that the record really would be taken. His taking of Humbles' record had brought new sponsorship requirements, including a week spent in residence at the Olympia Bicycle and Motorcycle Show, where Greaves was also introduced to His Royal Highness the Duke of Kent who congratulated him on his riding to date. One wonders at the mixed emotions felt by this fervently communist rider on being introduced to royalty, although records show that he held his tongue and even complimented the Duke on his apparent knowledge of bicycles.

The company Three Spires gathered previous record holders Planes and Humbles for a staged meeting with Greaves at the show. Unbeknown to the three riders, a fourth player in the year-mileage story was also in the building. The Frenchman René Menzies was up against the legendary Sid Ferris on an exhibition rollers match. Was this the point at which Menzies' interest in the year record was piqued?

By 8 November, Greaves had gone over the 40,000-mile marker and, with fewer than 4,000 miles to go, his name began to crop up as guest of honour at a number of end-of-year events. The general public and press were certain that Greaves was going to take the record. In an interesting interview with one magazine he gave further details of his vegetarian diet, including the fact that his reduced income had restricted his ability to 'explore the infinite number of vegetarian dishes that are available'. Greaves had tried many food combinations in order to sustain himself and come across many complications. At one point he was eating up to 2 pounds of dates a day, but found that these gave him blind boils, so gave them up. He eventually boiled his requirements down to a simple daily formula:

8 pints of warm milk
21 pounds of brown bread
¾ of a pound of butter
21 pounds of tomatoes
A little lettuce
Brazil nuts
Yeast extract

Despite only needing an average of 75 miles per day, Greaves continued to ride hard and, on Sunday 13 December 1936, despite missing twenty days of riding, he passed Nicholson's 1933 record of 43,996 miles. As was now tradition, a huge club run of cyclists was arranged to see Greaves pass this mileage at Hyde Park Corner in London. Marcel Planes and Arthur Humbles were invited to cheer Greaves over the line, and a detachment of Household Cavalry Guards was present, marching along the frost-bound roads with the 3,000 cyclists who'd turned out to celebrate the feat. Greaves completed his 44,000th mile at Speakers' Corner, requiring a team of police to clear a way through the cheering crowd and, after a few short speeches and photographs, he was whisked off to a reception at the Grosvenor Hotel.

A telegram also arrived from Nicholson in Australia to *Cycling* magazine:

Greaves c/o *Cycling*, London, congratulations record, Hope regain next year, Nicholson.

A reporter noted that the often truculent Greaves was not easy to interview, but had passed on the odd interesting fact, such as that he had gained 3 pounds in weight throughout his ride. Perhaps this was because, as Greaves enigmatically stated, foggy weather made him hungry. Another story tells of the teetotal Greaves being offered some champagne and meat – or 'proper food', as the benefactor presented them. Greaves retorted that, 'When I want to poison myself, I will do it properly with arsenic.'

Greaves was now front-page news, with the 15 December cover of *The Bicycle* magazine dedicated to his taking of the record, along with a full-page picture of him taken from the right and showing his good arm grasping his adapted bars of his Coventry Three Spires bicycle. He had resolved to continue riding for the remaining eighteen days of the year, setting himself a target of an additional 2,200 miles and a new total for future aspirants.

Greaves continued to ride as promised, laying plans for a final reception in Bradford. His PR team went into overdrive and informed the cycling and local press that his final ride of the year would take in Tadcaster, York, Leeds and then finish in Bradford town square. Yet again thousands of cyclists turned out to welcome their one-armed hero home. At ten minutes to midnight on Thursday 31 December 1936, Walter Greaves rode into the town square, having ridden 113 miles after a late start caused by attendance at a Bradford Elite dinner the previous evening. In front of a large crowd of well-wishers, he was met on the steps of the town hall by his sponsors and by the lord mayor, George Carter. Each presented him with a silver cup to commemorate the record, which Walter's son Joe still proudly displays upon his mantelpiece. The largest bears the following inscription:

> Presented to Walter W. Greaves by the directors of Coventry Bicycles Ltd manufacturers of Three Spires Cycles. In recognition of his wonderful achievement in bringing back to England the world's twelve months cycle endurance record. December 1936.

Greaves was also handed three cheques from his sponsors, totalling £150 – a decent chunk of money but meagre pickings for an entire year's work, given the exposure and coverage this tough, resourceful and unbowed rider had generated for them over the year. Greaves had represented his sponsors at a number of events, the largest of which was the Earls Court cycle show, and Coventry Bicycles had arranged a number of events, mainly in the south of England, where it had paraded Greaves and invited cyclists along to meet its record-breaker.

In 1937 Greaves became the second year-mileage rider to have his name and story inscribed within *The Golden Book of Cycling* and he managed to secure a position with Coventry Bicycles and the hand in marriage of his new wife, Beatrice Irene, or Rene for short. Apparently the two left the church under an arch of bicycle wheels and headed off to a honeymoon in Brighton, a luxury that Greaves would not have been able to afford prior to his record year.

Greaves made loose plans to attempt other records and mooted the possibility of an attempt at the Land's End to John o'Groats time, but these never came to fruition and his celebrity capital began to fade. Within a year his contract with Coventry Bicycles was at an end and Greaves was forced to look elsewhere for work. His new-found experience in the cycle trade kept him thinking about how he could improve the bicycle and, in particular, make it easier for riders to climb hills. He began to experiment with designs for shorter-wheelbase frames and designed a new gearing system that he'd planned to patent.

After his year-ride, Greaves had been banned from the amateur racing scene as having managed to attract sponsorship, he was deemed a profess-ional rider in the eyes of the Road Time Trials Association. He success-fully appealed against this ban and returned to racing. According to Aled Owen, a writer who has spent many years tracing Greaves' story:

'In late 1940 he appealed to the National Committee of Road Time Trials Association to be reinstated. In January 1941 he became the first to be re-admitted to the ranks of amateurs. It was generally accepted that Greaves had found himself forced to turn professional because of particularly hard times and the powers that be relented.'

Ever the antagonist, Greaves now leapt into the battle led by the British League of Racing Cyclists to re-establish road racing upon the British roads. The National Cyclists' Union had banned such racing in 1893, as it was afraid that were races to disrupt the path of the motorist, they would lead to an outright ban upon all road cycling. This ban had forced racing underground, with time trial courses identified by cryptic codes and races often being run in the very early hours of Sunday mornings. Greaves quickly became chairman of the BLRC, or 'the League' as it was known, and at the age of thirty-nine raced in one of its biggest showcase events: the Brighton to Glasgow race, held in 1945 and run in conjunction with the Scottish Cyclists' Union. This race was pivotal in British cycling and led to the formation of the Milk Race and ultimately the Tour of Britain.

Ninety-nine riders set off from Brighton, including twelve top French riders. Greaves finished over two hours behind the winner, taking twenty-second place out of only twenty-six cyclists to finish. This was a huge achieve-ment for the handicapped cyclist who went on to form his own cycle company and launch a Greaves-branded range of bicycles that including a 'King of the Mountains' model. A 1947 catalogue describes this bicycle as:

A road racing machine embodying many of the best features of continental design, plus some of my own refinements.

The catalogue is stamped:

Walter W. Greaves, Racing cycle Maker, 145 Whetley Lane, Bradford.

Greaves continued to be active on the racing scene and continued to grow his business until tragedy struck in November 1950 and the business was burnt to the ground. It was rumoured that the fire was started by the actions of a mischievous pet monkey named 'Tinkle', owned by Greaves and his wife. They had to be woken and dragged from the premises by the fire brigade and were lucky to escape with their lives. Greaves lost everything in the fire and his marital and cycling life went into decline as he was forced back on to the dole. A brief period running a cyclists' cafe did nothing to repair the damage and Greaves later served a period in jail for theft. This in part led to his divorce from Rene in 1956, which capped off his lowest point since taking the record.

Naturally, the ever-resilient Greaves bounced back yet again. He met and married Margaret Dyson, which led to the birth of his four children and to a succession of jobs as he fought hard to support his new family. He retrained as a blacksmith and, aided by his young sons, opened a forge. His wife Margaret was a musician and this clearly stirred something in Greaves, who began to compose and perform folk songs inspired by his life in the north and the surrounding mining communities. Greaves became popular on the West Riding folk circuit with his mixture of humorous songs and monologues, branding himself the 'singing blacksmith'.

Greaves remained a vegetarian and herbalist for the remainder of his life and his son Joe tells of him climbing the hills from his house at Keighley in search of a herb (broom) to fix a kidney complaint that had been troubling him. The resulting drink Greaves created cured him of the complaint, much to the surprise and astonishment of his doctor, who had been unable to find a cure. Unfortunately Greaves succumbed to Parkinson's disease in his early seventies and began to fall into decline. He repeatedly experimented upon himself with new herbal remedies but often caused himself more harm in his search for a cure. Greaves' health declined over a long period of eight years, and he eventually passed away at the age of eighty in 1987.

His family continue to live his legacy, with his grandchildren riding as keen racing cyclists and treasuring his year record artefacts to keep his memories alive.

With the passing of Greaves cycling lost one of its most colourful and interesting characters, and the year record said goodbye to the rider who had overcome the most to push the distance to new lengths. Greaves never once blamed his disability for his misfortune; quite the opposite

– he never attempted it hide it and many photos show him displaying his stumped arm as if it were the norm. Cycling forgets how pivotal Greaves was in escalating the battle of the year record. His overcoming of the distance with a single arm set the minds of many racing: if a one-armed cyclist could do it then so could they. He was, and still is, the perfect role model for any individual attempting to overcome adversity.

1937 –
THE 'CYCLING ASHES'

The 1936 ride of Walter Greaves triggered a cycling arms race that would push the distance record way beyond the reach of the enthusiast cyclist. Greaves had overcome physical adversity, a lack of funds and poor weather to take the record away from a seasoned professional rider and bring it back to British shores. This single act served to both inspire and irk the professional cyclists. Amateur cyclists now began to imagine themselves taking on the record. In return, professional cyclists haughtily declared that they, obviously, could do better.

During the final two months of 1936, when it became clear that Greaves was to take the record, a number of other aspirants began to appear. One of these, Ossie Nicholson, had good reason to do so. Having lost his hard-earned record, he was determined to take it back. Additions to his racing palmarès since his record-breaking year had been relatively meagre and it was time for him to step back into the international spotlight.

Another seasoned rider also came forward: René Menzies, who would have been made acutely aware of Greaves at the Olympia bicycle show in 1936. Menzies had been at the show, riding in a roller competition, and his interest must have been piqued by the unorthodox one-armed cyclist on a nearby stand who was closing in on the professional record.

Menzies was an unusual candidate for the cycling year record due simply to his age. At forty-eight years old he was some twenty years older than all of the previous holders – not that that was going to deter this Frenchman, who clearly had the necessary form. Menzies was of French descendancy, born in 1889 in Caen. He apparently caught the cycling bug at the age of six and grew quickly into the sport, winning the cycling championship of Normandy every year from 1906 to 1909 and, in 1910, adding the Vélodrome d'Hiver Paris Cup to his trophy cabinet. The Vélodrome d'Hiver was the brainchild of Henri Desgrange, the man credited with the founding of the Tour de France. The venue was a focal point for track racing in Paris, with the huge crowds attending the races often jammed shoulder to shoulder. The writer Ernest Hemingway, who lived in Paris at the time, was a frequent attendee at the six-day races held upon the track, writing in *A Moveable Feast*:

> I have started many stories about bicycle racing but have never written one that is as good as the races are both on the indoor and outdoor tracks and on the road. But I will get the Vélodrome d'Hiver with the smoky light of the afternoon and the high-banked wooden track and the whirring sound the tyres made on the wood as the riders passed, the effort and the tactics as the riders climbed and plunged, each one a part of his machine.

The 1914 Great War had clearly interrupted Menzies' racing, but not his cycling as he was drafted into the French Cyclists' Corps for the duration of the war, surviving with a Croix de Guerre medal for distinguished service. The war somewhat killed his enthusiasm for cycling, but, on relocating to the United Kingdom, he began to ride again and partake in a number of races, changing his focus from the track to long-distance events. The cycling press reported him to be of 'Scottish' extraction, although his documented racing career was exclusively in the south of England.

Menzies recorded many credible performances in club 100-mile and 12-hour time trials, the most notable of which was a win in the Norwood Paragon Open 25-mile time trial with a time of 1 hour, 10 minutes and 20 seconds. This win was clearly satisfying for Menzies as he beat the Olympian Horace 'Tiny' Johnson into fourth place. Tiny had won silver medals on the track in the 1920s in the men's pursuit and kilometre sprint and then gone on to become world sprint champion in 1922. At the time of this race in 1935, Menzies was cited as a professional riding for Westerly Road Club. This professional status was most likely a result of an advertising endorsement rather than riding as a career and likely stemmed back to his early racing days in France.

Menzies also continued to race in France as a veteran, with top-five placings in the Grand Prix Paris-Dieppe Veteran race in both 1935 and 1936. Here was a man who clearly knew his way around a bicycle and clearly had the pedigree to sustain pace over long distances. At his age the avenues open to Menzies' racing ambitions were probably starting to narrow, and the year record may have appeared tempting to a man whose speed was beginning to fade.

In December 1936 Menzies announced to the cycle trade and all that would listen his intention to smash the mileage record of Walter Greaves. However, his track record and previous achievements fell on deaf ears. The cycle industry reacted cynically to the appeals of Menzies for industry support. His age clearly counted against him and many thought that the mileage record was a young man's game and that a middle-aged rider would struggle to find the endurance and riding ability to cover such exceptional mileages.

Menzies had no choice but to start unaided and prove the industry wrong. His attack upon the record of Walter Greaves began at 7 a.m. on 1 January 1937 from the offices of the National Cyclists' Union in London. Menzies rolled up garbed in full racing attire and astride a Weaver bicycle equipped with a Smith's cyclometer. He had little support or funding for the year ahead and hoped to gather some through his performances upon his bike. At the time Menzies was married with a daughter and it may have been that he relied upon his wife to bring in a wage to support the start of his year.

Meanwhile, several hundred miles away in Birmingham, a man thirty years his junior was also planning an attempt.

Bernard Bennett was born in Birmingham on 4 February 1918, to John Pugh and Lilian Bennett. Growing up, he spent his teenage years in Balsall Heath, with the family remaining resident in the area up until his eighteenth birthday. The young Bernard was clearly influenced by the reports of the mile-eaters in the cycling press and in 1936 had undertaken a number of ambitious rides of his own, including a 378-mile 'jaunt' in twenty-six hours during the month of August. At the time he had no idea that within a few short years he would become one of the greatest, yet most-forgotten, endurance cyclists that England had produced.

Details of Bennett's early years remain scant. It appears that he had some form of financial support from friends or, more likely, family, as in November 1936 he quit his job and began to train. Bennett saw cycling as the perfect way to keep fit and, like many of the riders before him, saw the potential openings for a career within the industry, were he able to make his mark.

Bennett came to the record with a sense of realism. He understood that he was a mere youth and saw his attempt in 1937 as an apprenticeship year.

He knew that he was up against a seasoned professional in Nicholson and that Menzies was a hugely experienced veteran long-distance racer. Bennett spent December 1936 steadily increasing his mileage through daily rides. His aim was to reach a state whereby he could comfortably cover 150 miles a day, allowing him to exceed 50,000 miles for the year. In the main Bennett's attempt was welcomed by the cycling press as he was initially the only British rider stepping up to the mark, although the cartoonist Lewis cruelly represented Bennett as the baby of the pack in a cartoon that mocked all three riders. Bennett was pictured upon a child's bicycle, reaching out for a bottle of gripe water prior to starting his day and then having to explain to his mother why he returned home so late. Menzies was shown in bed speaking a mixture of French and English and Nicholson was depicted at the fictitious Australian town of 'Woorramoorraballoo-boolloboolloo'.

Bennett started 1937 with the lowest of expectations on his shoulders and it is unlikely that his ambition troubled the seasoned Ossie Nicholson, who had been quietly sitting in the wings.

Nicholson's 1933 record year had been relatively unsuccessful in lifting him from the shadow of Hubert Opperman. His subsequent racing pickings had been slim and his celebrity status had taken a nose dive when his supposedly unassailable record was beaten by over 2,000 miles by a one-armed vegetarian amateur – although Nicholson was generous in his acknowledgement of Greaves' feat as he knew only too well the rigours of rising each day to ride over 100 miles.

The Australian press were quick to point out that while Greaves had eclipsed the mileage of Nicholson, Nicholson's record of 366 consecutive centuries remained. The 'Cycling Ashes', as they became known in the Australian press, had returned to Britain and Nicholson was forced to react.

Consultations with Bruce Small of the Malvern Star cycle team led to firm plans for a 1937 attempt. Nicholson had a degree of confidence in this new attempt as he felt he'd approached the 1933 year with relative inexperience in endurance riding. The 1933 attempt had seen him go out far too quickly in the early stages in order to attack the mileage required. Nicholson had depleted his reserves at an early stage and found it very difficult to recover. This time he was wiser and was prepared to ride at a steadier pace in order to hit his numbers. He even planned to hold back on his tendency to hare off at over 17 miles per hour. His figures suggested that he could ride at an average pace of 150 miles per day and add a further 5,000 miles to the 1936 tally of Greaves. The *Sydney Referee* captured this new strategy well in a simple paragraph describing Nicholson's plans:

> The holding of this margin of reserve is very essential, for the constitution is not thus being pushed to its utmost and a rider, under these conditions, can provide his very best staying power.

Nicholson decided to use similar routes to his 1933 ride, probably with some reluctance as he'd not particularly enjoyed the mundanity of these roads and the abject lack of company upon them. Clearly the call of the record was strong enough to park these thoughts. As the start date grew near, Nicholson's ambition grew stronger and his planned tally was upped to a massive 60,000 miles for the year – just over 164 miles a day.

In the last two weeks of December 1936, Nicholson began to train in earnest, riding over 100 miles a day for the final fortnight of the year. His record attempt was scheduled to begin at 12.01 a.m. on New Year's Day 1937, apparently timed to avoid the holiday traffic that would build up later in the morning. His plan was to start 'big' but steady and get ahead of the other contenders as early as possible. This was clearly designed as much for his own motivation as the demotivation of the competition. Keeping track of the other riders' mileages would prove difficult as telegraph cables were the only mechanism available for getting up-to-date reports. Nicholson needed to know that he was on track to regain his record right from the start.

And so, as 1936 departed, three new contenders had arrived, each with their own inspirations and motivations: Bennett, the wet-behind-the-ears youngster entering into completely new territory as his own adventure in cycling; Menzies, the wizened ex-professional rider, inspired by Greaves to add one more trophy to his shelf in the twilight of his racing career; and Nicholson, the smarting Australian who'd seen himself and his country robbed of a world record by a disabled rider. The cycling mileage record had become a head-to-head race, with at least two challengers having known pedigree. Things had become serious as the competition evolved from the realms of amateur achievement to a mileage arms race played out across the press and telegraph wires spanning the globe. The *Kilmore*

Free Press in Victoria, Australia, affectionately dubbed it a 'triangular battle of mile piling'. The three riders set off with huge expectation resting upon their shoulders.

Nicholson had a six-hour start on Menzies (or fifteen hours if you consider the time difference), heading out on to the road as soon as the clock had struck the last chime of 12. His ride began from the same point as his 1933 ride, the Elizabeth Street post office in Melbourne, and, being New Year's Eve, his send-off was well supported, with a huge crowd turning out to see in 1937 and wish him well on his way.

As Nicholson headed out into the dark along the Point Nepean road – a route he knew only too well – he left behind a lucky mascot that had been presented to him by the president of the Mordialloc Carnival committee, possibly in irony: a baby tortoise with a ground speed some 300 times slower than Nicholson's own, along with a card bearing the inscription: 'From one great trier to another.' Nicholson also took with him a new nickname, 'The Tiger of the Road', which he'd gained as a result of his tenacity (and often foolishness) while racing, underlined by his 1933 ride. He'd not forgotten those who supported him on that record ride, and on his second day of riding carried a bunch of flowers all the way to Carrum in order to present them to his most ardent fan, the old lady in the bath chair. Nicholson also took with him a support crew. He'd clearly convinced Bruce Small that extra help and logistics would be required to bring the record back to Malvern Star. Small had agreed and provided Nicholson with a support car carrying food, spare bicycles and equipment.

Meanwhile, in London, René Menzies was on his way after a send-off at the NCU offices in Doughty Street, WC1 that contrasted hugely with the one given to Nicholson. Menzies' lack of sponsorship meant that his bicycle was a last-minute throw-together of old parts, quickly built into a 'Frankenstein's monster' by his friend, the mechanic Mr Weaver of Leyton. The lack of support also meant that Menzies was forced to use second-hand tubular tyres – not something to be recommended, given that every puncture would require an extended effort to fix and a subsequent loss of miles. While this bike was being built, Menzies had been unable to train and was forced to resort to long walks to get his legs into shape.

Menzies set off unaided and was waved away by his brother Maurice, a boy from the NCU offices, and a photographer and journalist from *Cycling*.

The weather was dreadful, as befits a British New Year's Day, and Menzies rode out of London in a rain storm. His first destination was Basingstoke.

Menzies' preparations had been rushed and he made the mistake of setting off without formally adopting the use of *Cycling*'s proven mileage-checking mechanism. Fortunately for him, an agreement to fall in line with the magazine's requirements put him back on the straight and narrow and *Cycling* agreed to credit him with these early rides and a subsequent mileage of 462. More immediately pressing was the fact that at his first ever food stop he ordered tea, cake and a sandwich before realising that he'd also neglected to bring any money with him. Luckily the bad weather worked in his favour and the cafe owner, impressed by his fortitude for riding a decent distance in the rain, let him off the bill. This was Menzies' only meal of the day, yet he still managed to ride an impressive 151 miles in eleven hours, finishing his ride at 6 p.m. outside the offices of *Cycling* in London.

As for Bennett, he was still lying in bed. His attempt would not begin until 3 January 1937 and, of all of the 1937 riders, his was the least advertised. It appears that Bennett set off from home with no publicity at all and the reasons for his late start are unclear. *Cycling* magazine reported his start a few days later and clearly stated that his tally would only be counted during 1937, so young Bernard started his record year two days in deficit to Menzies and Nicholson.

While Bennett was one of the three serious contenders in 1937, he was not the only youngster on the road. James Stewart, a Scottish amateur rider one year Bennett's senior, had set off on his own mission to overtake the record of Greaves. Stewart's goal was simpler than Bennett's: he wanted to quickly prove himself to the trade and gain sponsorship as a result. In late 1936 he'd lost his job and used the free time available at the beginning of 1937 to clock up 1,400 miles within sixteen days. This ended in a trip from Loch Lomond down to London in a hopeful quest to pick up sponsorship for the rest of the year. The penniless Scot spent many nights sleeping in the open on his way down, including one evening of luxury when he sneaked into the back of a furniture van. However, his quest was not rewarded and reports of his rides faded from the press as the disillusioned youth returned home without a contract.

Stewart was not the only wannabe to fall by the wayside. A cycling journalist from Gosport named Don Coster Graham popped up at the end of January and announced that he too was going to take the record away from Greaves – a somewhat optimistic claim as all of the other riders had nearly a month's start on him. However, he publicly stated that he would make up this deficit by riding more later on in the year, blissfully unaware that all three riders would be considering the same. Graham was sponsored by Ellimans Athletic Rub – a muscle rub that can still be purchased today – and appeared in an advert for them in a February edition of a cycling magazine. Records for Graham show him riding to just under 1,000 miles but he disappeared from the mileage tallies after February 1937, presumably returning to the comfort of the newspaper office.

The British-based riders began their years riding similar distances to each other. Menzies and Bennett were relatively level-pegging as the month came to a close at a daily average of about 140 miles with 4,138 and 3,674 miles respectively. Menzies reported that the weather had constrained his riding as he contended with continuous rain, snow and hail. At times he found the cold so intense that: 'I lost my temper with myself and cursed the universe in general and would swear like a mad devil especially when I encountered puncture after puncture in the slush and snow.'

After a month on the road Menzies was suffering financially and having to borrow money to keep himself going. He decided to ride from London to Birmingham in order to seek formal sponsorship from one of the cycling manufacturing companies and by chance encountered one of the Camillis brothers as he pushed up Potters Hill in Aston. Louis and Raimond Camillis had established the British Cyclo gear company a few years previously and would have been an ideal sponsor for the penniless Menzies. However, he quickly informed the tired rider that his firm was backing Ossie Nicholson. Menzies was distraught and close to tears but decided to retain a stiff upper lip and informed Camillis that he'd continue anyway. The previous month's riding had stiffened his resolve to see the year out. Camillis was impressed, so much so that he decided to back Menzies personally with a regular wage. He also committed to opening discussions within the business as to whether both riders could be publicly backed. The official sponsorship from British Cyclo never came, but the personal payments continued through the year, allowing Menzies to carry on.

Elated, Menzies returned to London, only to be hammered by the weather. He reached Hoddesdon in a state of near-collapse and had to be escorted back to Waltham Cross by riders from the Herts and Wessex Club, who cajoled the beleaguered rider down the road. Menzies stated that were it not for these riders he would have abandoned his year. He climbed off his bike at 11 p.m. and wearily sought out his trusted mechanic Mr Weaver. All of his wheel and bottom bracket bearings needed replacement. Menzies slept standing in the passage of Weaver's house as the mechanic got on with his task. Weaver was to prove instrumental throughout Menzies' year, selflessly repairing tubular tyres and other pieces of equipment, usually at very unsociable hours and short notice.

During his ride home Menzies had stopped at a cafe in Hoddesdon owned by Jack Newman. At the time he was so exhausted that he did not speak a word to the proprietor, as in Menzies' own words he was nearly 'all out'. This clearly had an impression on Newman, who invited Menzies to spend a week riding from his cafe. Newman clearly had the mind of a cyclist and began to advise Menzies on how to ride smarter in the winter conditions, and in particular how to avoid the headwinds. Menzies lapped up this advice, along with the food and chocolate that Newman would offer him daily. At the end of the week's stay Menzies asked for his bill, but the request was refused. It turned out that Newman was a cyclist of pedigree and had raced often in France where he'd received great kindness from all involved and he saw his support of Menzies as a repayment in kind. Menzies would make many diversions to Newman's cafe as the year progressed.

Over the pond Nicholson was upping the ante. Despite his plans to ride at measured pace, Nicholson had gone hard from the gun and had over 1,000 miles on both of his rivals at this point. A hot January and long days in the saddle had seen him shed over a stone and three-quarters in weight – a planned loss, with Nicholson purposely feeding himself up prior to the start in anticipation of losing weight in the early stages as he sought to quickly put the record beyond the reach of the others.

It seemed to be working. Nicholson had pushed himself hard and recorded a longest day during January of 178 miles. He averaged 153 miles per day for the first twenty-two days of the record. Riding in temperatures that often exceeded 100 °F in the shade, he'd had to deal with ferocious headwinds and periods of torrential rain, but, despite this, his first four days had been phenomenal and without precedent. Nicholson had clocked up 162.5, 157, 157 and 159 miles and ended his first week with an unofficial record for the highest ever total weekly mileage – 1,102.5 miles.

The riding then began to take its toll. This was not all Nicholson's fault. Bruce Small was driving Nicholson hard, trying to ensure that he stuck to a rigorous schedule to ensure that the record was regained, but which required a minimum of 124 miles per day. The team were determined that he would have a mileage buffer were anything to go wrong later in the record. This would prove fortuitous in February, but, for now, it was decided that he should back off a little and allow himself to recover.

After ten days he applied to the League of Victorian Wheelmen, the local cycle governing body, for the right to have his ride officially verified. It is not clear why he had not made the approach prior to his start. The other riders were being watched over by *Cycling* magazine – a respected publication but not an official cycling body – and Nicholson was clearly seeking to have his ride positioned as the only officially verified attempt. He was initially refused on a technicality but, after a second appliation, the League agreed to draft a set of rules to govern his ride's verification. True to form Nicholson and officialdom did not mix. The League was not happy with the process for mileage verification proposed by Nicholson's team and had mistakenly believed that the record was governed by the Union Cycliste Internationale, international cycling's governing body. The League threatened to report Nicholson to the UCI were these processes not improved. Consequently Bruce Small brushed them off and declared that the ride would continue with or without their blessing.

It seems that the lessons of the previous year had not been learnt, and Nicholson's pace and fatigue finally caught up with him. On 10 February 1937, a tired Nicholson crashed hard at Mordialloc in an attempt to avoid a lorry and suffered nasty road rash to the arms and legs. However, he felt that despite a little stiffness he was ok to continue riding. The next day at a lunch stop in Hastings his toe became increasingly painful. Nicholson sought out a doctor who examined him and to his horror found that the injury had turned septic. He implored the rider to abandon his attempt there and then but Nicholson ignored him and rode home, clocking a mere 74 miles for the day.

Back in Britain, after a strong start that closely matched Menzies', Bennett also began to have troubles. Late in January he suffered a jammed wheel and the ignominy of a train ride home. Two days later he reported further issues with his bike and on 29 January finally cracked and traded it in for a different model. The young lad must have been itching to give his new bike a really long test on the road, but 30 January saw his progress severely curtailed by a snowstorm that limited his day to a mere 39 miles. Bennett was struggling to find his pace during February and by the end of the month his daily average had dropped to 122 miles, a few short of the 124.3 required to beat the record of Walter Greaves.

The new bike didn't improve matters for Bennett as he rode into March. His mileage cards reported a broken chain, a bout of tonsillitis and three rest days at the beginning of the month. With these setbacks Bennett could not hope to compete with the mileages of Nicholson or Menzies. Bennett was typically riding from his home in Birmingham to Alcester and back twice a day, giving him a mileage between 115 and 160 miles, depending upon diversions upon the way. Menzies, meanwhile, had cranked up his efforts to a superb average of over 170 miles per day at this time in April, with Nicholson slightly behind on 156 miles but having shaken off the effects of his septic toe. Bennett began to take further rest days and it was clear that his objective was now solely the mileage of Greaves. He deliberately avoided sponsorship and endorsements as well in order to become classed as a true amateur. This would allow him to claim the amateur world record at the end of the year, were his mileage to be sufficient.

On 14 May Bennett and Menzies met on the road for the first time, at Aylesbury. Bennett had been heading towards London in order to carry out a mandatory fortnightly check of his mileometer at the offices of *Cycling* magazine. Menzies was heading in the opposite direction with his sights set on Coventry. The meeting was amicable and Menzies paid the young Bennett a sweeping compliment: 'When I saw he was just a "kid" and remembered my own bitter experiences with the vagaries of our climate, I think his performance highly commendable.'

Menzies was well able to pass praise at this point as his tally exceeded 19,000 miles, over 1,000 ahead of Bennett and getting closer to that of Nicholson. As May drew to a close Bennett did little to increase his mileage significantly and took further days off. Nicholson and Menzies were no such slackers and on 28 May *Cycling* reported Nicholson as having accumulated 22,695 miles – 1,124 ahead of Menzies but with the gap closing all the time.

Nicholson celebrated with a nasty crash on 1 June. A dog ran out in front of him and he swerved, jamming the front wheel of his bike into a tramline in Richmond. He was catapulted over the bars and sustained nasty cuts to his hands as he stretched them out to break his fall. Undeterred, he continued to ride after treatment but must have been wondering when his bad luck would finally end. In addition to his lorry-crash and septic toe, he had, in April, suffered a serious bout of tonsillitis which had apparently kept him from cycling for three days. Prior to that he'd reported sunstroke and a number of other crashes. Now, as the riders continued into June, things swung further against Nicholson. Melbourne was moving into the winter months and it was reported that Nicholson was having to contend with cold stinging rain being driven hard into his skin by 40-mile-per-hour gales rolling in from the Tasman Sea. Nicholson responded by continuing to ride in shorts, stating that this was his plan for the entire year no matter what the weather.

Over the other side of the world, Menzies was beginning to enjoy the fruits of summer. On 14 April 1937 Nicholson had been a colossal 1,600 miles ahead of Menzies, a total that would have seemed unassailable to some. Yet Menzies remained undeterred and increased his daily average accordingly, to an unheard-of 180 miles per day. On 11 June 1937 he was still in contention, with 23,950 miles showing on his cyclometer, compared to 25,044 for Nicholson – a difference of 1,094 miles.

Things were not looking good for the Australian, who became acutely aware of his rival set to overtake him. The Australian weather looked equally poor, with fog and frost hampering his progress. Victoria was experiencing one of its worst winters on record and Nicholson's will to ride the whole year in shorts was broken. A set of specially designed leg and arm warmers were constructed for him, and his team formulated a new diet designed to help him cope with the cold. With the impending overtake by Menzies spurring him on, Nicholson managed to average an impressive 178.65 miles per day through the awful weather. A cable to the UK reported that the plucky rider was 'thriving upon the solid punishment' and had managed to gain an additional 4½ pounds in weight during the month.

But Menzies took advantage of the British summer and its increased daylight hours, turning the tables on the Australian, who had been in a similar position at the start of the ride. As June faded into July, Menzies began to ride through the nights in an attempt to make up his deficit. Impressively, Nicholson responded in the same manner. Both men would have struggled with the low power of battery lights in that era, but Nicholson, still in the depths of the Australian winter, must have experienced a great deal more anguish given the longer winter nights and persistent lack of visibility due to rain and fog.

Now halfway through the year, the battle lines had been clearly drawn. Bennett's missed riding days had removed him from contention and it was a head to head between the experienced and extremely well-supported Australian and the veteran Frenchman, who was riding on minimal budget and left in the main to his own devices.

Nicholson's support gave him an unexpected advantage over Menzies. Bruce Small was in regular communication by wire with his London business interests, and this allowed the team to keep track of the mileages ridden by Menzies, which the Frenchman did not receive in return. As a result Nicholson's team were able to better pace him to stay ahead. Menzies had the more difficult job, relying upon infrequent updates of Nicholson's progress in the cycling press and having to ride on simple anticipation. All the Frenchman could do was concentrate on his own game and use the good weather of July and August to ramp his efforts.

And ramp them up he did. Menzies' intentions became clear in the first week of August with an unprecedented set of rides that had not been seen in the record before. From 3 August to 11 September Menzies rode repeated double-century rides in a valiant attempt to get ahead, completing thirty-seven doubles. This was despite significant problems with saddle sores which were beginning to cause him distress. By this time, Menzies was sponsored by Ellimans Athletic Rub and regularly appeared in magazine adverts to promote it. The rub was primarily sold for the purposes of massage, with claims that it could help increase a rider's potential for mileage. Perhaps the company had missed out on a marketing opportunity for another type of cream.

Yet Nicholson was not going down without a fight. Like Menzies, he committed to double-century days and quietly shattered the mileage record for a week, riding 1,466 miles between 8 and 14 August, including a 263-mile day, in winter. The Australians continued to monitor Menzies' progress closely and set Nicholson a similar schedule. This was leaked to the Australian press, who considered it unwise as it would weaken the rider. However, a newspaper report at the beginning of September stated that Nicholson was still looking strong despite the conditions and postulated that he could increase his mileages should he so wish. That wish became a necessity during September when Menzies appeared to abandon sleep and rode consistent seventeen-hour days with his rival firmly in his sights. Between 15 and 17 September Nicholson rode three 254-milers but, on 24 September, the gap was down to a mere 84 miles and it looked as if Menzies had achieved his goal. This must have proved an incredible morale boost for the French rider who three months previously had been some 1,600 miles behind. Nicholson, meanwhile, would have been looking at himself and his team and wondering what they could do in order to stave off the advance of Menzies. Then, as is often the case in cycling, fate stepped in.

On Saturday 25 September 1937 René Menzies was within four days of surpassing the record of Walter Greaves. He decided to repeat a favourite route of his via Girtford Bridge at Biggleswade and collided with a lorry. Menzies fell hard and broke his wrist, his bike landing beside him, seemingly irreparably damaged. Menzies sought help from a policeman, who used a police telephone box to put a call through to Menzies' brother Maurice. Maurice jumped in a car and rushed to his brother's aid, whisking him off to hospital.

Menzies' record attempt looked to be over. But, tantalisingly close to passing the previous mark of Greaves, Menzies was having none of it and persuaded a doctor to set his arm in splints and plaster it up in such a fashion that he was able to continue riding. He used a spare tubular tyre as a crude sling while riding.

Incredibly, he left hospital immediately, remounted and completed the day with 163 miles bagged on the damaged bicycle – a total of 44,833 for the year. Maurice then rushed the bike to the London offices of Rudge Whitworth, who by this time were supporting him with a new bicycle, where mechanics worked overnight on its repair and Menzies managed a credible 152 miles the day after, somehow managing to quickly adapt to a one-armed riding style. He was now better qualified than any to empathise with the achievement of Greaves the year before, but was without the advantage of the adapted bicycle Greaves had ridden – which makes the coming days' riding rather impressive.

Menzies was clearly determined to be the first to take the record, but Nicholson was right there with him. The cycling press had done its sums and worked out that both riders would ride past the 45,384-mile record on 29 September. The question was, which rider would be first?

On Tuesday 28 September 1937 Menzies was on the road at 3 a.m. and pedalled for twenty hours in order to record a 247-mile day. This was the mark of a man who had put aside a serious injury in pursuit of his goal. It was also a requirement of his bicycle sponsor, Rudge Whitworth, who had anticipated his breaking the record the very next day and arranged a reception to accompany him towards the mileage of Greaves.

Then, early on Wednesday morning, a telegram was received from Australia stating that Nicholson had done it. At 3 p.m. local time in Melbourne he rode – for the third time in his career – through a paper banner declaring him the year record holder. A crowd had gathered at the Melbourne showground to watch him ride his 45,384th mile. He smashed through the paper banner erected across the track – which had Greaves' previous record mileage scrawled across it – and a laurel wreath was presented to him by Joyce Barry, a record-breaking Australian cyclist in her own right.

It looked as if the Australian had taken the record. But time differences needed to be taken into account – Melbourne was nine hours ahead of London and therefore Nicholson had a head start. When the news arrived in the UK urgent phone calls were made to Menzies' usual stopping-places to alert him and tell him that he needed to speed up in order to break the record. Even AA patrolmen were alerted to look out for the rider. All eyes were on the clock, knowing that Nicholson had hit the target at 3 p.m. Eventually he was found and accelerated towards his target, passing the mark of Greaves at 1.40 p.m. and claiming the record.

In absolute time Nicholson had been the first to reach the mark, yet Menzies had done it faster. It had taken Nicholson 271 days and 15 hours to reach the mileage; Menzies had been over an hour quicker, taking 271 days, 13 hours and 40 minutes. This was based upon the competition beginning after the last stroke of midnight on New Year's Eve. Recall that while Nicholson had set off at one minute past midnight, Menzies had started later, at seven in the morning, and had thus ridden the distance even faster in absolute terms, giving him two claims to being the fastest to the new record.

A car picked Menzies up from his checking point and drove him directly to Cockfosters, where he was met by a bevy of cycling girls, clubmen and riders upon single-wheeled ordinaries who accompanied him to Alexandra Palace for an official reception. Previous record breakers Walter Greaves and Arthur Humbles were there to greet him, as was another famous old timer, Mr S.F. Edge, who presented the Frenchman with a cup with two sashes attached – an English Union Jack and French Tricolore. Menzies' sponsor Rudge Whitworth and Mr Camillis of British Cyclo were also on hand to lap up their share of the reflected glory. Camillis must have been pleased that his personal investment had paid off.

Greaves' record had been broken, but, with three months of riding to go, there was still everything to play for. It was clear that Greaves' mark was going to be beaten by a huge margin at the end of the year. Both Nicholson and Menzies were averaging well over 5,000 miles a month and figures in excess of 60,000 for the year started to look achievable. Nicholson now appeared to have the upper hand, with the weather in Australia improving and the days getting longer. Menzies was still injured as his arm was taking a long time to set, more than likely aggravated by his continuing long days upon the bicycle. Adding to his disadvantage was the approaching British winter. The days were drawing in and the weather turning for the worse as he rode into his second spell of winter for his record year.

Many expected Nicholson to pull away by some margin, but the dogged Frenchman with his arm in a sling fought his way through a series of colds and poor weather to stay in touch with the Australian's ever-increasing mileage. A month after passing Greaves' record, both riders had exceeded 50,000 miles and the gap between them was only 163 miles in Nicholson's favour. November saw Nicholson crash yet again and require medical attention, while Menzies was hampered by fog and long periods of heavy rain. Menzies was also experiencing other difficulties that his predecessor Greaves would certainly have empathised with. During one particularly windy day he suffered a puncture just as the rain began to fall heavily. He struggled to fix it with his large oilskin cape billowing around him and his broken wrist making his grip weak, hampering his attempts to loosen the wing nuts of his wheel. But still the battle continued and amazingly Menzies fought back and ate into Nicholson's lead, unknowingly taking advantage of the Australian's curtailed mileage on the day of his fall and reducing the gap to a mere 58 miles. And at the end of the month Menzies got his reward for his perseverance and temerity as *Cycling* magazine announced that on 27 November 1937 Menzies had taken the lead with 55,567 miles, 21 ahead of Nicholson.

Menzies had taken the lead by reviewing his choice of routes, favouring rides such as the road from London to Portsmouth, which was lit most of the way to Guildford, saving his batteries and allowing him to ride at a faster pace.

The weather appeared to become kinder to Menzies as he entered the final month of the year and continued to lead Nicholson, with the gap varying between 100 and 150 miles. Or so he and the British press thought. There appears to have been some last-minute gamesmanship by the

Australians in a clever attempt to rob Menzies of the prize. Through the first weeks of December *Cycling* had reported Nicholson's mileages that had been cabled over from his sponsor Malvern Star. These clearly showed the Australian lagging behind the Frenchman. However, on 17 December, a cable put Nicholson ahead with a figure of 59,781 – a massive 616 miles up on Menzies' total, which stood at 59,165. These revised figures were published in the 22 December magazine, giving the poor Frenchman only nine days to make up the deficit – around an extra 68 miles per day. *Cycling* reported that they were seeking urgent clarification as it could have been that the revised figure was a mistake. Sadly it wasn't and Menzies appears to have been lulled into a false sense of security, believing that he simply had to maintain his current daily average of 150 miles to take the prize.

Over a period of some three weeks while this misinformation was propagated Nicholson had covered some extraordinary distances knowing, via Bruce Small's London links, that he was the one who had the lead. To compound the torture the Australians neglected to cable Nicholson's mileages before 31 December, leaving a huge degree of uncertainty as to whether or not Menzies had the record.

Regardless, the smiling and resolute Frenchman rode into London and up to the doors of the Horticultural Hall in Westminster as the last bells of 1937 began to toll. He headed a large band of club cyclists from Ealing Cycling Club and was flanked by his daughter on one side and a triumphant Bernard Bennett on the other. Bennett had cause to celebrate, as he had passed Greaves' record distance on 18 December and thus become the amateur world record holder, having completed his year with no support or sponsorship at all. Bennett had ridden a steady 45,801 miles, putting him nearly 15,000 behind his fellow competitors but 417 ahead of Greaves. He was rightly honoured that evening for an amazing achievement for one so young. In recognition of this, Menzies had ridden to Birmingham the day before and on the final day of 1937 the two riders had cycled from Birmingham to London together.

Menzies' final tally for 1937 was 61,561 miles. He spoke a few words as he was hauled to the stage at a huge party at which he was guest of honour. This was a 'super do' for cyclists hosted by Claud Butler and attended by over 5,000 riders who jammed the hall to watch Menzies and Bennett be presented with golden armlets by the Cyclo gear company, which had sponsored Menzies for a large portion of his ride. Cruelly, Menzies only now learnt that Nicholson had ridden 1,294.6 miles further than he had.

Cyclists had ridden from all over the country to attend and they listened ardently as Menzies relayed the frustrations and toils of his year. He told of how he was unsure as to whether the 60,000 mile distance was even possible upon the bike; he told of the loneliness of the life upon the road, his only interactions being with those who signed his mileage cards. He also told of the frustrations of riding from London and having to enter and leave the city hampered by heavy traffic on most days. Then he announced his intention to carry on. Aware that Nicholson was to claim the record for that year, Menzies advised that he was to continue to 100,000 kilometres and set a new benchmark for the fastest time to that distance. He intended to cross the channel and complete the remainder of his ride in his native France, finishing in his birthplace of Caen. Sadly, Nicholson's total mileage for the year meant that he had already achieved this feat, further confounding the agonies poured upon Menzies.

Nicholson's final mileage for the year was initially announced as 62,855.6 miles. His performance had been incredible. He'd suffered injury, accident and poor weather throughout his second year-record attempt and had, once again, finished as a mileage record rider. He finally climbed off his bike at Mordialloc, regaining his title having apparently ridden for forty-eight hours non-stop in an attempt to push the distance beyond the reach of other aspirants. He was accompanied by a group of Tasmanian cyclists as a guard of honour, in recognition of his birthplace.

It transpired that a clerical mistake had set Nicholson's record figure too high and the official mileage for the Australian was finally agreed to be 62,657 after an extensive audit carried out by the Australian cycling authorities. These figures were confirmed by Mr Drake, the Malvern Star representative in the UK responsible for feeding Bruce Small details of Menzies' progress. Drake had been accused of being responsible for the misinformation concerning Nicholson's early December figures. He in turn entirely refuted this and chose to point the finger squarely at the arithmeticians operating within *Cycling* magazine.

The British press was somewhat muted in its praise of Nicholson, possibly due to the issues with his mileage figures near the end but more likely down to the fact that the record had once again left British shores. Despite being of French descent, Menzies had been adopted by British cyclists and was clearly seen to be representing British interests throughout the year. Instead of praising Nicholson, the magazines chose to laud cycling in general and used the huge mileages of the riders to underline the fact that it could not and should not be considered a dangerous pastime. The health benefits were clear as all three riders had completed the year having adapted well to the rigours of long-distance riding and were looking remarkably fresh as a result. The new record was also positioned as a testament to the reliability of the bicycle and its equipment as very few motorists had completed comparable mileages within the same year. Finally they underlined the safety of cycling as a pastime, commenting that two riders in different climates, riding through all ranges of weather and on all types of road surface, had survived relatively unscathed despite averaging around 170 miles per day.

One journalist put it to the cycling public that the days of these records being beaten by high margins were over. In his view the limits were close to being reached. He had no idea of what was yet to come.

Nicholson deserved more praise from the British press. He was the first man to attempt the year record twice, and the only man to take it twice. But he was never to repeat it. After his second record success he returned to his career as a professional cyclist, which he continued well into the 1940s. During his 1937 year he had set an unofficial record for the highest mileage ridden in a week, riding 1,466 miles in August. This had not entered the Australian record books as it had been verified by a committee set up specifically to monitor the year, rather than a formal cycling-records body. So, in May 1938, Nicholson set out for Adelaide to attempt to beat a figure of 1,449.3 miles set by W. Humphreys. Nicholson's Malvern Star team had set out a 36-kilometre (22.37-mile) course around the town and over the period of a single week Nicholson completed the circuit sixty-seven times, setting a new world record of 1,498.75 miles. Malvern Star quickly rushed out a set of postcard prints to commemorate his record.

Sadly this was to be Nicholson's last record and his impact upon the cycling world subsequently began to fade. His mammoth year of slow and steady riding had robbed him of the speed that he used to display when track racing. He continued to compete throughout 1938 but results were lacking. His most notable appearance being a six-day race in Sydney where Nicholson's greatest impact was his voice. The length of the races meant that mornings were usually a slack period where riders ceased hardcore racing and lazily rode the track in an attempt to recover. The bored riders would look for any entertainment to keep themselves going, sometimes reading newspapers on the bike. The boredom clearly got to Gino Bambagiotti, an Italian racer who urged Nicholson to sing in order to entertain them. Nicholson obliged and his voice clearly went down well with the assembled riders and crowd as he went on to sing on radio shows and appear in numerous stage productions, including a stint playing Henry VIII.

The irony of his representation as the wife-discarding English monarch is not lost as Nicholson was a known philanderer, having abandoned his first wife in 1933 and embarked on numerous affairs as he travelled as a cyclist and entertainer. In his later years he was finally caught out and, in 1940, served a brief prison sentence for bigamy. Eventually he returned to his first wife Annie and lived for a while in Richmond, working within the cycle trade as a mechanic and builder. But he could not leave his philandering ways behind and in the 1950s left to move to New Zealand and settle down with a new wife, Nancy. His final years were spent working as a sales representative before passing away at the relatively young age of fifty-seven in 1965. The death of the great cyclist went unnoticed by the cycling community.

Without the powerful Australian's tenacity and determination the record would probably have grown incrementally year on year, by perhaps a few thousand miles each time, to a figure nearer 50,000 miles. Nicholson's Herculean battle with Menzies had driven the record over 17,000 miles further than the year before. One only hopes that there was some cycling representation at his graveside as he was waved away from this world. To this date no memorial to this great Australian cyclist remains, save a few words written about him online.

Menzies' post-1937 cycling career would prove more successful than Nicholson's. After losing the record to Nicholson, a lesser man than he might have packed up his disappointment and gone home on New Year's Day to lick his wounds. Menzies, however, was made of stronger stuff. Nicholson had robbed him of the year-mileage prize and also the 100,000-kilometre record, but Menzies had spotted another prize – the 100,000-*mile* record – and, unlike the Australian, he continued to ride on New Year's Day. He decided to keep going into 1938 and subsequently make a second attempt to take the year record away from Nicholson. He had managed to recruit additional sponsors to help him on his way, with the Rudge Whitworth bicycle company formalising their relationship with an agreement to continue its sponsorship. The plan to ride in France was resurrected and Menzies crossed the channel early in 1938, spending much of March riding around the Cannes and Nice area. At the beginning of the month he had added nearly 10,000 miles to his 1937 total but eventually found the winds and hills of the south of France a hindrance to his stated aim of close to 200 miles per day. He packed up and rode north to Calais, arriving back in England some time in April 1938.

On 13 May 1938 he had amassed 21,768 miles, over 2,700 miles ahead of his total ridden the previous year and on target to exceed the record set by Nicholson. But in June he suffered yet another setback after being run down by an RAF car near Hitchin, which subsequently left the scene without stopping. Menzies was quite badly hurt, with road rash on most of his extremities, but, as per 1937, he simply dusted himself off, remounted and completed the day with 186 miles in the bag.

The strong yet diminutive Frenchman continued to hammer out the miles upon the British roads he loved for a further two months. On 18 August 1938 Menzies left Percy's Cafe in Welwyn Garden City at 9 a.m. and rode to Girtford Bridge, from where a band of cyclists accompanied him into central London to the Rudge Whitworth premises on Tottenham Court Road. He was joined there by Lilian Dredge, who had recently set a women's Land's End to John o'Groats record and the pair rode into Soho Square together, a moment that was captured on a Pathé news reel. Menzies' cyclometer showed that he had ridden 100,010 miles in 587 days, therefore setting a new record and benchmark for the fastest to gain 100,000 miles. At forty-eight years old the charismatic Frenchman had finally established a world record. However, he'd decided to end his attempt to take the year record away from Nicholson, probably down to either fatigue or a belief that it was out of reach given his current averages. Instead he was to join the Cyclo gear company and help them promote their products via a tour of the British Isles.

Like Nicholson, Menzies made a brief return to racing after 1938. He featured in a number of time trials and placed a strong second in the 1939 Paris-Dieppe veterans' race. Also like Nicholson, Menzies' marriage fell apart, at the end of 1939, although it is unclear as to whether this was down to his absence through cycling or other reasons.

After the war he attempted to race as an amateur, but his previous sponsorship prevented this and no British club would accept his entry. Menzies was undaunted and, in 1950, he rode a 24-hour race unofficially, waiting for the last man to go and then setting off in pursuit. At the age of

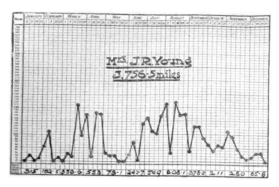

Mrs. J.R. Young
3,756.5 miles

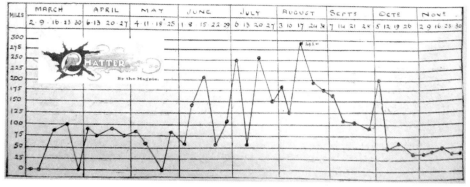

Top left Harry Long, who recorded a mileage in 1908 of 12,940 miles. *Cycling*, 27 January 1909.
Top right An example of a completed mileage chart, in this case showing Mrs J.R. Young's 1902 mileage of 3,756.5 miles.
Centre 'Chatter' by 'The Magpie' *(inset)*, and H.E.S. of Sleaford's 1901 centuries chart. Both from *Cycling*, 21 December 1901.
Bottom left John H. George, winner of America's 1897 mileage competition.
Image: Century Road Club of America manual, 1898.
Bottom right Harold Freeman. *Cycling*, 24 January 1903.

Top left The cover of *Cycling*, 3 January 1912, showing pentagenarian W.R. Wells of the Bath Road Club, who covered over 30,000 miles in 1911 as part of the magazine's century competition.

Top right Mrs A.M.C. Allen, winner of the Johnson Century Medal in 1897.
Image: Century Road Club of America manual, 1898.

Bottom Edward 'Teddy' Hale, pictured in *Cycling*, 5 August 1899.

PROOF

of the great wearing qualities and all-round reliability

OF THE

EADIE Coaster

The Original British Coaster with the never-failing brake.

34,366 Miles
IN TWELVE MONTHS

by Mr. MARCEL PLANES on a bicycle fitted with an EADIE COASTER HUB, the most perfect combination of brake and free wheel.

Mr. MARCEL PLANES says:—
"I find the Eadie Coaster an ideal brake. It always answers readily to my requirements, giving me the utmost confidence to ride down the steepest hill. The free wheel is all that can be desired."

The Eadie Coaster contains "the brake which always acts," and the free-est of free wheels. The brake is most powerful, it can be immediately applied by the slightest backward pressure of the pedal. Every cyclist should make sure of "always cycling in safety" by having it fitted to either his new or old machine.

Write for latest Descriptive Leaflet.

The Birmingham Small Arms Co., Ltd.
2, SMALL HEATH, BIRMINGHAM.

The Eadie Coaster.

Marcel Planes, winner of "Cycling's" Century Competition, who rode 100,000 miles in seven years on a bicycle fitted with an Eadie Coaster.

Top Portrait of Marcel Planes, from the 6 December 1911 issue of *Cycling*.
Bottom left A family portrait of Planes. *Image courtesy of the Planes family.*
Bottom right A 1912 advert for the Eadie Coaster hub, featuring Marcel Planes.

Top left A strong team of century riders, pictured in the 6 September 1911 issue of *Cycling*. L–R: H. Morris, W.G. Brown, W.R. Wells, A.D. Munro, Marcel Planes and R. Clements.

Top right An unconventional bicycle out on the road. *Image courtesy of the Planes family.*

Bottom Planes' checking card from 11 December 1911, showing 102 miles ridden and the note '*Hale's century record passed.*' Photo: Dave Barter/Planes family archive.

Left Planes' eighteen-carat gold medal, which he received as winner of *Cycling*'s 1911 century competition, and which is still treasured by his family. *Photos: Dave Barter/Planes family archive.*

Right An advert for Mead Cycles featuring Planes. *Image courtesy of the Planes family.*

Top A.A. Humbles leaving Trafalgar Square, London, at the start of his record attempt.
Photo: Douglas Miller/Topical Press Agency/Getty Images.
Bottom Humbles, prior to commencing his 34,367th mile in the company of thousands
of cyclists at Hyde Park Corner on 11 December 1932.

100 MILES A DAY FOR 1 YEAR

ONLY *Quality* CAN MAKE IT POSSIBLE....

The world is choosing Hercules. Day after day, many more Hercules are sold than any other make. Why? Because Hercules quality created a world-wide demand. A world-wide demand

lowered production costs to a minimum. Lowered production costs bring the Hercules Roadsters, Light Roadsters and Racers to you, at prices far below those of any other make of same quality.

'Popular' Hercules costs £1 less than other makes of similar specification. It has Dunlop roadster tyres, Dunlop rims and a Dunlop waterproof saddle. All usual bright parts are chromium plated.

'POPULAR' MODEL
£3.19.9
OR ON EASY TERMS

These prices apply only to England, Wales and Southern Scotland.

YOUR LOCAL DEALER HAS THESE GREAT SPORTS MODELS

MODEL 'O' RACER — CASH PRICE **£4.3.6** OR EASY TERMS

MODEL 'E' RACER — CASH PRICE **£4.19.6** OR EASY TERMS

and the famous
EMPIRE CLUB RACER — CASH PRICE **£5.15.6** OR EASY TERMS

Hercules
CHROMIUM PLATED BRITISH CYCLES

From any of the following dealers:—
T. G. HALL, 25 and 27, BARTON ST., Gloucester.
A. J. HERBERT, 11, BRISTOL RD, Gloucester.
GOUGH'S, 26, LONDON ROAD, Gloucester.
A. WILLIAMS & CO., 32, WESTGATE ST., Gloucester.
TOM SIMS, 143, BARTON STREET, Gloucester.
SILVEY BROS., THE GARAGE, SAUL, Gloucester.

Albert Arthur Humbles

in an endeavour publicly to demonstrate what an ordinary clubman could do on a clubman's machine, covered 36,007 miles from January 8th 1932 to December 31st 1932, thus beating the 21-year-old record for twelve months riding of 34,366 miles established by Marcel Planes in *Cycling's* Century Competition of 1911.

Humbles had no special training for the ride, although it was undertaken professionally and constituted a full-time occupation. His daily average throughout the year was 100.3 miles, the longest ride in any one day being 172 miles and the shortest 35 miles. Although his usual routes were out from London along the Great North Road, the Cambridge Road and the Newmarket Road he toured England and Wales for considerable periods, visiting places so far apart as Alnwick, Clovelly, Bury St. Edmunds and Bere Regis.

He actually broke the previous record by riding the 34,367th mile at the head of a gigantic club run of over 3,000 cyclists through Hyde Park, London, on December 11th 1932.

A.A. Humbles.
Club:- Ingleside C.C.
Date:- January 18th 1933
Age:- 22.

'Its staying power is invaluable'

says A. A. Humbles, the cycling year's mileage record holder

"Cycling" photograph

"I have been fortunate to break the World's Endurance Cycling Record of 34,366 miles for one year's riding, and my 36,007th mile was completed at the N.C.U. London Centre Reunion.

I have found during 8 months' riding out from home and back that a breakfast of Quick Quaker Oats every morning has provided a good foundation for hard training.

I am glad to say that not once have I been forced from my machine through illness. Most days I started between 8 and 9 o'clock in the morning, doing 50 miles before another meal. *The staying power of Quick Quaker is invaluable.*"

Signed A. Humbles.

Quick Quaker
MADE IN CANADA
Quaker Oats Ltd., London.

Top left Humbles in an advert for Hercules' Empire Club Racer. From *The Citizen*, 22 April 1932.
Top right An image of Humbles in *Cycling* being greeted by members of Gloucester City Cycling Club on the completion of six months' riding.
Bottom left Humbles' entry in *The Golden Book of Cycling*. Image courtesy of The Pedal Club.
Bottom right Humbles in a 1933 advert for Quaker Oats in the *Nottingham Evening Post*.

NICHOLSON'S SECOND WORLD'S RECORD

5000 CHEER GREAT CYCLIST

(By Stan. Mullany.)

On Monday last, at 1.35 p.m., Ossie Nicholson, the Tour de France rider, succeeded in smashing the world's 12 months record of 36,007 miles which stood to the credit of A. A. Humbles of England. Outside the "Malvern

"Ossie" Nicholson, who established a **world** cycling record **for one** year.

AMAZING YEAR'S CYCLE RIDE

Nicholson's Great Achievement

Top left News of Nicholson's 1933 record-breaking ride in the 4 November 1933 edition of the *Frankston and Somerville Standard*. *Image: National Library of Australia.*

Top right Nicholson's record-breaking ride, reported in the *Northern Star* on 3 January 1934. *Image: National Library of Australia.*

Bottom Nicholson receives a trophy from Ralph Small after passing Humbles' record, in this photo from *Cycling*, 12 January 1934.

A terrific action shot of Walter Greaves from the Modern Records Centre archives at the University of Warwick. *Photo originally published in Cycling.*

TWO VEG. MILE-EATERS GET TOGETHER

A. W. BRUMELL *Encounters* W. W. GREAVES

WALTER GREAVES NEARS THE FINISH

Join Him at Hyde Park and Ride with Him the Mile that Breaks the Record

WALTER GREAVES, the one-armed Yorkshireman, is expected to break the world's year mileage record of 43,996 miles, set up by the Australian rider, Ossie Nicholson, on Sunday next, December 13. Up to last Sunday he had covered 43,184 miles and, in spite of snow and rain, he is still going strong. In order that all interested cyclists can give him a welcome that such a ride deserves, arrangements have been made for Greaves to ride the mile that breaks the record around Hyde Park, finishing at the Speakers' Gate, where he will be received by many notable people and be presented with a commemorative trophy. Cyclists are invited to assemble inside the park, at Hyde Park Corner, at 9.15 a.m.

Greaves is riding a Coventry Three Spires bicycle with Safety Spokes, Middlemore saddle and Dunlop tyres.

Walter Greaves—a "Cycling" portrait.
A41

Walter Greaves on his Coventry Three Spires Bicycle

Top left An invitation in the 9 December 1936 issue of *Cycling* for cyclists to join Walter Greaves as he rides his record-breaking mile on 13 December 1936.
Top right Greaves and A.W. Brumell in the 25 February 1936 issue of *The Bicycle*.
Bottom left Walter with his son Joe. *Photo courtesy of Joe Greaves.*
Bottom right Greaves' record-breaking ride on the front cover of *The Bicycle*, 15 December 1936.

CYCLING

JANUARY 6, 1937.

45,383.7 MILES

THOUSANDS GREET WALTER GREAVES AS HE ENDS HIS GREAT YEAR'S RIDE

"It is a magnificent feat, especially for a rider with only one arm"— Lord Mayor of Bradford

Greaves to Write the Story of His Remarkable Ride in Next Wednesday's "Cycling"

Mr. F. W. Hawkins (Coventry Bicycles, Ltd.) handing three cheques to Greaves. An exclusive "Cycling" photograph taken at 1 a.m. on January 1, 1937. The three cheques are £100 from Coventry Bicycles; £25 from TriVelox Gears, Ltd., and £25 from Middlemore Saddles. The three cups seen in the picture are also from the same companies.

THE momentous year of 1936, a year that will be long remembered in history, had but ten minutes still to expire when Walter William Greaves, the 30-year-old one-armed Bradford vegetarian, rode to the Town Hall Square at Bradford, to end his year's mileage record ride. Since January 6, when he started out to beat the year's record then held by Ossie Nicholson, the well-known Australian with 43,996 miles, Greaves has ridden 45,383.7 miles. He passed Nicholson's record on December 13.

Lord Mayor's Greeting.

Thousands greeted the record-breaker when he arrived at Bradford, and stalwart policemen had to shoulder a passageway through the eager crowd in order that he could reach the steps of the Town Hall, where the Lord Mayor, Alderman George R. Carter, awaited to congratulate him. "It is a magnificent feat, especially for a rider with only one arm," declared the Lord Mayor amid cheers.

The previous evening Greaves had attended the Bradford Elite dinner and consequently he had not started his last day's ride quite so early as the others. Nevertheless he had still ridden about 113 miles.

A10

After the Lord Mayor, on behalf of the Coventry Bicycle Co., the TriVelox Gear Co., the Middlemore Saddle Co. and Mr. W. Bains, the well-known Bradford cycle agent, had presented Greaves with four silver cups, the record breaker was taken to a nearby hotel where Mr. F. W. Hawkins, on behalf of Coventry Bicycles, the TriVelox Gear Co. and Middlemores, presented him with a cheque for £100 and

two for £25 each. Greaves, it will be recalled, rode a Coventry "Three Spires" bicycle, equipped with a TriVelox gear (78 ins., 73 ins., and 66.6 ins.) and Middlemore saddle.

When he began his ride Greaves was unemployed. Now, as well as receiving prize money and a salary throughout his ride, he has been given a year's contract with Coventry Bicycles, Ltd. Ever since he started Greaves's mileage

The scene at the steps of the Town Hall, Bradford, just after Greaves had finished his ride on December 31. The record breaker is seen just behind the cup. The Lord Mayor of Bradford is standing next to him, hidden by the crowd.

Greaves' year record reported in the 6 January 1937 issue of *Cycling*.

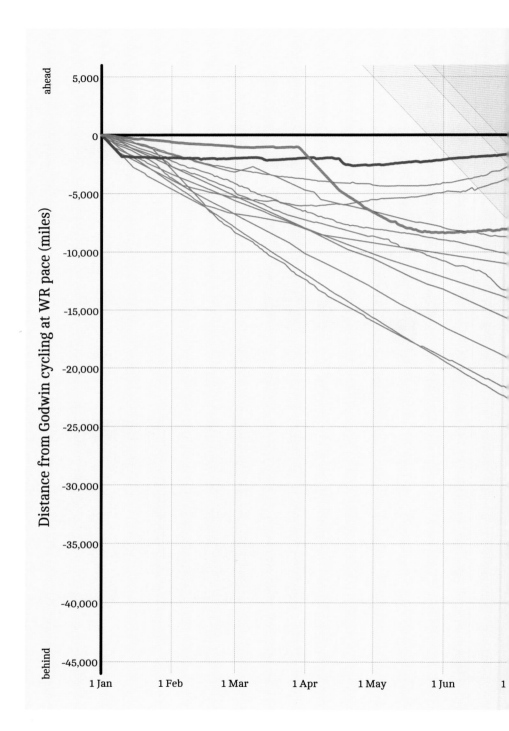

A graphical visualisation comparing the mile-eaters' calendar-year performances against Godwin's 1939 record. Also shown is the mileage to date of Steve Abraham (red line) and Kurt Searvogel (blue line). *Graphic by Jo Wood, Professor of Visual Analytics*

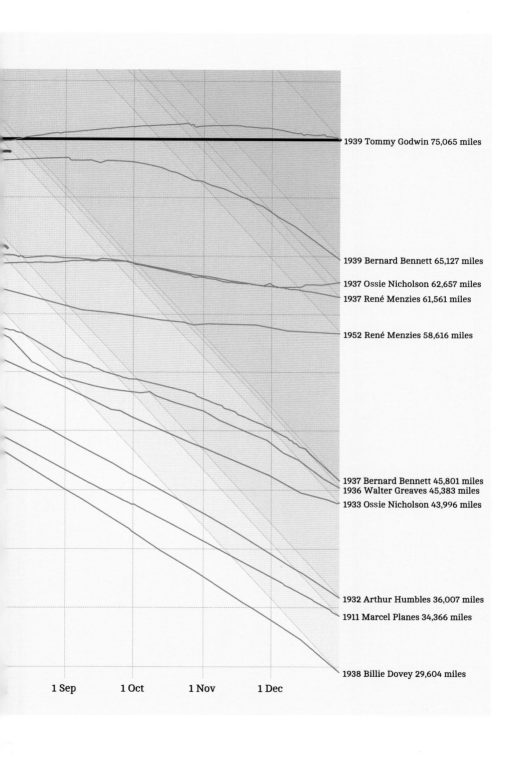

1939 Tommy Godwin 75,065 miles

1939 Bernard Bennett 65,127 miles

1937 Ossie Nicholson 62,657 miles
1937 René Menzies 61,561 miles

1952 René Menzies 58,616 miles

1937 Bernard Bennett 45,801 miles
1936 Walter Greaves 45,383 miles
1933 Ossie Nicholson 43,996 miles

1932 Arthur Humbles 36,007 miles

1911 Marcel Planes 34,366 miles

1938 Billie Dovey 29,604 miles

1 Sep   1 Oct   1 Nov   1 Dec

HOWEVER THE BABY OF THE PARTY IS LITTLE BERNARD BENNETT OF BIRMINGHAM —— EQUIPPED WITH A FEEDING BOTTLE OF GRIPE WATER

THIS TINY TOT SETS OFF EVERY MORNING ON HIS KIDDIECAR AND DOESN'T COME BACK UNTIL HE HAS DONE A HUNDRED AND FORTY MILES OR SO.

WHEREVER HAVE YOU BEEN? IT'S HOURS PAST YOUR BEDTIME!

AW! I MET SOME O' THE BOYS

B. BENNETT, BRITISH CYCLIST.

Top left Ossie Nicholson, pictured in *The Cyclist*, 5 January 1938.
Top right René Menzies, pictured in *The Cyclist*, 5 January 1938.
Centre The cartoon of 'baby' Bernard Bennett, which featured in *The Cyclist*.
Bottom left Scottish amateur James Stewart, one of the contenders who fell by the wayside in 1937.
From *Cycling*, January 1937.
Bottom right Bennett's checking card from 25 January 1937, as reproduced in *The Cyclist*.

THE BICYCLE: January 4, 1938   17

Sunday in Hyde Park. A. J. Denny, managing director of Rudge-Whitworth Cycles, congratulates Menzies

CLAUD LETS IN IN WITH A BANG!

L. CAMILLO

With GAY at the Horticultural Hall

H. S. DRUCE

H. R. HORDEN (Brooks Saddles)

G. A. HOFFMAN (Sister Smith's and Rudge-Whitworth's)

Outside the new Horticultural Hall. Left to right, Miss Menzies, Rene Menzies and Bernard Bennett

Syd Ferris (left) hands over the lucky-number prize, a C.B. Tandem, to the fortunate winner. In centre is Claud Butler

Entering Hyde Park on Sunday

CLOSING SCENES OF MENZIES' RIDE

Menzies' ride featured in a splash in *The Bicycle* on 4 January 1938.

OSSIE NICHOLSON'S RECORD RIDE

Daily Average, Month by Month

CHECKED by a special committee under the direction of Mr. G. R. Broadbent, of the R.A.C.V., Ossie Nicholson's daily averages per month during his record-breaking ride, make very interesting reading. They are as follows :—

January	4671.1 (150.71)	July	.. 5339 (172.23)
February	4279.6 (152.84)	August ..	5973.6 (192.7)
March..	4841.7 (156.16)	September	5760.8 (192)
April ..	4279.8 (162.21)	October..	5271.6 (170)
May ..	4968 (160.26)	November	5527.8 (184.26)
June ..	5359.5 (178.65)	December	6075 (196)

A total of over 170,000 miles was covered between the three contestants who put up such remarkable performances in last year's long distance rides. Bernard Bennett (amateur) notched 45,801 miles, Rene Menzies (British professional record holder) 61,561 miles, and Ossie Nicholson (Australian professional, and world record holder) 62,657.6 miles.

While a different make of machine was used by each rider, it is interesting to note that "Cyclo" three-speed gears were used by all three.

A recent picture of Ossie Nicholson, holder of the year's mileage record with 62,657 miles. Details of his daily averages for each month are given alongside

Rene Menzies, the 48 year old cyclist who, on Wednesday last, reached the amazing total of 45,384 miles ridden since January 1st, and so broke the world's annual mileage record with over three months to spare.

He used a Rudge Whitworth bicycle, fitted with a Cyclo Gear and Constrictor tyres.

45,384 miles in 272 days

Full Story on Page 7

Top Ossie Nicholson's record ride, as featured in *Bicycling News* on 10 February 1938.
Bottom René Menzies. *The Bicycle*, 5 October 1937.

Billie Dovey in Trafalgar Square. *Photo: Cycling/Fleming family archives.*

THOUGHTS OF A YEAR RIDER

BY
BILLIE DOVEY

The Rudge-Whitworth girl rider who is out to cover a minimum of 25,000 miles in a year to demonstrate the health benefits of cycling for women, describes a few impressions obtained during her days awheel

Billie Dovey, posts a checking card to *Cycling* from West Wycombe.

AN interesting question was recently asked by a non-cycling acquaintance who said, " Why do you hold your handlebar like that?" " . . . like that . . ." being the familiar " on the tops " position. I explained to my friend that most experienced cyclists were able to obtain two, if not three, positions on a dropped bar. Having satisfied him that I was not suffering from back-ache, it did occur to me that more than a few women riders do not appear to be as comfortable on their machines as they might be. I have always maintained that when positioned holding the " drops," this should give the maximum comfort for riding mile after mile, and be one's main position.

Almost Disaster.

Rather appalling is the manner in which private cars are allowed to park at shopping centres. After having ridden for only two weeks, I was slowly climbing a hill, made harder by a strong head-wind, when an off-side door was flung open in my path. Fortunately I did not swerve, but managed to stop against the side of the car, to watch a large lorry rumble past where I had been riding. I dismounted, and spoke to the car driver, and almost immediately received a command from the same " gentleman " to go to that mythical place of torture. . . .

The car number I carefully noted at once, but what could I do in the matter? This sort of thing I know happens to cyclists every day. It is no doubt individuals of this type only who would have the public believe that . . . cyclists are the biggest nuisance on the road. Even when approached in a civil and ordinary manner, wishing to point out the fallacy of his action he has not the decency to even listen.

Did you know that most married male tourists admit that their cycling holidays are much more enjoyable when spent with their wives?

The reason divulged to me by much-travelled experts was that their partners nearly always managed to pack the things they need (all of them!) . . . and better. Pyjamas would be housed in a rubber-lined sponge-bag. When " he " washed, the flannel was always there, and not at the bottom of the touring bag. Shaving tackle, etc., would be neatly enclosed in another sponge-bag. These, incidentally, only cost sixpence, and have a multitude of uses.

I suppose now there will be an avalanche of protests from the great " unmarrieds " that they can do without the bother of a wife on tour! Well, here's praise for the girl friend who reminds you that some of your kit was left in the bathroom, and has the pluck at breakfast-table to tell you that you've left shaving-soap behind your ears!

Whether cycling in Herts, Essex or Surrey, it is always noticeable how the workmen on roadside repairs will shout a greeting. I have on occasions ridden past twenty or more men—the " Good morning! " call is passed along the line, and is sometimes akin to being welcomed by a guard of honour.

In the majority of cases each has his bicycle—still the handiest means of transport!

I found Kent—perhaps not in the grandest of humours, for the week spent in visiting this county was one of high North-East winds, drizzle and lack of sunshine. What I saw brought on the longing that " some day " I would have to return thoroughly to explore the lesser byways.

I loved Sandwich, with its quaint narrow streets, and also Shoreham—sleepy and unspoilt. It is, of course, very satisfying to see places like these mid-week, for I can well imagine the same atmosphere does not prevail at times when many scores of other travellers decide to visit these well-known spots.

Club Assistance.

At Dover I was rendered valuable assistance by two members of the Dover Cycling Club re routes, accommodation, etc., which I shall always associate with the name of that town. Taking their names and addresses before entering upon the Sussex part of my tour, it was not over-surprising that one of them had actually been christened Gordon Goodfellow by his parents!

Males are said to be more successful than women because of their persistence and tenacity of purpose. In which case, I ought to have handed a bouquet to each of the two very charming " boys " from the East Kent D.A. of the C.T.C. who rode in from Margate, and insisted on taking me out to supper!

A 43

One of Billie's 'Thoughts of a Year Rider' articles in *Cycling*. This one in the 6 July 1938 issue.

Top left Billie in an advert for Cadbury, 'an emergency meal for all travellers, particularly cyclists who are often off the beaten track.'
Top right A Malvern Star advert featuring Pat Hawkins, in the 16 August 1941 edition of the *Daily News*.
Bottom Billie – smiling, as ever – out on the road. *Photo: Cycling/Fleming family archives.*

Top Billie out on the road. *Photo: Cycling/Fleming family archives.*

Bottom It was a great pleasure to be able to meet Billie in 2014 and to talk to her about her 1938 year and her love of cycling. *Photo: Dave Barter.*

Top Tommy Godwin out on the road.
Bottom left Godwin signing his checking card in front of witnesses.
Bottom right Godwin in an advert for Dunlop tyres in the 10 January 1940 issue of *Cycling*.

T. E. GODWIN RIDES 75,065 MILES

Stupendous New Year's Mileage Record

IN spite of the weather conditions, which must have prevented many from reaching the meeting place on time, hundreds of cyclists, some in uniform, rode with Tommy Godwin through Hyde Park, London's famous park, on Sunday morning, the last day of the year, to celebrate Godwin's feat of having ridden 75,000 miles during the year.

Starting from Hyde Park Corner, the monster club run rode round the banks of the Serpentine to Marble Arch, where Godwin, looking as fresh and as fit as any of the clubfolk accompanying him, was presented with a laurel wreath and a yellow jersey bearing the words " Year's Mileage Record, 75,065 Miles." This was the total Godwin intended to complete that day, which meant that he had still 55 miles to ride before midnight that night.

From Marble Arch Godwin rode with an escort to the Grosvenor House Hotel where, before a little band of enthusiasts, including Marcel Planes, the man who won *Cycling's* Century Competition in 1911 and so set up the first year's mileage record, Godwin was invited by the Editor of *Cycling* to sign the Golden Book of Cycling. Calling upon the assembly, which included the holder of the Land's End to John o'Groat's record, S. H. Ferris; L. Hartwell, London manager of Raleighs and Sturmey-Archer Gears; E. V. Mills and W. G. Paul, world's tandem record holders; C. F. Davey, Godwin's manager; F. Keller, advertising manager of Raleighs and Sturmey-Archers, and several prominent London clubmen, Mr. Hartwell said that Tommy Godwin had beaten the previous year's record, put up by Ossie Nicholson, an Australian, in 1937, by 12,048 miles. " Even to experienced cyclists Godwin's feat of having ridden an average of 205 miles for 365 days is looked upon as an amazing performance," declared Mr. Hartwell, who added that it was early in Godwin's ride that he decided to fit a Sturmey-Archer four-speed hub gear to his Raleigh bicycle. Mr. Hartwell thanked the Editor of *Cycling* for checking Godwin's ride. " This is Godwin's 5,001st signature I've seen

Marcel Planes congratulating Tommy Godwin in Hyde Park on Sunday.

this year," said the Editor of *Cycling* when asking Godwin to sign a page of the Golden Book of Cycling. He revealed that Godwin had sent him five postcards every day and checking cards containing 10 daily signatures. Telegrams of congratulations were read from G. H. B. Wilson, managing director of Raleighs,

and A. Frazer of New-Hudsons and Bernard Bennett, the young Birmingham rider, who finished up the year with a mileage of 65,127. After signing the Golden Book of Cycling, Godwin set out to ride his remaining 55 miles. The following morning he was up early—he is carrying on to ride 100,000 miles in 500 days.

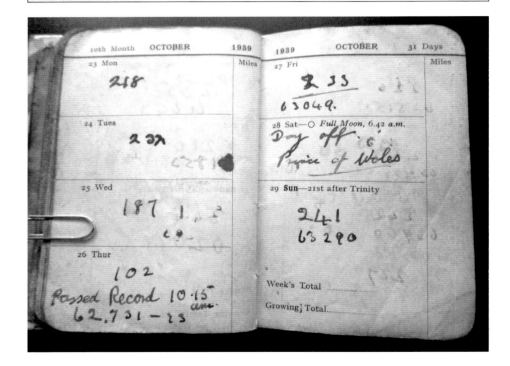

Top Tommy's record ride is reported in the 3 January 1940 issue of *Cycling*.
Bottom Tommy's diary from late October 1939, showing his daily mileages and the day he broke Nicholson's record.
Photo: Dave Barter/Godwin family archive.

HOW I RODE 75,000 MILES IN THE YEAR

"My STURMEY-ARCHER 4 SPEED GEAR saved ⅓ of the effort"

says TOMMY GODWIN

Tommy's mileage increased from 156 miles per day to over 200 when he fitted the Sturmey-Archer 4-speed Gear ....a step up of over 33⅓%
In 11 months Tommy subjected his Gear to something like **10 years' normal wear**! Yet never once did it falter. "I'd never have succeeded without it," says Tommy. "I regard the Sturmey-Archer 4-speed Gear as a necessity for all cyclists."

YOU ALSO CAN
SAVE ⅓ OF YOUR EFFORT
For every mile you travel without a Sturmey-Archer 4-speed Gear, you can cover ONE MILE AND A THIRD when you fit the Gear—and with the same effort! That's the difference it made to Tommy.

★ *EFFORT WITHOUT STURMEY-ARCHER COVERS 3 MILES*

★ *SAME EFFORT WITH STURMEY-ARCHER COVERS 4 MILES*

STURMEY-ARCHER
STURMEY-ARCHER GEARS LTD., NOTTINGHAM

Top H.J. Brueton presenting the New Hudson cup to Bernard Bennett at the end of his ride, while J.B. Bayliss looks on. *Cycling*, 3 January 1940.
Bottom Godwin in an advert for Sturmey-Archer in the 17 January 1940 issue of *Cycling*.

Top left Godwin reaches the 100-000-mile mark at the Paddington track on 13 May 1940.
Top right Godwin's mileometer showing five zeros, as he passes the 100,000-mile mark in May 1940.
Bottom *L–R:* Tommy Godwin, Neil Hemmings and Gordon Jones in Whitchurch, Shropshire, c.1957.
Photo: Hemmings family archive.

sixty he recorded a massive 412 miles. As the record for that year was Bob Mynott's 459.50 miles, Menzies' total no doubt put a large number of his younger competitors to shame.

He didn't stop there. Just before midnight on New Year's Eve 1951 the sixty-two-year-old Menzies caught a taxi to Parliament Square in London and set off for a third attempt at the year record. His target was not the full record, which at that time had been set by Tommy Godwin in 1939. Menzies was simply determined to beat Nicholson. His stated aim was to ride beyond 62,657.6 miles on the same bicycle that he had used some fifteen years earlier. Only a few friends and a reporter were present to see him off and wish him luck and the roads were covered in winter sleet. Menzies led a tiny band of cyclists around Parliament Square, past Hyde Park Corner and then dropped them all as he upped the pace and headed for Marble Arch. They briefly regained contact before Menzies headed off in search of a post office to send his inaugural mileage card. The riders did not see him again that day as he'd hared off west, eventually arriving at Wolverhampton with 121 miles upon the clock. The magnanimous Tommy Godwin wished Menzies well on his attempt and cordially offered Menzies a bed and food for the night were he to stray over into the Stoke area. Godwin also stated that were Menzies to go further than his target distance and encroach upon his own record, he might be tempted to have a go again himself.

Later that month Menzies crashed and broke his collarbone. This prevented him from riding for nearly three weeks, after which he was pictured outside the offices of *The Bicycle* magazine holding his machine aloft as evidence that the injury was mended. His mileage to 18 February was 3,900, some 2,700 miles behind where he needed to be in order to keep track with Nicholson's figures. Yet still he rode on, tackling yet another terrible British winter and riding through near Arctic conditions only too aware of the deficit that his injury had created. In order to keep his mileage high he began to sleep on the roadside, often by accident. On one occasion he had been riding with his cape on to escape the rain and gently dozed off in the saddle. Fortunately he fell on to a grassy verge, without disturbing his sleep at all. He was awakened by a concerned passer-by who thought he'd found the body of an injured cyclist and was about to call 999 before prudently deciding to prod the sleeping Menzies with his toe.

Menzies even considered following the 1952 Tour de France caravan as part of his year until Jacques Goddet, the race organiser, heard of his plans and sent an urgent cable back to the UK:

'Menzies – don't be a fool. Stay where you have roads like a velodrome. Don't you know when you are well off?'

This was a clear reference to the mountains of the Alps and Pyrenees.

The Tour plans were not followed through, but Menzies did cross the channel during his year – on a quest for a beret. Menzies was always seen riding with a black beret atop his head and had asked his new wife to dye a spare that was beginning to lose its colour. The blue dye had run out of the hat in the rain and completely covered Menzies face. He'd not been able to acquire one in the UK and thus decided a trip to France was in order, finding a new beret in Saint-Étienne.

Menzies was quick to return to the UK, visiting Scotland and most of the English counties as part of his riding year. In November a gale blew a tree branch into his path, smashing his wheel and injuring his shoulder. Resolute as ever, Menzies carried his bicycle by foot for seven miles to Bawtry to seek a repair. Despite this, he had ridden 48,920 miles in 292 days by the time winter arrived, along with its icy roads, fog and cold. This hampered Menzies and it was now clear that he would have to ride into 1953 in order to go past the total of Nicholson. Undeterred, he celebrated the New Year with a ride down to the Pyrenees.

By this time Cycling magazine had ceased formally verifying year mileage records. Therefore, Menzies' ride had been overseen by The Bicycle magazine and, as a result of his injury and subsequent inability to ride in January, they had agreed to effectively 'neutralise' twenty-four days of 1952 as part of his count. He therefore planned to finish his year on 24 January 1953 after two days of riding around Hyde Park.

The weather forced him to take the train home for a large portion of his French itinerary. He arrived back in the UK and rode from Newhaven to London. On the Thursday before his planned finish his cyclometer showed a value of 62,433 miles, 224 short of the total of Nicholson. But Menzies was clearly anxious to get it done and rode 204 of these before 9 a.m. on the Friday morning, clocking up his 62,658th mile at 10.16 a.m. Menzies had cocked a snook back in time to the younger Nicholson and shown that he had always been capable of beating the Australian, and still was now, at the age of sixty-three. After a hastily organised press conference Menzies retired to bed with a cold.

The next day, Menzies was back on his bike for a planned reception around Parliament Square. At 11 a.m. on Saturday 24 January 1953 he rode the final miles of his most outstanding year. Of all the mile-eaters none but he had found the will to take on the record three times and nobody had ever even conceived of an attempt beyond their thirtieth year. This resolute and cheerful Frenchman had taken on nobody but himself and the ghost of Nicholson's record in his quest to better his mileage. While the calendar year record had eluded him due to injury, he had beaten Nicholson over 365 days and in his own mind put to bed the frustrations of 1937.

Marcel Planes, now a sprightly sixty-two years old himself, turned out to accompany Menzies over his final miles. Tommy Godwin sent his own personal tribute: 'I would like to express my congratulations to Mr Menzies on such a wonderful feat – in my estimation he is a real King of the Road, and I welcome this opportunity to pay tribute to this fine sportsman'.

Menzies was accompanied at the reception around Parliament Square by a number of other cyclists, some of whom had ridden overnight to see him finish with a final mileage reading of 62,785 miles. Fittingly they stopped in Dean Street for a glass of red wine. This was the area that Marcel Planes had ridden from daily in 1911 as part of his own record attempt. Remember also that the two riders shared similar French heritage and one wonders with which language they conversed as Planes relayed his hearty congratulations.

Menzies carried on riding for the rest of his life and had planned to undertake a tour to France in his seventieth year. Sadly, he was mortally injured in an accident with a car on Boxing Day 1971 while riding around Hyde Park Corner, a location intrinsically linked with many of the year-record riders. Again the cycling world quietly waved goodbye to one of the greatest endurance riders it had ever known.

Menzies strength had lain not only in his legs but, as he had repeatedly demonstrated, also in his character. His will to return to the unfinished business of 1937 and – despite yet another serious injury – conquer his opponent while in his twilight years is unprecedented. The press often commented that this great man lived for one thing only: his days upon the bike. And while it is tragic that he lost his life to an accident, it is also fitting that he met his end doing the thing he loved most and that he was, at that time, planning yet another long-distance riding adventure.

BILLIE DOVEY –
THE 'KEEP FIT' GIRL

P rior to 1938, endurance-riding headlines had been dominated by men. This was at a time when the mainstream cycling press was still undecided on the place of women within cycle racing and competition. But women were beginning to have their say. Some truly great female riders were emerging and beginning to attack records that had been seen as the domain of the men. Sixteen new women's place-to-place records had been set in 1937, along with the creation of a series of female-only time trials. Momentum was beginning to gather around female cyclists. It was time for women to redress the balance and put female cycling properly on the year map.

Lilian Irene Bartram was born on 13 April 1914 to a Camden-based tool-maker and his wife Julie. She was to be the first of three children conceived by the couple, all of them girls. Her name proved to be a bit of a mouthful for those around her and so Lilian soon became Lillie, which morphed further into 'Billie' as those around her confused the first and last letters of her name. An apparently studious child, she worked hard at Lyulph Stanley Central School in Camden before leaving at the age of sixteen to become a secretary.

Billie discovered cycling at the age of eighteen after a chance meeting at a youth club with a young lad who taught her to ride a bike. In her own words: 'I couldn't ride a bike at the time, he used to take me out on the Barnet bypass in Mill Hill London in the evening and teach me how to ride this bike. He used to ride about a metre from the kerb and I had to stay in this gap.'

While the relationship with this lad did not last, the relationship with the bicycle did and Billie became besotted with cycling. She began to use her bicycle to commute to work and its benefits in terms of health and adventure had become clear. Billie's passion was bolstered by her involvement in the Women's League of Health and Beauty, an organisation founded by Mary Bagot Stack in the 1930s. Mary believed that women held the key to the improvement of the world around them and preached a vision of 'a league of women who will renew their energy in themselves and for themselves day by day.' She trained a network of female fitness instructors to spread the message of the 'Women's League' and the membership grew rapidly to over 166,000 by 1937. Billie was inspired and felt that she could do something to spread the word about cycling.

She made it her mission to tell others, especially women, about cycling and as a result wrote to a large number of companies with her idea for cycling promotion. The rides of Bennett, Nicholson and Menzies had started a thought process in Dovey's mind and she wanted to set herself up as a showcase rider, riding her bike every day for a year. Each month she would ride at least 2,000 miles and aim to complete the year with 25,000 miles upon the clock. Billie had no particular ambition to set a women's record (although, as one had never previously been officially recorded, she would do just that). This was to be an altruistic mission to spread the word rather than a personal ambition to become the best.

In late 1935 Lilian Bartram became Lilian Dovey after meeting and marrying her husband Fredrick in Hendon. Fredrick, a keen cyclist who worked as a chartered accountant, clearly supported Billie's cycling ambitions and went on to manage her diary and engagements through-out her record year.

At the time Billie was a member of the North-Western Road Club and mixing in some esteemed female cycling company, including E. Rolph – a rider who'd spent the previous year fighting it out on various place-to-place records under the auspices of the recently formed Women's Road Record Association. Using her cycling knowledge, contacts and secretarial skills to good effect, Billie wrote to all of the major cycling companies and explained her mission. Eventually her tenacity paid off and, at the age of twenty-three, Billie received sponsorship from Rudge Whitworth, the sponsor of René Menzies, who agreed to provide her with a new bike and the requisite support to begin her ride. In return Billie was required to travel the country stopping at the Rudge Whitworth dealerships and giving talks along her way. Word then got out and Cadbury was brought on as an additional sponsor, with Billie appearing in an early set of adverts promo-ting its chocolate as an 'ideal emergency meal for cyclists off the beaten track'. The company provided Billie with unlimited supplies of chocolate for her ride, a benefit that would be the envy of many a modern-day sweet-tooth.

Cycling magazine was approached and asked to verify Billie's ride using the process that had been tried and tested since 1911. This would require the submission of mileage cards and a regular visit to the offices of the magazine for a mileometer check. The magazine labelled her the 'keep fit girl' and somewhat offhandedly labelled her task a 'year's cycling propaganda ride'.

Not long after midnight on 1 January 1938 Billie left Claud Butler's party at the New Horticultural Hall in London, where Bennett and Menzies were still celebrating the end of their attempts, and began her ride. Giving up her job as a typist and leaving her husband at home to act as her manager and co-ordinator, she set out to tour Great Britain. Her mission: 'to demonstrate that cycling is a simple and easy method to keep fit'.

Billie had no ambition at all to set a cycling record: 'It was just an idea I had, I didn't set out to attempt a year record. At the time there was a lot of publicity about the Women's League of Health and Beauty, an organisation concerned with women's health and fitness. I was so besotted with cycling that I thought "well you could keep fit by riding a bicycle". I had this idea that I could do just that.'

Billie maintained this modesty throughout her year, clearly set on a mission in the service of cycling, rather than attempting to benefit from it.

Billie's first week got off to a reasonable start, totalling 459 miles. This was slightly down on the average required to hit 25,000 but remember she, like all of the other British riders, began in winter, and the reduced daylight hours and inclement weather would have been a factor. She started riding locally and her routes and mileages were recorded as follows:

Date	Route	Mileage
1 January 1938	London (Westminster), Mill Hill, Aylesbury, Mill Hill	71.6
2 January 1938	Watford, Rickmansworth, Denham, High Wycombe, Princes Risborough, Wendover, Amersham, Chalfont St Giles, Rickmansworth, Watford, Mill Hill	80.3
3 January 1938	Welwyn, Hitchin, Baldock, Royston, Ware, Hatfield, Mill Hill	77.2
4 January 1938	Woodford, Bishop's Stortford, Stansted, Woodford, Mill Hill	75.2
5 January 1938	St Albans, Hockliffe, Leighton Buzzard, Hemel Hempstead, St Albans, Hatfield, Barnet, Mill Hill	72.0
6 January 1938	Stanborough, Hatfield, Potters Bar, Barnet, Mill Hill	35.4
7 January 1938	Stevenage, Hatfield, Barnet, Mill Hill	47.3
	Total	459

Interestingly, Billie was not alone out on the roads mile-munching. An amateur cyclist and Liverpudlian, R.A. Cheesbrough, had decided to take on Nicholson's record in the same year and, like Billie, set out on 1 January. Cheesbrough managed to clock up an impressive 1,166.5 miles in his first week, despite being hit by a car which had breasted a canal bridge too quickly. The accident was made worse by the fact that Cheesbrough wasn't even cycling at the time but was searching for a spanner that had dropped from his bag. For some inexplicable reason he grabbed the front bumper of the car and was dragged down the road for 80 yards. Fortunately he only suffered cuts and bruises, but the subsequent loss in mileage left him down on Nicholson's average by 5 miles a day. The plucky Liverpudlian continued to ride despite suffering back pain, but things got worse and on 9 February 1938, already several hundred miles behind Ossie Nicholson's pace, it was reported that he had a poisoned toe and had been ordered to rest by his doctor. He valiantly battled on through February, but things were getting worse and between 5 and 18 February 1938 he was forced to rest for five days. He finally packed in his attempt later that month as it was clear his foot was getting no better and Nicholson's mileage was moving ever further out of reach as he recuperated.

1938 was clearly a bad year for male cycling mileage-record aspirants. A Mr William T. Holt of Radcliffe (Lancashire) also set out for glory. He was hit by a car on the same day as R.A. Cheesbrough and ended up hospitalised in Banbury. Three days later he lost control on tramlines, crashed and was left with neuritis that rendered the lower portion of his right arm temporarily useless. William's bad luck was compounded by the fact that he was just about to receive sponsorship for his year's ride. The offer was now put on hold as his backers sought to assess how his injuries would heal. Despite the setbacks he kept riding one-armed, and by 7 March 1938 had amassed a total of 6,700 miles as he fought his way back into contention, with most of his riding reported as being upon the Lancashire roads with the occasional trip to the Midlands. However, he looks to have given up shortly after this last report as no mention appears to have been made of his attempt again.

One man would fare slightly better in 1938. Remember that René Menzies was also out on the roads. He succeeded in his attempt to get to 100,000 miles, although he too failed in his year attempt and only rode 24 miles on 1 January as a rest day before cycling 111 miles in the UK and then heading over to France.

Three weeks into her ride, Billie was still going strong. She'd managed to maintain a daily average of 71 miles and was still riding around an area centred upon her home in Mill Hill. Then came a big day. On 6 February 1938 she rode her first century of the year. Setting off from Cobham she rode via Guildford, Elstead, Odiham, Bagshot and Windsor before finishing in Mill Hill with a grand total of 107 miles for the day. Clearly gaining a taste for the hundred-milers she knocked off another two weeks later, this time heading east from Mill Hill and riding 108 miles. It appeared that cycling agreed with the young rider, who reported that rather than wasting away, she was actually gaining weight. On 23 February she was 3 pounds heavier than when she started her ride (muscle we must assume, although it could also have been down to Cadbury's sponsorship of unlimited supplies of chocolate).

Billie's agreement with Rudge Whitworth was demanding from the off, with her sponsor requiring that she represent them at many engagements during her ride, often on a daily basis. The first documented occasion was when she was presented as a guest to the annual dinner of the Vegetarian Cycling and Athletic Club – the same club to which Walter Greaves had belonged. Other presentations were lower key, sometimes simply a meeting of local cyclists at a Rudge Whitworth dealership. Rudge Whitworth relished the early attention that Billie was receiving in the press and contacted its entire dealer network, urging them to get in touch and book an appointment with Billie for the purposes of 'local publicity'.

March 1938 saw Billie's campaigning really hit her stride when she wrote a full-page article in *Cycling* magazine extolling the virtues of cycling and imploring more women to join her on the road. The article underpinned Billie's no-nonsense approach to life that clearly remained with her throughout her life. Her headline ran: 'Wanted – 1,000,000 more women cyclists', and the article debunked the myth that women would find riding a bike difficult and made it clear that there were many female-specific bikes to be had from a variety of bicycle manufacturers. She went on to detail her straightforward logistics for cycling to work, such as storing clothing to change into, and highlighted the London bus strike as a clear example of female emancipation, with many women taking to their bikes to get to work. However, my favourite quote outlines the fact that in 1938 women were still very much seen as the fairer sex and little else:

Others still consider it 'not becoming' or perhaps 'unladylike' although generally these Victorian ideas are just about as dead as the proverbial door nail.

The appearance of we wheel-women matters more than we sometimes imagine. The ever critical public notice us as we pass through village, town and hamlet, so during 1938 we must do our best to look as clean and healthy as possible when riding, in order that we may attract more and more of our sex to pedal their way to fitness and social enjoyment.

Winter was clearly kind to Billie as 23 March 1938 found her ahead of her 25,000 mile schedule with a daily average of almost 73 miles. She was still riding locally, with most of her days reported as ending in Mill Hill and the same familiar towns frequently recorded upon her mileage cards – Wendover, Hornchurch and St Albans. Billie did not always ride circular routes and occasionally used public transport to return home. On 8 March she rode from Mill Hill to Wantage via Reading, recording her third century at a distance of 110.8 miles.

By the end of the month Billie's ride was starting to attract attention beyond the coasts of Great Britain. An invitation was received from Ireland inviting her over to spend time in the Dublin area, although the trip never happened and it is likely that Rudge Whitworth saw little benefit in her making the trip as the majority of its dealerships were located in Great Britain. The company was very much focused upon developing direct sales, particularly to the growing contingent of female cyclists. Its preference was for Billie to make appearances at venues where its bikes could be purchased there and then.

At the end of March Billie left the North-Western Road Club and announced her affiliation with the Southern Ladies' Road Club instead. This club had been recently formed by Florence 'Flossie' Wren, a racing cyclist and wife of the well-known frame builder Cyril. Billie now represented female cyclists both in actions and affiliations.

April saw Billie spread her wings further and really ramp up her daily average. She started touring the West Country, visiting locations such as Swindon, Marlborough and Glastonbury, and as far afield as Taunton. On 15 and 16 April she rode her first back-to-back centuries, with a ride of 106.2 miles followed by one of 100.5. Her daily average was now up to 80 miles and she was starting to very definitely prove her point that women can easily adapt to regular cycling and gain fitness as a result in performance alone.

On 4 May 1938 *Cycling* magazine announced Billie's first national tour schedule. She was to give talks throughout early May in locations ranging from Guildford to Portsmouth. Each location would have been at a Rudge Whitworth dealer where Billie would present herself at 7 p.m. and give a talk concerning her ride. This clearly benefitted her sponsors as the question of 'which bike?' would ultimately come up during the evening. But Billie wanted to do much more than advertise bikes and, through a letter to *Cycling* magazine, asked that cycling club folk could attend so that she could spread her healthy living message further.

Around this time a Miss Evelyn Hamilton set out to ride 10,000 miles in 100 days and, from 7 to 13 May, had clocked up an impressive 763.5 miles. Billie's enthusiasm for female mile-munching was clearly contagious. Hamilton was still going strong after twenty-one days with 2,259.9 miles in the bag. After forty-nine days the total was 5,218.1 and, after ninety-one days, 9,737.9. Hamilton reported her quest to be completed on 24 August when her letter saying thank you for all of the support she had received from the cycling community appeared in *Cycling* magazine. Hamilton had apparently far exceeded her original 10,000-mile target.

Billie had also hit 10,000 miles, on 12 May as Hamilton was starting her ride. In doing so she also moved 1,000 miles ahead of her initial schedule. Billie's ride gathered further press attention in June 1938 as, in a forthright interview in *Bicycling* magazine, she described her motivations for riding 75 miles each day. The interview gave an insight into the kind of determination and zest for life that Billie possessed:

> I am now engaged in the most enjoyable occupation I have ever had, for instead of tapping a typewriter under a glass roof, I am now healthfully pedalling a bicycle around every day.

Clearly Billie was no shrinking violet content to bear the drudgery of an office job day in, day out. She went on to describe the challenges she had faced in her first five months of riding, including strong winds:

> So far my ride has been generally blessed with fine weather, but there have been strong (aye, very strong) winds for several of the days.

She also detailed her diet, which was almost vegetarian with the staples of fruit, eggs, milk and brown bread responsible for powering her ride.

Billie's interview further underpinned her determination to spread the word about cycling. The fact that she was going to set a record was secondary; she saw great importance in engaging with non-cyclists to extol the benefits of moving to two wheels:

> Every day I come into contact with all types and classes of people, and it is to these, in the course of conversation, that I advocate cycling, if necessary defend cyclists, and generally do my best to get the game appreciated a little more.

Billie reached her half-year target with three weeks to spare, hitting 12,500 miles on 9 June 1938. At the end of the month she had covered 14,516 miles and was now comfortably ahead of her planned 75-mile-a-day average. Her exploits were starting to make news in the national press, who had picked up her story and were reporting her progress in a positive manner:

> [Billie's] pioneering effort should do much to encourage many more women to take to riding bicycles.

> Mrs Dovey's excellent health is exemplary of the good health obtainable by women who ride bicycles regularly.

> [Reference] her idea that physical fitness in women is improved by daily cycling. Mrs Dovey is a strong recommendation for her theory.

Billie's ride was now gathering serious attention and her sponsor Cadbury took out a full-page advert in *Cycling*, with Billie praising chocolate as a 'hunger-knock' remedy. Three pages later there she was again, advertising Ellimans Athletic Rub, just as Greaves and Menzies had done, the company always quick to associate itself with any of the successful endurance riders.

In an article in *Cycling* magazine published in July 1938, Billie gave further insight into her experiences out on the road. Her frustrations are all too familiar to the modern cyclist. She mentions incidents of poor parking by motorists that caused her a number of close shaves, and she talks of almost being 'doored' and subsequently receiving abuse:

I dismounted and spoke to the car driver and almost immediately received a command from the same 'gentleman' to go to that mythical place of torture. The car number I carefully noted but what could I do in this matter? This sort of thing I know happens every day. It is no doubt individuals of this type only who would have the public believe that cyclists are the biggest nuisance on the road.

Luckily, Billie's experiences weren't all bad, and she fondly recounts being serenaded by a line of twenty workmen, each uttering a cheery good morning as she passed down their line.

July saw Billie head further north and increase her daily average to 97 miles per day. Yorkshire was graced with her presence, followed by Durham and an excursion into Scotland to Edinburgh. Then, to prove her fitness message further, Billie made her way home with an incredible 189-mile ride from York to Mill Hill in order to keep a promise to attend a Cyclists' Touring Club West Met. Ladies rally the following day. Leaving York in pouring rain, she rode the first 100 miles in oilskins, fighting a strong crosswind. Fortified by a tea stop at Fuller's in Girtford Bridge she completed the ride that evening and made her appointment.

Determined not to continuously seek easy terrain, Billie sought out a number of hilly routes as part of her tour. Now, as she progressed northwards, Billie attempted some serious hills, with Buttertubs Pass and Lythe Bank in Yorkshire appearing on her mileage cards. Throughout her ride, Billie rode a three-geared bicycle with gears of 60, 66 and 74 inches, with most of her riding being done in the middle 66-inch gear. For these hills, she made the concession of lowering her gearing accordingly – to 54, 63 and 70.

Billie toured Scotland for three weeks in August with her husband Fredrick, who had temporarily put on hold his role as her organiser in order to join her on the bike. They covered 1,657 miles north of the border before Billie began her ride home, via Newcastle, Lancashire and Birmingham. She was still giving her evening talks, which were proving to be very popular and were even attended by sailors from the Argentinian destroyer *San Juana* – one of whom returned home with a newly purchased Rudge-Whitworth bicycle.

Billie's campaign continued throughout the month. She wrote a letter that appeared in *Cycling* urging female cyclists to ride bicycles to work.

Her letter spoke of the derision she had personally received for arriving at work on a bike, and of how she fought this derision with persistence, travelling to work day after day in the same manner. After a while, derision had turned to curiosity and then envy as co-workers admired her healthy appearance.

By 1 September Billie had broken the 20,000-mile marker and it was becoming increasingly clear that she would end the year having ridden further than her target of 25,000 miles – which had also been Harry Long's total in 1910. As the month progressed, Billie ventured back up north, touring round Hebden Bridge, Scarborough, Newcastle, Whitley Bay and Northumberland. She then headed south again and was welcomed into the Potteries region of Staffordshire by the lord mayor of Stoke-on-Trent, Alderman G.J. Timmis. He took Billie on a tour of the Imperial Pottery works, after which she remounted and continued on her way, knocking up a creditable 90 miles for the day.

September proved difficult for Billie, weather-wise, with persistent rains and wind hampering her progress. However, as she repeatedly demonstrated, she was made of stern stuff and took her bike into the hilly Lake District for a meeting with the Barrow Wheelers at Ulverston. She then headed south to Clitheroe and into North Wales, maintaining a gruelling schedule. An October article in *Cycling* magazine entitled 'A Day with Mrs Dovey' described how Billie would complete her household tasks in the mornings, before she heading out to ride an average of 83 miles each day at a pace noted to be 12 to 15 miles per hour. Then, in the evenings, she would give talks at Rudge Whitworth dealers. Even these could be energetic – one October engagement, at the Royalty Theatre in Chester, saw Billie give a demonstration on stage with her bike on rollers.

In October, the weather turned worse still, confining Billie to the roads around her home in Mill Hill. In preparation for winter, she now changed tyres from high pressure Dunlop Silver Sprite tyres to lower pressure Endricks. Towards the end of the month, Billie passed a huge milestone, completing her 25,000th mile on 28 October and thus reaching her stated target. As was common among mile-eaters, she decided not to stop but to continue to the end of the year, now with a loose aim of hitting 30,000 miles.

The cycling press, with whom her persistent message and high-mileage efforts were clearly starting to resonate, applauded her efforts. Her mission was definitely reaping press rewards and starting to propagate messages combining both women and cycling, such as the following observation made by a journalist following her progress:

There are few things free in life, yet to a cycling woman two of them – fresh air and a pleasant English countryside – are hers to the full to take and explore.

Early November saw Billie at the Earls Court cycle show, meeting other cyclists and representing her sponsors while still continuing to rack up her daily miles. She would ride in the morning, arriving at the stand at 4 p.m. each day to meet the public and show off her record-breaking bike, a female-specific design that was now getting a lot of attention.

A week later Billie was back on the road. She had spent fifty hours at the show representing her sponsors, which must have been tiring, but not as tiring as her ride to the Potteries in order to attend the North Staffs CTC dinner. Accompanied by Lilian Dredge (a notable record-breaking cyclist who'd set the women's Land's End to John o'Groats record at 3 days 20 hours and 54 minutes on 26 July that year) she faced 80-miles-per-hour gales and encountered several blockages, including dropped telegraph wires and trees. Being cyclists, they were able to easily skip round these and managed to reach their dinner, which they attended and then turned round to head back to London for another dinner engagement at Olympia.

Dredge had become a regular companion on the road for Billie after riding over to one of her presentations and announcing that: 'I thought I'd like a ride, so I came down to see you. I read in *Cycling* that you were down this way. Actually, I'm looking for a companion on my training spins … ' This was a huge compliment to Billie's efforts as Dredge was a world-class rider who'd sought her out as a potential training partner. The two ladies covered many thousands of miles out on the road together, which spared them some of the boredom of long solo rides.

Dredge's company kept Billie's mileage figures relatively high despite the onset of winter, and at the end of November she had 27,723 miles to her credit. As she moved into December her mileage began to drop against previous averages, but this was due to two considerations. Firstly, the weather had deteriorated significantly and the December snow and ice were hampering her progress. The second, and greater, reason was that Billie had now achieved her personal ambition to put cycling, and specifically women's cycling, properly upon the public agenda. She was now recognised as a record-setting cyclist in her own right, having, by demonstration, shown that there was only benefit to be had from long days out on the road. Billie was now being actively sought out as a speaker at prominent cycling events and her column inches were increasing, benefiting both her own cycling sermon and the public exposure of her sponsors Rudge Whitworth. She broke further ground in December, not only by continuing to ride but by being selected as the guest speaker at the Southgate Cycling Club annual dinner. The club was a well-established but very much male-dominated club and Billie's appointment as speaker was heralded as a minor record by the cycling press. A few days later she redressed the balance as a guest of the Southern Ladies' club.

The 21 December issue of *Cycling* reported that Billie would complete her year at Claud Butler's New Year Party at the Horticultural Hall in Westminster. This was a prestigious annual event attended by thousands of cyclists. Prior to this Billie would ride to Broadcasting House for an appearance upon the *In Town Tonight* show.

At the end of December Billie gave a long eulogy to the press concerning her year and talked of the friends she'd made out on the road and the amazing places that she'd managed to visit. It's worth noting that she was the only year-record cyclist since Walter Greaves to actively seek out hillier terrain. Billie's ride was not only about accumulating miles, it was about accumulating experience and sharing this with a wider audience.

Billie had also benefited from the support of, and association with, previous record breakers, which gave her further publicity and credibility. She had shared a stage with René Menzies and Bernard Bennett on a number of occasions, such as the Cyclist's Rally at Silver End in Essex in June 1938 when she and Bennett gave talks concerning their long-distance rides and signed autographs for a number of the assembled throng.

By the latter part of the year Menzies had finished his 100,000-mile ride and returned to cycling for the fun of it. Billie encountered him later in December, lying down in a verge with a recumbent bicycle next to him. She invited him home for a cup of tea, marvelling at his 'ankles up' riding all the way home: 'People stared at René's feet in mid-air and I laughed when I dropped back a little to see what a recumbent cyclist looked like from behind.'

On 31 December, Billie rode her final miles towards the Horticultural Hall in London to finish her year. Her mileage total was recorded at 29,603.7 miles, the poor weather in the last few weeks of the month leaving it frustratingly short of a round 30,000 miles. Her final mileage card was signed by Harry England, the editor of *Cycling* magazine and she was presented with a bouquet and commemorative armlet by René Menzies as Claud Butler's 'do' applauded the young lady who had tenaciously grabbed cycling by the ears and turned its head to view women's cycling as an equal in what had always been a male-dominated sport. She said a few simple words, so indicative of the mission of one who'd simply set out to spread her passion for cycling with all who would listen: 'My mileage should not be judged by the miles, because it was a year of cycling as we know it.'

Billie then enjoyed the rest of the festivities into the early hours before dashing across to the premises of local cycle dealer T.A. Ley, where she had an appointment to see the rider Tommy Godwin off on his 1939 record attempt.

In January 1939, a post mortem of Billie's year was published in the form of a medical report. This had apparently arisen after her husband Fredrick had contacted an acquaintance and medical professional, Charles Fearnley, to request that he give her a massage earlier that year. Fearnley agreed, but Billie did not make the appointment until 13 December 1938. Fearnley was shocked by the picture of health that Billie presented, married with the lack of musculature that he'd anticipated. He'd clearly expected her to reflect the physique of the male racing cyclists of the time, with protruding muscles and huge calves. He coyly noted that:

'The curve of her limbs is daintily feminine … exactly the same is true of the calf; the sweet curve of femininity, yet definite delineation upon contraction. I could not help remarking, somewhat indelicately, I fear, that she had a nice leg for a stocking, thinking to myself that those legs had not graced a pair of silken hose for nearly a year.'

These words may seem somewhat misogynistic to a modern reader, yet this was exactly the kind of message Billie wanted to be relayed to a wider female audience. The message was clear: cycling had in no way destroyed her femininity, it had enhanced it. Ladies who took to the bicycle would not find themselves transformed into the muscular racing cyclists the press often portrayed. She was evidence of this. Fearnley then paid tribute to her year, clearly segmenting her efforts from those of the previous generations of female racing cyclists:

'Billie Dovey's [year] has been ordinary "sensible" safe cycling day in day out, not so much to prove the limit of feminine achievement but to show the illuminating number of hours one can beneficially and enjoyably spend awheel without so much as approaching over strain.'

And this tribute alone should underline Billie Dovey's rightful place in cycling history. The fact that she set a verified and official benchmark of 29,603.7 miles for the women's cycling year record is secondary. Billie was the first woman to put cycling's benefits at the forefront of her own personal ambition. She did this consistently throughout her year and beyond with her public messages always focusing upon the gifts cycling had given to her rather than her own contribution to cycling herself. This endeared her to a cycling press that had become somewhat weary of the egos that floated around the sport and who had reported her ride positively from the start.

While much of the cycling press and public focused upon Billie's ride as an 'exhibition', one other female cyclist saw Billie's ride as a personal challenge. Australian Pat Hawkins was nine years younger than Billie. She began competitive cycling in 1939 and within a year had set the women's distance record for the week, managing to ride 1,546.8 miles in seven days. The record had previously been at 1,438.4, held by Valda Unthank. Pat, who was only eighteen years old at the time, beat it by over 100 miles in a fully supported attempt run under the auspices of Bruce Small's Malvern Star bicycle company – the same company which had previously supported Ossie Nicholson in his two record-breaking years. Ossie had ridden 1,507.5 miles in his biggest week in 1937 to take the men's record. Pat had taken not only the women's record but also snatched the men's away from Nicholson.

On 1 February 1941, at the age of nineteen, Hawkins set out at noon to take on Billie's record over a twelve-month period and apparently got off to a flying start. Within thirty weeks of riding she was 633 miles ahead of Billie's running total. Yet disaster beckoned from the wings as Hawkins' mother died and she herself suffered a serious road accident that saw her hospitalised. Hawkins wanted to abandon the attempt, but her friends and family urged her to continue as she had amassed nearly 25,000 miles in less than eight months and was clearly on track to take the record.

Hawkins continued to ride and in October 1941 claimed a series of records. She took Marguerite Wilson's 300-mile record in 15 hours 45 minutes (1 hour and 24 minutes quicker than Wilson). She then broke her own week record with an astonishing 1,912.1 miles. Finally, she took Billie's 365-day record and, by 18 October, had amassed some 30,705.5 miles.

Hawkins ended her year with a claimed mileage of 45,402.9 miles. Incredibly she had only ridden for 302 of the 365 days and thus clocked up a daily average of 150 miles, way in excess of anything that had ever been ridden before by a woman. Hawkins had apparently managed to fit her riding around her household chores – as Billie had – and her record year was initially celebrated as a huge success by her sponsors and the cycling press. But later that month things began to unravel. Hawkins' ride had been overseen by a committee in a similar manner to that of Ossie Nicholson. They had reviewed her mileage cards and tally sheets and found a number of inconsistencies. It appeared that a time had been incorrectly entered upon Hawkins' record sheet on 30 January 1942, two days before the end of her ride.

Hawkins had been followed by committee members during the last twenty-four hours of her year. She had ridden 311.4 miles – a triple century in a time many men would have envied – and the committee had verified every single mile of this ride. Yet the 30 January inconsistency meant the committee could not fully validate her entire year and as such her record would not stand. Bruce Small issued the following cryptic statement:

> A time which appeared incorrect was shown on a log sheet submitted by Miss Hawkins for Friday January 30th, two days before the finish of the record. Exhaustive enquiries were immediately made by us, and the result of the enquiries was handed to the committee. The committee's statement was made after further investigation.

Hawkins' year was subsequently struck from the record. No more detail was ever released and her sponsors were quick to distance themselves from it by accepting the decision of the committee. Exactly what Hawkins had done wrong in her record-keeping and the extent of it will never be known. She faded from the cycling scene almost immediately and never gave a public statement covering her version of events. It is difficult to reach an opinion on Hawkins' record year as the public details of it are sparse. Her week record in 1940 appears to have been properly supervised and adjudicated, so there is no doubt that she had the mindset and endurance necessary to spend long days back-to-back in the saddle. However, the near silence in the press after her year was discredited appears to hide deeper issues that will now never surface.

Billie, meanwhile, became a regular feature at prestigious cycling events beyond 1939, including being an active participant in the 1939 ride of Tommy Godwin. She made plans to set out on a cycle tour across the USA, but Hitler's invasion of Poland put paid to that. During the war she returned to office duties, working for an aircraft company, but was also formally engaged by Raleigh to represent them in the press, which explains her association with Tommy Godwin throughout his riding year. Billie also stepped up her cycling with a move on to three wheels, taking the women's 25-, 50- and 100-mile tricycle records in the 1940s.

Her marriage to Fredrick Dovey did not stand the test of time and they eventually divorced after the birth of their only child, Llewellyyn Stafford, who was born in 1942. In 1953 Billie married George Fleming, a racing cyclist with a huge reputation. Fleming was another signatory to *The Golden Book of Cycling*, which cited his racing achievements on the road and track. He was credited as the first man to ride 25 miles in under an hour, during a holiday in Ireland where he recorded a time of 57 minutes and 56 seconds. Billie and George spent many happy years together, continuing to ride into old age and carrying out long cycle-tours, including an epic ride across the mountains of the Pyrenees. George passed away in 1997 leaving Billie to while away her final years in Devon.

Of all the cycling year-record holders, Billie is the only one that I was able to meet. In 2014 I was commissioned by *Cycling Weekly* magazine to interview her prior to her 100th birthday. I met Billie at the age of ninety-nine, a few weeks before her centenary. She was living in a care home at Abbotsham in Devon and we chatted in her room with a view over a sunlit lake and its resident wildlife. On meeting Billie I was immediately struck by the no-nonsense approach of the petite lady with the steely eye who remained true to the ethos and purpose of the ride she had undertaken some three-quarters of a century previously. To her it had seemed the obvious thing to do. She refused to focus on any hardships and continually steered the conversation back to the positives of her ride. She'd clearly loved every minute of it and still retained a passion for the sport to which she had given so much.

The hours I spent with her were fascinating and humbling, and her modesty and refusal to portray her year as a great achievement were striking. It's worth repeating a number of our discussions in Billie's own words. I began by asking her about her bike:

'It was a Rudge Whitworth fitted with a three-speed cycle derailleur gear, you don't want more than three gears do you?'

I mention to Billie that some modern bikes are equipped with thirty-three. She tells me that you can't tell the difference between them and three is plenty, thirty-three is ridiculous.

'The Rudge Whitworth was a great bike, I found it really comfortable to ride even on long 100-mile-plus days.'

Billie then went on to tell me about the roads and riding conditions in 1938.

'There was less traffic of course, other than that, well, roads are roads! In fairness the road surfaces were similar to those encountered today but the lack of traffic made cycling a lovely experience. My average was about 81 miles per day but in the summer I rode further in the better weather and longer days. One day I was in York, woke up in the morning and said to myself, "I think I'll ride home today and set off back to Mill Hill." I ended up riding 196 miles. I loved it. I was completely self-supported throughout the record and just used to go into cafes or shops to get some food. I didn't carry any water with me at all, just a saddle bag with some clothes and tools.'

We then spent time discussing the comparison between riding on the roads in 1938 and present day cycling. I enquired as to whether at the age of ninety-nine she still had a keen interest in cycling.

'Oh yes! The last big thing I did on my bike was in 1957. George and I went to the Pyrenees and cycled over the whole mountain range from the Atlantic Ocean to the Mediterranean Sea, including all of the classic mountain passes. The Tourmalet was my favourite, you never think you're going to reach the top. We spent two weeks in the mountains and finished with a week's holiday by the sea. I still watch the Tour de France and other events. I think modern cyclists have a harder time than we did due to the traffic on the roads. More people were riding to work in those days but I think it's starting a bit more in London now with people commuting. I wouldn't want to ride there though.'

We discussed the areas of the UK that Billie had most enjoyed and which places she had visited.

'There weren't any worse ones, everywhere was interesting because you have a bike, you can discover things. My greatest discovery was possibly Yorkshire and the countryside there, over Sutton Bank. I'm looking forward to seeing the Tour there in 2014. I got as far as Loch Lomond in Scotland. One evening the Glasgow Wheelers invited me to their club run and we went out for a ride; on the way back from the cafe we were coming down a long hill into Glasgow, I was in with the group and didn't see a pile of grit. I rode straight into it and fell down within this group of men. I felt a right twerp.'

Ultimately Billie had set out on a mission to highlight the benefits of cycling and specifically promote it in a female context. I was keen to understand whether Billie thought the campaign had been a success and asked her view.

'It's hard for me to say. People were very enthusiastic about my ride and people would often come and see me in the evening when I gave a talk at a shop or village hall. I'd tell them how nice it was to ride a bike – it keeps you fit, doesn't make any noise!'

Billie's parting words were some advice for any cyclist wanting to take on the record, words that I'm sure would have been echoed by all the riders that came before and after her.

'The only thing I could say to that is that you have to really want to do it. Whatever the weather is that morning you have to put your clothes on and get on and ride the bike. It's not funny walking out in the pouring rain and getting onto your bike. You really have to hold the determination to want to do it. You will have bad days, but the good days make up for all of the bad ones.'

At the end of our interview Billie handed me an envelope that contained a few photos taken during her record year. That was all she appeared to have kept in order to remember her amazing performance. I had them mounted in an album and added a series of press cuttings that I'd collected to give her a more permanent memory. On 13 April 2014 Billie Fleming celebrated her hundredth birthday with her family, including her younger sisters who were now in their nineties. Billie phoned me shortly afterwards to thank me for the album and tell me that she'd had a wonderful time and achieved yet another life ambition of reaching the age of 100. Sadly Billie passed away less than a month later, on 12 May 2014.

Cycling had lost another of its great ambassadors, yet Billie was to leave behind a legacy of which she would be proud. Later that year Hertfordshire-based cyclist Anne Hunt set up the Billie Fleming Tribute Ride, urging female cyclists to spend at least one day in the saddle in 2015 in recognition of Billie's contribution to female cycling. The tribute has been a huge success, as each day another rider takes to the roads in order to promote women's cycling in a manner in which Billie would most certainly approve. The ride does not seek to break any records, it's simply there to recognise the huge contribution to female cycling that Billie Fleming made.

TOMMY GODWIN –
THE UNBREAKABLE RECORD?

In 1938 the British roads and long-distance cycling belonged to Billie Dovey and her heartfelt mission to further the cause of women's cycling and fitness. The failed attempts of Cheesbrough and Holt were the only real markers in the men's record, with Menzies retiring exhausted but satisfied with his 100,000-mile effort. However, Dovey's achievements throughout the year had helped to keep the embers glowing and three contenders stepped forward to attempt the record in 1939.

Bernard Bennett was the obvious choice for the betting man. He'd taken the amateur record two years previously and now knew exactly what was required of him if he wanted to mount his bike daily and rack up big miles in all weathers.

In 1937, despite taking the amateur mileage-record title, Bennett had become somewhat lost in the melee of journalistic excitement surrounding the huge mileages of Nicholson and Menzies. But the then-nineteen-year-old's achievement was not lost on potential sponsors watching from the wings, who clearly saw potential in the young rider and quickly put deals in front of him. At the end of the year Bennett had announced that he believed he had the mettle to take the professional record from Nicholson and had been snapped up by local Birmingham-based bicycle manufacturer New Hudson and offered a professional deal. He now had a shiny New Hudson 'Featherlight Club' at his disposal and was pictured with his new sponsor outside its Birmingham offices, replete in a New Hudson jersey. He was to spend a year training, in preparation for a full-on attempt on the record in 1939. The cycle company set up a nationwide tour for Bernard in 1938, similar to Billie Dovey's, and predicated upon his promotion of cycling as a 'visible demonstration of his perfect condition and astounding reliability, easy running and durability of the modern bicycle and its equipment.'

Like Dovey, with whom he occasionally crossed paths, Bennett was to spread the message of the health and financial benefits of cycling as a mode of leisure and transport.

His tour began in February 1938 and was labelled the 'Fitness' Tour of Britain. He began in the home counties, travelled as far north as Scarborough and then across the country to Blackpool, before heading back south and into the western counties. (It appears that New Hudson did not include Wales or Scotland in its own definition of 'Britain'.) Just like Billie, he gave presentations at cycle dealers stocking his sponsor's models.

As planned, the 1938 tour enabled Bennett to further hone the art of long-distance cycling and eradicate a number of issues that had dogged him during his 1937 record attempt. Now classed as a professional rider, Bennett's confidence was high. Any attempt he made would have to surpass the mileage of Nicholson – which was over 15,000 miles further than Bennett's own amateur total – but Bennett had the New Hudson bicycle company providing logistical and financial support. He'd had another long year in the saddle and he had befriended René Menzies and formally recruited him as an adviser and coach for his new attempt. Who better to guide the young Birmingham lad than the wizened Anglo-Frenchman who had come within a whisker of taking the record himself?

The second rider making plans for 1939 was Richard (Dick) Victor Edward Swann. Swann also had his eyes on the prize and had decided to set out riding as an amateur. Brighton-born Swann came from a long lineage of racing cyclists. His great-grandfather had raced high-wheel bicycles as a professional in the 1870s, and his grandfather had also raced. Sadly, shortly after Swann was born in 1917, his father died at sea in World War I. He lost his mother to an illness and, after being looked after by various family members, wound up in an orphanage.

Swann's own cycling career began when, as a thirteen-year-old, he began work in an ironmonger's shop, a job which came with a single-speed delivery bike. Shortly afterwards, having moved to London and started work as an apprentice in the printing industry, Swann began his racing career, riding for the Actonia Cycling Club in time trials and closed-circuit track races. The club was based in Acton in London, with club runs leaving Acton Town Hall every Sunday and a very active racing and social scene. Swann excelled on the track, primarily at the distance of 1 mile, apparently thanks to an explosive start that would later see him moved back behind the start line in handicap races. (Swann had a secret weapon in his cycling coach and mentor, Freddie Wild. Swann was of slight build and Wild was a huge northern policeman. In Swann's own words: 'A push-off from him was worth 20 yards.') Swann was also active on the cyclocross and roller scenes of the 1930s – again short and explosive events that did not usually require effort lasting longer than an hour.

Why Swann decided that he would have a stab at the year record is unclear. He had little relevant experience and did not appear well-suited to the challenge. But the interest around the 1937 and 1938 rides had clearly whetted his appetite and, like Bennett in 1937, he had decided to set off unaided with no publicly stated sponsorship or means of financial support.

It was the third newcomer, however, who was the most interesting: Thomas Edward Godwin, or Tommy, as he had become known. Unlike Swann or Bennett, Godwin had real racing form and came to the record with a set of legs that were used to riding long distances at high speed. He announced his candidacy for the mileage-record crown in December 1938, with a press release outlining his plan on 17 December – exactly the same day as Bennett published his. This must have unnerved the young Bennett, who had previous experience of competing against true racing cyclists in Nicholson and Menzies. Yet again he was up against a rider who had a house full of trophies and an extraordinarily hard will to win, bred, in Tommy's case, from a difficult childhood.

Godwin's childhood was not a happy one, and was fraught with difficulty from an early age. He was born on 5 June 1912 in 12 Talbot Street, Stoke-on-Trent, the first son of Thomas Henry Godwin and Sarah Rowley. His parents had married the previous year, after Tommy Senior returned from India, where he had served as a member of the Labour Corps. Between 1913 and 1916, Tommy saw the arrival of three further siblings: his sisters Alice, Adeliene and Nora. When World War I broke out, Tommy's father was sent to fight in France, leaving his young family behind, and, while he was absent, both Adeliene and Nora sadly succumbed to diphtheria. The impact of these deaths must have played hard on the young Tommy, who would have borne direct witness to the grief of his mother.

Things did not improve after the war ended. By the time Tommy was twelve, his family had expanded further, with two more siblings, and his father was struggling to make ends meet. Thomas Godwin had been seriously injured in France, with bullet wounds and gas gangrene. When he was demobbed in 1924 there was little support from the state and, with his military career over, work was hard to find. He was only able to scratch out a living as a general labourer and must have felt a huge responsibility to help support the ever-expanding family around him. Unfortunately Thomas and his wife sought solace in drink and the young Tommy was often to be found sitting outside the Bird in Hand public house looking after his siblings as he waited for his parents to emerge. The children were often forced to beg for food from customers.

Tommy also had a crippled half-sister who needed looking after. Named Elsie, she was the daughter of his mother Sarah born before she had married Thomas Henry. At the age of five she was run over by a rag-and-bone cart, leaving her with a badly twisted foot. Even though she was Tommy's elder sister, his protective brotherly instincts meant that he spent his early years fighting off bullies who tormented Elsie about her profound injuries.

Here we can see the formation of the character that would drive Godwin into his racing career. This was a young man devoid of privilege and living within an environment where every single penny counted. At an early age he found himself caring for a sister and a drunken father with disabilities and so, wearing shoes borrowed from neighbours, he set out to find work in order to help contribute to the family income.

Godwin started working in a local grocery store, often paid in food as the owner was aware that any money he earned may be diverted by his parents into drink. He was required to use a bicycle – provided by the shop – to make deliveries to customers. This was no racing machine; it was a heavy utility cycle replete with carriers and a large basket upon the front. His sister Edna fondly remembers how the young lad quickly took to the bicycle and used to give her thrilling rides around the Stoke area, him pedalling furiously and her sitting in the basket.

It wasn't long before Tommy began to expand his cycling horizons. At the age of fourteen he found out that a local cycling club was running a 25-mile time trial. This piqued the interest of the teenager, who clearly saw youth as no barrier to cycling success and asked the store owner whether he could enter the event and race upon the shop cycle. The owner agreed and between the two of them they removed as much weight from the bike as possible, including the heavy delivery basket. Godwin borrowed a set of shoes from a neighbour and entered the event. To this day the details, his time and his placing cannot be verified, yet many who knew Godwin recall that he won the event, at the age of fourteen, in a stated time of 1 hour and 5 minutes.

This time is very unlikely to be correct as Godwin's official race results show his fastest times ever were around the 1-hour 2-minute mark, and they were ridden at the peak of his adult career. What is certain is that this race ignited a passion within the young lad, who joined the North Staffordshire Cycling Club at the age of fifteen and went on to have a racing career in which he would be hailed the seventh-best amateur rider in Great Britain.

Tommy's racing achievements as an amateur rider were vast. A quote from George Hemmings, who knew Tommy throughout his later days as a racing cyclist, described a drawer in Godwin's sideboard stuffed full of medals and small trophies that Godwin had won in various races up to 1939. Various sources have stated that this booty amounted to over 200 different awards from separate races, although nobody knows the exact number.

Godwin excelled in time trials. In the 1930s, mass-start road races were effectively banned from British roads and cycle racing was composed almost exclusively of measured-distance time trials. The first official record I can find of Godwin's prowess is dated September 1931, with Godwin, at the age of nineteen, placing fourth in the Nottingham Wheelers' annual 25-mile time trial with a time of 1 hour, 6 minutes and 19 seconds. He was riding as a member of the Potteries Cycling Club and the time was enough to ensure that his club took the team prize. Tommy's first win recorded in the national press was a 30-mile time trial run by his own club – on 27 May 1932. Godwin stormed home in 1 hour, 17 minutes and 45 seconds, twenty-four seconds ahead of F. Brown, who'd beaten him by a good two minutes at the Nottingham time trial the year before. Later in 1932, Godwin placed third in the Potteries' 100-mile time trial and second in the national Clarion 50-mile event. Not only was the young rider getting faster, but he was adapting to the more demanding long-distance events.

By the end of the 1932 season, Godwin was winning more and posting ever-faster times. His best time was a 1-hour, 4-minute and 12-second win at the Altrincham Ravens' 25, nearly a minute ahead of the second-placed rider. However, it was in the Manchester Wheelers' 12-hour, in August, that Tommy showed he had the real credentials to become an endurance rider. A 12-hour race is all about pacing and stamina with riders competing around a measured course to see who can ride the furthest in a fixed time period. The event was won by Frank Southall of Norwood Paragon, an Olympic cyclist with a huge pedigree that included numerous track records and the world unpaced hour record. He recorded a distance of 233 miles 6 furlongs and 163 yards. Godwin placed a creditable eighth with 218 miles 5 furlongs, meaning he had sustained a speed of over 18 miles per hour for twelve hours.

It's worth noting that Godwin, riding as an amateur, was entirely self-supported at these events. Often, club riders such as he would make their own way to the events by bicycle before competing. This would require an early start and sometimes a ride in excess of 70 miles before the rigours of competition itself. The riders would then have to turn tail and carry any winnings home – which could be a joint of meat or a large trophy.

The next year, 1933, proved to be Godwin's most successful and he became a real contender for the coveted Best British All-Rounder (BBAR) title, a national competition based upon average speed across three specific race disciplines: 50 miles, 100 miles and a 12-hour competition. By June 1933 Godwin held third place, one above the legendary Frank Southall, with an average speed of 23.041 miles per hour. Southall had won the race every year since its creation by *Cycling* magazine in 1930. Godwin posted a time of 2 hours, 10 minutes and 12 seconds in the 50-mile time trial, at the Dukinfield 50 event run by the East Liverpool Wheelers. He was one of four riders that smashed the course record that day, but was unable to take the outright win as the local rider L.J. Ross took this honour – maybe knowledge of the course had weighed in his favour.

Unfortunately, Godwin was not able to maintain his third place. Southall took the title once again, with Godwin finishing a creditable seventh – a prestigious honour for the twenty-one-year-old rider and effectively anointing him the seventh-fastest man in the country. He finished the year with an average speed of 21.265 miles per hour, based upon his results at the Dukinfield 50, the Bath 100-mile (a time of 4 hours, 4 minutes and 6 seconds) and a distance of 232 miles in twelve hours at the Manchester Wheelers' event.

Godwin raced the whole season for the Potteries CC and helped the team take the honours at a number of events that year. Yet, for some reason, in November 1933, the club decided to expel Godwin. A committee meeting was called and he was invited to attend to present his defence. Godwin declined and was summarily dismissed from the club with no reason given to the inquisitive press. Godwin simply transferred his loyalties to the Birchfield CC racing team and continued to compete throughout 1934 and 1935, mainly in 25-mile time trials, managing to drive his time down to 1 hour, 2 minutes and 31 seconds, which won him the scratch race held by the Dublin Harps in Ireland.

Godwin moved north to race in 1936 and entered a number of events for the Derby Ivanhoe team, He frequently placed well but was unable to repeat his 25-mile time from the previous season. In 1936 he moved further south in search of work, appearing briefly as a rider for the Watford Cycling Club, before leaving to join the Rickmansworth club. He continued to compete in the BBAR competition and at one point in 1938 was twelfth in the national table, but was clearly struggling to find the form that had seen him in the top ten five years previously. He briefly overturned the form book in August 1938 with his fastest ever 50-mile ride in a blistering 2 hours, 8 minutes and 25 seconds to take the win in the Vegetarian Cycling Club 50, despite an altercation with a car halfway along the course which cost him twenty seconds.

Despite his continuing good form, it must have been clear to Godwin that he was never going to top the leaderboard in time trialling. The bar was continually moving beyond his reach as younger riders pushed harder and harder to evermore impressive standards. Godwin's 2-hour 8-minute 50-miler was impressive, yet in the same year Harry Earnshaw rode the same distance nearly four minutes faster, winning the BBAR competition with an average speed of 22.627 miles per hour, almost one and a half miles faster than Godwin's best year. Tommy knew that if he wanted to leave his mark upon the cycling landscape he'd need to look elsewhere. His opportunity came after a chance meeting in a pub in 1938.

Godwin had become a strict vegetarian, apparently after a stint working for a Burslem piemaker where he saw the myriad of offal and fat used in the construction of a pie. This put him off meat for life. Godwin was also a confirmed teetotaller; after a childhood witnessing the damage his parents had wrought via their excessive drinking, he made an immediate decision that he would never do the same. In 1938 he was lodging in Rickmansworth with the Robbins family, when two brothers from that family introduced Godwin to the local cycling club. One evening the brothers invited Godwin to join them in a visit to their local pub (Godwin later told his friends that the two brothers, both being over 6 foot 5 in height, rested on the bar like 'herons'), and introduced him to a cycle dealer from the area, Mr T.A. Ley. As the teetotal Tommy drank his hot water or lemonade, the conversation turned to the year mileage record and the fact that Ossie Nicholson had taken it back to Australia. Ley persuaded Godwin to take on the challenge himself and offered him support and a bicycle. All Godwin had to do was ride.

This was a tempting offer for the twenty-six-year-old racer. Work was hard to come by in 1938 and his current racing career was starting to wane. Here was a discipline that he should be able to adapt to, given his experience in riding long-distance events and the journeys by bicycle he had to make to get to them. Ley's sponsorship would allow him to focus on simply riding, and taking the record would elevate him to first in the world rather than seventh-best in the country.

Godwin proved an equally tempting proposition to Mr Ley. Here was a chance to promote his cycle business, Ley Cycles, nationally and launch a new range of bicycles trading off Godwin's feats. He quickly sketched out plans for a new range of cycles branded with Godwin's name in order to capitalise upon the press that would undoubtedly arise as a result of the attempt. A deal was struck. The exact details of this have never been revealed, but must have been lucrative enough to allow Godwin to leave his job (he was then working as a railway telegraphist) and concentrate on riding his bike for 365 days instead. Ley Cycles was run from a shop on The Broadway in Northwood Hills in Middlesex. It was a relatively small, family-run company and it appears that My Ley had taken a significant risk in deciding to support Godwin, effectively adding the equivalent of a another salary to the business for a whole year.

Ley Cycles designed two machines that were to carry the Godwin name. The first was named the 'Tommy Godwin Mass Start' and was to be sold as either a frame only or complete bicycle. It was designed for racers and was a relatively expensive model, priced at 14 guineas for a complete bicycle and 7 guineas for the frame-only model (14 guineas would be around £750 in today's money). The 'Tommy Godwin Track' model was also planned, although the exact details of this model are unknown. Details of the two bikes were announced a month into Godwin's year, but the machine he set out on was a custom model, presumably assembled to his own personal specification.

Godwin's Ley 'TG Special' was constructed from lightweight steel based upon the company's existing 'Continental' machine. The frame was made from Reynolds 531, a type of steel tubing still in use on modern bicycles today. His wheels were 27 inches in circumference, slightly smaller than a modern 700cc road cycling wheel. The bike featured a Brooks leather saddle and was fitted with a Sturmey-Archer three-speed hub gearing system. Before this bike Godwin had primarily ridden bicycles with a fixed gear for most of his racing and thus who knew what extra he could do with three gears and a freewheel?

Godwin began to prepare for the year in December 1938, steadily increasing his mileage throughout the month and putting in long rides of up to

170 miles. An announcement was made to the press in the middle of the month in which Godwin stated that his intention was to ride some 200 miles a day in four shifts of 50 miles, beginning at 6 a.m. each day. This would see him end the year with 73,000 miles upon the clock – a massive jump up from Nicholson's current record. Godwin somewhat optimistically hinted that he might attempt a number of Road Records Association place-to-place records during the year.

Godwin wanted to ride these shifts as quickly as possible in order to give himself a decent recovery period each day. The plan was to base himself in Hemel Hempstead, where he was currently lodging, and begin the year riding in the area.

Meanwhile, over in Birmingham, Bernard Bennett was making an announcement of his own. His intention was to set off in the early hours of 1 January and ride a swift hundred miles from his home during the night, prior to a formal send off at 12 noon at a reception hosted by his sponsors.

The stage was now set for the next fixture in the cycling ashes. Could England re-take the cycling mileage record honours from Australia? And if so, which rider would prevail? Swann, Godwin and Bennett all came from different cycling backgrounds. Godwin was the elder, more experienced racing man looking to elevate himself to national honours. Bennett was the youthful cycle tourist who'd already made a successful attempt and possibly had the greater experience, while Swann was the short distance sprinter with no record at all of endurance riding.

Huge excitement began to gather in the British cycling communities as clubmen and women across the country heard news of the 1939 attempts. The launch points and times for Godwin and Bennett had been widely distributed and a number of cyclists made plans to ride out and cheer these two riders along their way. Swann, meanwhile, being bereft of formal sponsorship, made no such announcement and suffered a more low-key send off as a result.

The British weather clearly did not share the same enthusiasm for the riders as the public did. The early hours of 1 January 1939 were seen in by rain, which fell persistently from midnight onwards. Bennett's launch event had been tabled for midday at the Black Horse Hotel in Northfield. He left his Birmingham home at 4.30 a.m., waved off by his mother, father, uncle and a journalist from *Cycling* who took a photo of the young rider covered head to foot in wet weather gear, complete with rain cape and sou'wester. The journalist described Bennett as 'bubbling with cheerful-ness', although the picture tells a different story, with apprehension written all over the rider's face. Still, Bennett rode through the rain and the dark for 95 miles, via Gloucester, Tewkesbury, and Droitwich, to the hotel where he was met by his New Hudson sponsors and the deputy lord mayor of Birmingham. The weather had brightened up a little and a number of cyclists had made their way over to offer their encouragement.

By now, Bennett had been able to dispense with the cape and cap, but kept the rain trousers on to keep the road spray from his legs. His stated target for the year was 68,000 miles, an average of some 186 miles per day. His plan was to base himself from home and ride each day in two large loops, returning home for a meal in the middle of each day. As part of his preparation he'd been conditioning himself to longer rides and had under-taken a trip to John o'Groats and back from Birmingham. The training appeared to have helped on his first day, as, despite the poor weather, he achieved a total mileage of 162 miles.

Bennett had a thirty-minute head start on Godwin, who left his lodgings at 5 a.m., impatient to get some miles on the clock before his own planned official send off, also at noon. He too suffered in the pouring rain, yet managed to clock up 82 miles of his own before arriving at the Ley Cycles shop somewhere close to midday. Godwin was greeted by a huge crowd of more than 200 cyclists, including a very nervous policeman who had to be dissuaded from calling for backup after having become convinced that he was witnessing a riot in the making. A large number of clubmen had ridden many miles to wave Godwin off, including a member of the Swindon Wheelers who offered his services were Godwin to stray into Wiltshire.

Godwin's friend and cyclist of huge reputation, Jimmy Carr, had ridden all the way down from the Stoke area on a tandem. He and his stoker had planned to escort Godwin back to Stoke-on-Trent that day. Apparently they were staying in the same lodgings as Godwin on New Year's Eve and had expected to ride with him to the planned send off. However, when they awoke Godwin had already left, clearly anxious to begin his year as he meant to go on. Unlike Bennett, Godwin had not set out in heavy waterproof gear and arrived at his official start in cycling tights and a heavy sweater bearing his sponsor's logo. Fortunately the weather began to improve and the assembled crowd watched as Godwin posed for photographs with Captain George Eyston before continuing on his ride. Eyston was a well-known racing driver who had claimed a succession of land-speed records in the 1930s, having taken them from Sir Malcolm Campbell – Godwin's sponsor Mr Ley must have had some influence to convince Eyston to appear at the send-off. Eyston offered Godwin some 'words of encouragement' which, sadly, were not recorded.

If Eyston had taken a glance at Godwin's mileometer he may have found the figure higher than he'd expected. Godwin had only ridden 82 miles to the start at The Broadway, yet his mileometer read 155 miles – he had been testing it prior to his start on 1 January and put 73 miles on to the clock before starting his record attempt.

Also present that morning was the rider with the most recent experience of riding throughout the year, Billie Dovey – who must have had bags under her eyes after making her way from 'Claud's do' in central London in order to see Godwin off. She pinned a sprig of white heather to Godwin as a symbol of good luck, which complemented a small lucky silver horse-shoe that he wore around his neck. Godwin then headed north out of Northwood Hills, accompanied by Jimmy Carr and many of the cyclists who had ridden over to see him off. Local residents must have stared out of their windows in bemusement as the peloton of clubmen wound their way out of town. Meanwhile, Mr Ley returned to his shop, anxiously hoping that his investment would pay off. The launch of his new brand of bicycles relied upon Godwin's success and significant media attention. Godwin certainly did his best to put his fears to rest on the first day, ending with a mileage of 234.

The initial enthusiasm of the three record aspirants was soon dampened by the British weather, which did not improve from its poor start on New Year's Day. The first casualty of the 1939 attempts was Swann. He managed to stay upright for six days before crashing heavily on Handcross Hill and injuring both his ankle and knee. His injuries were clearly serious enough for a doctor to order him to rest for a few days. Swann announced with some swagger that he would comply, 'But, by Gosh! I'll make my erring legs work hard afterwards to make up for the lost miles.' Brave talk from the rider who had only covered 939.6 miles in those first six days; an average of 156.6 and behind the averages of both Nicholson's record (170) and Godwin (179.4). Swann's words turned out to be hollow. He never returned to his attempt, possibly down to his injuries proving insuromountable in such a short period. Following his withdrawal, Swann somewhat enigmatically appeared to attempt to erase it from his cycling palmarès, rebranding himself as 'Dick' Swann and quietly dropping the 'V.E.' initials from his name. He went on to serve in the British Army during the war, organising clandestine track races across the UK during various postings to Dover, Glasgow, Bristol and Leeds. He continued his enthusiasm for cycling while fighting abroad and managed a number of cycle tours around Africa during lulls in the fighting. After the war Swann stayed with cycling, racing in almost every cycling discipline there was and continuing to do so into his sixties. He became a cycle-journalist and wrote extensively about long-distance cycling, but never once mentioned his own failed attempt in 1939. He was instrumental in the resurrection of the Century Road Club in America which had previously suffered a dwindling membership and fought passionately for black and female riders to be included in its membership. And, despite a brief career as a minister in the church, he apparently punched an official who had made a poor job of race organisation. Dick Swann passed away in September 2003 after one of the most colourful careers in cycling.

Bernard Bennett was having a torrid time, apparently suffering the worst of the weather. In the first three days he'd only managed an average of 138 miles per day and had already lost significant time after a crash had smashed the rear wheel on his bike and he'd had to wait by the roadside for a willing helper to arrive with a spare. The crash had been caused by snowfall which had built up on the roads in the Birmingham area, turned to ice and made riding conditions extremely difficult for the young rider. The ice was compounded further by dense fog and subsequent reduced visibility. Bennett must have had to use all of his powers of concentration simply to remain upright. In the following two days his riding was curtailed further by the weather, with his planned daily average of 186 pared down to 48 and 68 miles respectively.

Nicholson's record was beginning to slip away from Bennett before the first week was even over. By 7 January he'd only recorded 598 miles, a long way behind the average required to beat Nicholson and barely half of the 1,165 clocked up by Godwin. The terrible weather would have given Bennett every excuse to call it a day, but he was reported to be in good spirits and advised that he'd always planned to 'go easy' at the start. Things deteriorated further for Bennett as the weather refused to let up and he began to suffer. Yet more crashes caused a leg strain that required medical attention, further reducing his riding time. The leg strain began to cause problems with his knees, a sensation that many cyclists will know only too well. Bennett's doctor advised a week off riding, but Bennett ignored this advice and struggled on, trying to keep his record dreams alive.

Godwin was clearly not on a go-easy strategy, despite the conditions. The poor weather in the Midlands area had seen him retreat back to his base in Hemel Hempstead, but the entire country was soon in the grip of a ferocious winter. The whole of the south of England suffered snow cover and extremely low temperatures that caused the roads to ice over. Godwin ventured out undeterred and suffered two crashes within his first two weeks, injuring his knee. One of these crashes had been caused by a lorry that had overtaken him and cut in too close, clipping his front wheel and forcing him off the road. Godwin had hit a tree with the crown of his head and was dragged to a nearby garage in a semi-conscious state. It took three hours to bring him round properly and get him back on the road. He still managed to end that day with 168 miles. Four days later, during a ride to London for an important meeting with *Cycling* to have his cyclometer readings verified, he had his second crash. Setting out early to clock up a few miles in the Berkhamsted area, Godwin crashed on ice, subsequently turning up at the magazine's offices an hour later covered in cuts and bruises. Yet, somehow, Godwin found a way to maintain a daily average within reach of the Nicholson record.

It's worth taking a moment to consider just what Bennett and Godwin were going through. During January the riders would have had approximately eight hours of daylight available in order to complete their rides. To beat Nicholson's daily average of 170 miles in daylight would have required an average speed of 21.25 miles per hour, clearly not feasible on icy roads. A figure closer to 14 miles per hour would have been more likely in the poor conditions, meaning that five or more hours would be spent riding in the dark. Godwin and Bennett did not have the luxury of high-powered cycle lighting enjoyed by modern riders, and street lighting was nowhere near as well developed as it is today. Their hub-powered dynamo systems would have dimly lit small patches of road and made it difficult to see and avoid black ice.

Add to this their personal logistics: at the start of their attempts both riders had limited support from their sponsors and would have been required to carry and find most of their food out on the road. Godwin told of using cafes for most of his meals and carrying chocolate as his primary means of energy food. Bennett took a different strategy of riding close to home and relying on his family to sustain him through regular food stops. This self-support also meant fixing punctures and other mechanical issues while trying to keep warm. In the absence of the mobile phone, major problems required a trudge to the nearest town in search of a phone box or a hopeful roadside wait for an AA patrolman or other friendly face.

Self-support also meant seeking out individuals at each major turn in order to sign mileage cards – cards which then had to be kept safe and dry as they were the only records of the riders' miles. Postboxes and stamps had to be found during the day in order to send these cards to *Cycling*.

Finally, and perhaps of particular importance in the winter, modern cyclists benefit greatly from technology in the form of weather forecasts. As we set out on the road we are aware of forecasted wind directions and weather conditions, sometimes even in real time. This allows us to adapt our rides accordingly, maybe altering direction to make the most of a following wind or avoiding an area that is forecast to be hit by storms. Godwin and Bennett had to rely upon the radio for their information and in the main would not have been able to make plans based on reliable weather forecasts as they simply did not exist to the extent we know today.

Fortunately, both riders enjoyed the support of an enthusiastic cycling community which willed them on. Godwin would have had particular support, as he was a well-known face on the cycling landscape after his long racing career. He even had a network of riders keeping him informed of conditions in their particular areas, allowing him to travel to places where roads were deemed to be rideable. One story tells of a particularly harsh day where Godwin was boxed in due to snow and ice and forced to ride up and down a single section of road while a team of cycling enthusiasts worked hard to clear the way as best they could. Godwin clearly made better decisions on where to ride than Bennett during January.

Amidst the excitement and support for the riders, there were still occasional voices of dissent. One came from the president of the North Road Cycling Club, W.C. Frankum. At the annual dinner of the Century Road Club he had been given the honour of proposing the toast, subsequently taking the stage to say a few inflammatory words concerning Bennett, Godwin and those before him. Frankum referred back to the riders of 1911, questioning whether the current riders were doing themselves or the sport any good by undertaking such massive rides and appearing to imply that the current riders were not suffering the same conditions or riding in the same spirit as those that had set out in 1911.

Maurice Draisey, the Century Road Club secretary, reinforced Frankum's view with his own statement that he: 'considered the modern year's mileage record attempts to be ridiculous'. Was this sour grapes from the organisation that had been formed as a direct result of the year record competition run by *Cycling* magazine in 1911? Only from some; the opposing view also existed within the club. A.H. Glass stood and retorted that he disagreed with these views. He felt the riders were suffering similar road conditions to those who had set out pre-war and clearly supported their attempts. The debate is interesting when compared to those who today make similar remarks concerning modern attempts being 'too easy' while harking back to the riders of 1939.

By the end of January both riders were down on their planned schedules. The weather showed no signs of improvement and Godwin continued to tangle with the traffic. Riding near Bicester a car drove into the rear of his bicycle, wrecking the wheel and curtailing his day's riding to 136 miles but fortunately leaving Godwin unscathed.

Godwin ended the month with 4,773 miles and an average of 154 miles a day. His last Sunday was mired by illness, reported in the press as both a chill and stomach trouble. He only managed 109 miles that day. His attempt at the cycling year record had got off to a miserable start, yet he had still clocked a January total higher than any rider before him had managed.

Bennett, meanwhile, was a long way behind with a grand total of 2,686, an average of 86.6. It looked to be all over for the young rider, but he remained convinced that as the weather improved he'd be able to catch Godwin and overtake Nicholson.

The mileage cards submitted by Bennett and Godwin would tell an incredible story – if they could be found. No copies remain after *Cycling* – by this time renamed as *Cycling Weekly* – cleared out their archives into a skip in the 1990s. It appears that the stored mileage cards of the riders are now rotting in a landfill somewhere. Were they to have been kept, we would know exactly where Bennett and Godwin fought with the roads during those winter months. The best information we have is gleaned from the reports that do remain from the cycling press of 1939, and the limited testimonies of the riders themselves. In Godwin's case we also have a further insight – a mileage diary which he kept during the record attempt. Godwin was member number 876 of the Cyclists' Touring Club and as such had a CTC diary for recording his cycling on an annual basis. Godwin kept few mementoes from his 1939 ride, but did hold on to his diaries, subsequently passing them to George Hemmings who held them after his death.

The first insight offered by these diaries is the stresses and fatigue suffered by Godwin right from the start. He clearly had no time to sit and write notes in detail after each day's ride, instead barely scrawling a single number on to each page – his calculated mileage for each day. Some of these numbers are incorrect and do not tally with the official mileages recorded by the press, possibly due to the fact that Godwin started the year with 73 miles already on his clock. At the end of each day he would have had to subtract this and the previous days' total from the number displayed at the end. In his tired state it is understandable that mistakes were made. These compounded one another and he had to go back and alter figures on previous pages, with the diary showing a myriad of crossings out, corrections and pencil marks. There are three distinct sets of figures throughout: those written in pencil, which I believe are the original numbers, a set of figures in blue pen that are often incorrect and were probably early attempts at corrections, and a set of figures in a black ink that are his definitive figure, some clearly completed retrospectively. Some pages show smudged ink, due to water getting on to the pages, and others show untidy writing and crossings out in frustration – the scrawled arithmetic of a rider who must have wanted nothing more than food and some sleep.

Godwin's diaries also show that he was unable to settle into a rhythm during the first month of his ride. The ambitious plan for four shifts of 50 miles had been destroyed by the weather and he only made the 200-mile target twice during January. Some days he struggled to scratch over 100 miles.

Years later Jimmy Carr was interviewed by the *Staffordshire Weekly Sentinel* and spoke of his experiences hosting the shattered Godwin, who would turn up at his house after a long day out in the inclement weather:

> Many a time Tommy turned up here completely exhausted and we had to bathe him and put him to bed. Sometimes he was so wet

that we had to take his clothes off and wring them out. The water poured from them.

The interview also detailed days in which Godwin would be the only road user brave enough to face the icy conditions and often fell many times throughout his ride. At this point in the year he must have been giving serious thought as to whether he'd made a sensible decision to attack Nicholson's record without the full professional support that the Australian had enjoyed.

Both riders had some catching up to do, as did Godwin's sponsor T.A. Ley. Godwin's bike repairs had started to add up and Ley needed to make sales of the newly launched 'Godwin' models to recoup his costs. At the beginning of February Ley announced in *The Bicycle* magazine that the new range was ready and interested cyclists could apply for a catalogue directly from the shop. The business was clearly hoping that this announcement would kick-start a flurry of orders.

During February the snow and ice began to abate and both riders started to settle into their task. Bennett continued to circle the Birmingham area while Godwin started to venture further afield, making his first visit to the Sussex coast for the year with a ride south to Brighton and Worthing. Godwin also managed to find time for two cycling dinners, the first at his Rickmansworth club, where he apparently received fifteen awards won at club events the previous year, and the second as guest of honour at the Somervale Cycling Club in Somerset. The month appears to have passed without significant incident for both riders. Godwin had missed his January target, but beat Nicholson's January total by some 237 miles and in February topped him by a further 136. In the last week of February Godwin had ridden 9,188 miles, putting him behind his schedule by some 915 miles but 236.3 ahead of Nicholson. Bennett was a long way back on 6,801, 2,150 behind Nicholson's pace and 2,387 behind that of Godwin.

At this point the gap between Bennett and Godwin seemed insurmountable, despite the younger rider being the more experienced in the year-mileage game. However, Bennett now reached for his address book and called René Menzies, who began to offer advice and, more importantly, to pace Bennett in his quest to reel in Godwin. The strategy began to pay off immediately as Bennett increased his mileage figures towards the end of February before pushing even harder into March where he managed to eclipse Godwin's figures for the month by 146 miles. He was now on 12,485 miles, some 2,277 behind Godwin's 14,762.

It was April 1939 when Menzies' influence began to show most clearly. He accompanied Bennett out on a number of his rides, chivvying him along from a motorcycle sidecar. The worst of the winter was now over and increasing daylight meant that Bennett was able to spend long hours out on the road in his determined fight to claw back the deficit to Godwin. He was still basing himself at his Birmingham home, but riding further afield, including a number of stints of 200 miles to London and back. March had seen the longest ride of the battle to date, with Bennett notching up a day of 263 miles, riding south from Birmingham on to the flat roads of the Somerset levels before returning home. In April, Bennett's intentions to take the record were made abundantly clear. Despite it being one of the shortest months of the year, Bennett rode 6,671 miles, an average of 222.37 per day, and took another 1,041 miles out of Godwin's lead. At the end of the month his running total of 19,156 put him within 1,236 miles of Godwin, who'd been riding a steadier average of 188.9 miles and had recorded 20,392 miles for the year thus far.

A real battle was starting to unfold and Bennett's determination to succeed showed that he'd learnt from his 1937 effort and developed a hardened fighting spirit. On his previous attempt, he had slackened off somewhat as Menzies pulled ahead. But now, with his mentor shouting in his ear, he was determined not to let this happen again. Both riders were now ahead of Nicholson's running total and, with the onset of spring and summer, it was likely that they could stay ahead.

Godwin was not resting on his laurels. He'd also been increasing his daily averages through March and April, aided by the addition of an extra gear to his bike. He'd started the ride using a three-speed Sturmey-Archer hub. In March, Sturmey-Archer persuaded him to install its very latest model, which added an extra gear. Godwin's mileages began to increase and a number of press articles attributed this to his additional gear. It is more likely that this increase was down to the improving weather and increased daylight, but Godwin was true to his sponsor and maintained throughout the year and beyond that the extra gears had indeed aided him. Sturmey-Archer had developed the hub after Hubert Opperman started breaking numerous records using a rival four-speed Cyclo gear mechanism. The company needed a four-speed offering of its own and hence the new system was born with an extra low gear to help with hills. Godwin had apparently made a brief sojourn to Wales, but like Humbles before him decided that, even with his extra gear, the hills restricted mileage too much and so he quickly returned to his own stomping ground and remained mainly within the flatter regions of the London–Stoke and London–Lincoln corridors.

Going into May 1939 Bennett seemingly had the advantage, probably thanks to the pacing provided by Menzies. Godwin's sponsor, Ley Cycles, appeared to be having a tough time of it. While the cycling public had clearly got behind Godwin, the orders for the new range of 'Tommy Godwin' models must not have reached expectations. Ley's advertising dried up and friends of Godwin later reported that it was having difficulty funding the ongoing needs of Godwin's ride – primarily bicycle components, and also possibly an allowance for food and lodgings. The exact details are not known. But what is clear is the fact that Bennett's enhanced support was allowing him to edge ever closer to Godwin. Godwin's friends began to feel a need for a larger firm than Ley to step in, and approaches were made to a number of manufacturers to explore whether they would consider taking over or adding to the support of Godwin's year. One of the companies approached was Raleigh.

Raleigh's view of the cycling media differed to Ley's. In sponsoring Godwin, Ley Cycles had hoped to sell large volumes of bicycles in order to recoup its costs. This in turn required media exposure and advertising to raise awareness of its models and it is possible that Ley expected immediate results before Godwin had ended his ride. Raleigh took a different approach, evidenced by figures held within its archives. The company knew that bicycle sales were stimulated by coverage and advertising within the mainstream press. It also knew the cost of this advertising based upon page rates. Raleigh spent significant amounts of money placing adverts, but also significant amounts of time seeding press articles that mentioned its name. It attached a precise monetary value to every column inch that name-checked Raleigh and created reports that highlighted the value of this PR activity. Raleigh saw that Godwin's coverage in the press would continue to grow if he kept on track to take the record. It was able to calculate the value of this coverage and hence decide that taking over Godwin's sponsorship would benefit the company financially. This proved to be exactly the case, as a report in August 1939 by one of its marketing staff details. The company had analysed seventy-five clippings that mentioned Godwin and Raleigh in the same article and valued this coverage at £200 (close to £9,000 in today's money). Not a bad return over a three-month period.

Of course, Raleigh was a giant when compared to Ley Cycles and was able to take such a strategic decision. Ley was crippled by the need for short-term growth and subsequently released Godwin from their agreement, allowing him to become a Raleigh rider. It is unclear what happened to Ley Cycles as a result, or whether any of its planned 'Tommy Godwin' models saw the light of day. At least one model was constructed and this was the machine that Godwin rode up until 27 May. Whether this machine survives somewhere is unknown. Maybe Mr T.A. Ley took it back in an attempt to cover his losses. Or maybe Godwin, with his generous nature, gave it away.

Godwin's move to Raleigh transformed his year and allowed him to level the field against Bennett and his support from New Hudson and Menzies. Raleigh immediately engaged ex-racer Charlie Davey to take over the direct management of Godwin's remaining year and help him with pacing. Raleigh also provided Godwin with a new bicycle, a Raleigh 'Record Ace' fitted with the same Sturmey-Archer gears that Godwin had enjoyed on his Ley. The new bike would not have offered any real advantage over the Ley as the tubing, geometry and components were similar, but Raleigh also provided a spare bicycle and roadside support, allowing Godwin to significantly reduce time wasted at the roadside while dealing with repairs or punctures. It is likely that this had formed part of Bennett's advantage in the previous months, as Menzies would have had access to New Hudson components and more than likely carried spare wheels and accessories in the motorcycle side car.

Charlie Davey would have been the ideal coach for Godwin for a number of reasons. Firstly, he had a huge racing pedigree that would have commanded instant respect from Godwin, who'd climbed the racing ladder himself. Davey had raced at international level, having come to cycling in his teenage years. Like Godwin, Davey had quickly shown a talent for racing – he had raced and won numerous long-distance time trial events and represented Great Britain at the Stockholm Olympic Games in 1912, partaking in a 200-mile time trial and finishing in a hugely creditable 11 hours, 47 minutes and 6 seconds. After the Olympics Davey fought in the war before returning to track racing. He eventually turned professional and took a number of UK place-to-place records, including Land's End to

London, which he rode in 17 hours and 29 minutes. Secondly, Davey was a committed vegetarian and as such would have been sympathetic to Godwin's dietary requirements in an age when vegetarian alternatives were not as freely available as they are today. But Davey's greatest skill was in management. At the age of fifty-three his professional racing career was behind him and so he'd turned to management in the 1930s, managing the riders Sid Ferris and Hubert James on their various record rides while in the employment of Sturmey-Archer. Davey would have empathised with Godwin's task and also understood how he functioned as a cyclist. He would have had the support networks and contacts within Raleigh and Sturmey-Archer to make things happen.

An event was hastily arranged to alert the press to Godwin's change in sponsorship and, on 27 May 1939, Godwin became a Raleigh/Sturmey-Archer rider under the stewardship of Charlie Davey. The change proved to be pivotal, as at this point Bennett had closed the gap and was a mere 817 miles behind Godwin's total. Davey took tight control of the reins and Godwin's first period of professional support and pacing began.

Godwin set out his intentions clearly at the end of May, with a 308-mile day on Wednesday 31 May. His diary incorrectly marks this as 309 miles, but a handwritten note states: 'First time over 300 miles.' The day before that, he had covered 220 miles, riding at an average speed in excess of 16 miles per hour for close on twelve hours in order to achieve the mileage.

The pivotal day in the battle between Bennett and Godwin arrived in June 1939. On 19 June Godwin rode 258 miles, while, over in the west of England, Bennett had notched up a day of 259.5 miles. The mileages themselves were of little consequence – the key was that, by this point, Bennett had cut his deficit to Godwin's total mileage to only 587 miles. Bennett's team had clearly been keeping an eye on Godwin's mileages and would have been ensuring that their young rider did just a little bit more the next day. These cheeky extra miles had the desired effect and Bennett was now in striking distance of Godwin. This was all the more remarkable as Bennett had lost four days earlier in the year to bad weather. Had he managed to ride each of these, he would probably have been on level terms. Godwin and Davey knew that something extraordinary had to be done in order to fend off the younger challenger. Bennett had shown that he now fully grasped the art of high mileage riding and equally he was not prepared to crumble from the challenge of a more experienced rider as he had against Menzies in 1937.

On 20 June Godwin fired his first warning shot, riding 295 miles – some 40 miles further than Bennett achieved that day. Then, on the summer solstice and after only a few hours' sleep, Godwin rose before the sun and completed a ride that still remains a pinnacle of achievement in the history of the cycling year record, tallying a massive 361 miles in one day. This represents an average speed of over 15 miles an hour in a twenty-four-hour period. Allowing for three to four hours' rest, stops and feeding, we see that Godwin's average speed would have been somewhere close to 18 miles per hour and held for twenty hours. Godwin's diary modestly records the feat with the simple note: 'Largest miles per day', but the figure '361' is written three times and underlined once. Davey and Godwin had used the longest day of the year to huge effect and started a clear campaign to crush the hopes of Bennett – who thought he had done enough by riding an impressive 294 miles of his own that day. Godwin arose the next day and rode 291 miles of his own, sending a clear message that his huge mileage the previous day required little recovery.

Bennett fought hard for the remainder of the month to stay in contention and even began to claw a few miles back in the final week, but Godwin now had the bit between his teeth, riding an average of 292 miles per day for the rest of the month. Both riders finished the month having smashed Nicholson's record for the highest ever monthly mileage out of the park. Bennett had now ridden 33,894 miles and Godwin 34,610. Their daily averages were unprecedented, with both riding over 250 miles a day that month. Their June totals were huge and very close to one another, with Bennett leading with 7,762 and Godwin 101 miles behind. But Godwin and Davey had halted the encroachment of the determined Midlander, with Godwin holding a lead of 716 miles at month end.

The record does not tell us exactly how the two riders achieved these massive numbers, but we should remember that both riders now had motor-vehicle support and coaches on hand daily to ensure that they were out on the road early and riding as many miles as possible without the distractions of sourcing food or dealing with mechanicals. Godwin and Bennett were clearly aware of one another's tallies and were attempting to go one better the next day if possible. The press made brief remarks about the riders seeking out roads with a large amount of lorry traffic, possibly to benefit from a brief draft in the slipstream of a passing vehicle. The support vehicles were probably not used for drafting – it seems likely that support from them took the form of encouragement, a process Davey would have been familiar with from his support of Road Records Association riders in place-to-place record attempts, which involved driving ahead to planned meeting points ready to hold up a bottle or food.

Word of the progress of the two English riders reached Ossie Nicholson in Australia and he began to consider the fact that his record was under serious threat. While he had managed to increase his mileage in the later part of the year it was clear that the battle on English soil was likely to drive each rider harder over the summer months with both clearly on track to eclipse his total. The British press received word that Nicholson was starting to train for a 1940 attempt. As it turns out this was bluster from Bruce Small, Nicholson's manager, in an attempt to distract the two English riders, who ignored it and fought on into the good weather of July 1939, when, yet again, the monthly record mileage took another hammering.

Both riders continued to amass huge daily averages for the first two weeks of July: Bennett riding 277 per day and Godwin 276. Then Godwin took the initiative, with an incredible three days between 12 and 14 July when he rode 314, 307 and 305 miles respectively. He eschewed almost all sleep in the process, reputedly using hedgerows and fields to grab the odd hour's rest when he fell exhausted from his bicycle.

These mileages began to raise eyebrows in *Cycling*, which had yet to spend proper time with the riders out on the road and understand just how the figures were being achieved. Harry England was subsequently despatched to spend a day out with Tommy Godwin – who responded by knocking out his second most impressive day of the year. On 21 July 1939, exactly one month on from his massive 361-mile ride, Godwin rode an equally impressive 348 miles. The details of this day remain the only record we have of his hourly splits. Godwin was out on the road at 5 a.m. and pedalled nearly continuously for twenty hours at an average speed of 17.4 miles per hour. (*See Figure 1.*)

What makes this even more impressive is the fact that Godwin had ridden over 300 miles a day for the previous four days. (*See Figure 2.*)

Including his 21 July ride, he averaged 323.6 miles a day for five days. He had ridden 4,046 miles in two weeks. The 2015 Tour de France route was 2,088 miles long and took three – Tommy rode nearly twice the distance in less time and with no rest days. The day after his huge fortnight, Godwin recovered with a mere 238 miles, and built up to another 300-mile-plus spurt

Hour	Distance (miles)	Cumulative (miles)
5 a.m.	16.8	16.8
6 a.m.	16.8	33.6
7 a.m.	16.7	50.3
8 a.m.	10.9	61.2
9 a.m.	10	71.2
10 a.m.	20	91.2
11 a.m.	21.8	113
Noon	13.3	126.3
1 p.m.	19.7	146
2 p.m.	12	158
3 p.m.	23	181
4 p.m.	12	193
5 p.m.	19	212
6 p.m.	24.3	236.3
7 p.m.	13	249.3
8 p.m.	16.3	265.6
9 p.m.	20.5	286.1
10 p.m.	22.1	308.2
11 p.m.	18.8	327
Midnight	21	348
Total		348

Figure 1: Tommy Godwin's hourly splits for his 348-mile ride on 21 July 1939.

Date	Mileage
8 July 1939	253
9 July 1939	243
10 July 1939	301
11 July 1939	239
12 July 1939	314
13 July 1939	307
14 July 1939	305
15 July 1939	236
16 July 1939	230
17 July 1939	313
18 July 1939	316
19 July 1939	333
20 July 1939	308
21 July 1939	348
Total	4,046

Figure 2: Tommy Godwin's daily mileages, 8–21 July 1939.

between 26 and 30 July in which he recorded 306-, 301-, and 339-mile days.

These figures were the ultimate undoing of Bennett. He had been leaving home between 3 and 4 a.m. each day, riding at a steady pace of 14 to 15 miles per hour for nineteen to twenty hours and arriving home somewhere around 10.30 p.m., but Godwin's three- to four-day surges were applying a pressure that the Midlander could not react to. Bennett's daily averages in the order of 270 to 280 miles were just not enough to counter the 100- to 120-mile advantage that Godwin gained over that period.

As the month of July came to an end the deficit between Godwin's and Bennett's had grown to 1,156 miles, with the two men totalling 43,193 and 42,037 respectively. Meanwhile, Harry England had returned to the offices of *Cycling* and raised a real concern.

England was in no doubt that the mileages being reported were genuine, but was concerned that what had begun in 1911 as a competition for amateurs had now morphed into a professionally sanctioned race upon England's roads. England saw that the systematic pacing of Bennett and Godwin had potential to escalate out of control, with both riders being driven to injury or incident by their respective team managers. He saw that the high mileages could only be sustained by either dangerous speed or sleep deprivation and thus decided that the magazine needed to take action. England was faced with a difficult decision as the original rules of the competition had not forbidden pacing by team managers. Equally Nicholson had clearly enjoyed the support of a full-time coach throughout his record year in 1937. Were England to ban it outright he would run the risk of the two riders and the cycling public crying foul and blaming *Cycling* for the subsequent failure of the riders to bring the record back to British shores.

England decided upon a more diplomatic solution. He contacted both Raleigh and New Hudson and raised his concerns. It was likely that he emphasised the issue of the competition becoming an unofficial 'road race', which in 1939 was still banned by the National Cyclists' Union. This would have caused both manufacturers to think carefully about their positioning, as being seen to promote road-racing directly could have had a detrimental effect upon their brands.

Raleigh and New Hudson spoke over the phone at the end of July and arranged to meet in order to draw up loose terms for their riders' management over the rest of the year. However, they were clearly rattled by the approach of England as an immediate announcement was made via *Cycling* on 2 August 1939.

'Godwin and Bennett to Ride Unpaced,' ran the headline. The two manufacturers had agreed that the riders would continue for the rest of the year unpaced and unaided. *Cycling* welcomed the announcement:

> Quite obviously the public highway was no place for a ding-dong everything-allowed race of this nature.

It's worth reflecting that this decision would probably have come relatively easily for both manufacturers. The British riders were so far ahead of their Australian rival that New Hudson and Raleigh were highly confident that their riders would surpass the record mileage. The total mileages at this point were: Godwin, 43,736; Bennett, 42,467; and Nicholson (in 1937), 34,209. Regardless of which rider ultimately took the honours for the year, both manufacturers could claim that their bicycles were record beaters. The frenetic pacing of April to August 1939 had done its job and New Hudson and Raleigh could leave the two riders alone to fight their own individual battles against each other. The dropping of pacing also gave the record rides more credence in the public eye as one journalist commented:

> There is always an atmosphere of artificiality about records established with the assistance of pace.

It's probably a fair analysis to say that the riders welcomed this development as much as the cycling public. They had both been driven to extraordinary lengths to get to this point and their long averages over the summer months were taking a toll. However, Godwin had been unable to resist one final cheeky dig at his rival. On 1 August 1939 he rode 308 miles, his final 300-plus day of the year.

The month-end figures for August show the profound effect that pacing had had upon the two riders. Godwin finished the month with 7,367 and Bennett 6,642, both at least 1,200 miles down on the previous month's totals (close to 40 miles a day on average). Still, even left to their own devices, the riders were managing to average over 214 miles a day and also managing to stay incident free, with neither recording any crashes or serious mechanicals for the month. On paper it looked like they would cruise to the finish line, with the record being taken much earlier than expected.

Unfortunately 1939 was to be a troubled year and on 1 September Adolf Hitler directed his armies into Poland, causing the United Kingdom to declare war upon Germany two days later, on 3 September 1939.

This had an understandably profound effect upon both riders. Bennett climbed off his bike for the day and recorded no miles whatsoever. He was either glued to the radio listening to developments or perhaps inconsolable as he saw yet again his aspirations pulled out from underneath him. Godwin's daughter Barbara tells a different story for her father. He did set out on his bike but apparently threw the machine into a hedge in a rage when he was told that war really had been declared. At this point in the year both men had so much to lose; they had dedicated eight months of their lives to riding almost non-stop and dealing with every obstacle placed in their paths. Now there was a seemingly insurmountable barrier. War had the potential to curtail their riding completely and both knew only too well what it would take for them to restart and rebuild all over again. Godwin ended the day with 159 miles, his shortest ride since 30 April and clearly a reaction to the terrible news.

Of the two riders, Bennett's attempt was the most at risk. Conscription to fight was now enshrined in law by the National Service (Armed Forces) Act of 1939, which allowed the government to call up any male resident in the UK aged between eighteen and forty-one. Conscription was usually carried out in waves, with the younger men called to fight first, and the first wave of conscription covered those aged between twenty and twenty-three years of age. On 3 September 1939, Bennett was twenty years old and Godwin twenty-seven. Bennett looked likely to be called up first, with Godwin caught in subsequent waves. It would have been tempting for Bennett to call it a day, as he was now a long way behind Godwin's mileage and likely to be sent to fight in the near future. However, he – and Godwin – decided to keep riding and it was not long before both riders were compelled to modify their bicycles. Blackout regulations meant that all lights had to be screened during the hours of darkness and these regulations covered bicycles as well as cars. The regulations read as follows:

In the case of lamps carried by pedal cycles:
   a) The upper half of the front glass must be completely obscured.
   b) The lower half of any reflector must be treated with black paint or otherwise rendered non-effective.
   c) Panels or windows provided for the emission of light, other

than facing to the front, must be completely obscured.

d) All other apertures such as those provided for ventilation purposes, must as far as practicable, be screened to prevent the emission of light, particularly in an upward direction.

e) The light emitted by the lamp must be white.

Rear Lamp:

Every bicycle, tricycle etc., must, when on a road during the hours of darkness, carry a lamp displaying to the rear of the vehicle a red light so screened and dimmed that no light is thrown above the horizontal and no appreciable light is thrown on the ground.

These restrictions had a big impact upon the two riders, who were about to enter the winter months when the days shortened and the hours of riding in the dark increased. The front light restrictions made it much harder for them to see the road ahead. The rear restrictions made it harder for them to be seen by vehicles approaching from behind. Both increased the probability of crashes.

The riders also now needed to carry gas masks as the threat of air raids upon the country began. This added to their burden as the masks were cumbersome and not easy to strap to the bicycle.

Up until this point Godwin had been riding a black Raleigh 'Record Ace' bicycle. He'd also been hit by a car and a lorry and thus decided to take no chances with the further restrictions upon his visibility. Godwin had his bike enamelled white and even stated in an interview that he'd whitewash himself if that was what it took to be seen out on the roads. This had limited success, with a Raleigh press release reporting that in one September week Godwin had two very near misses with cars and was knocked off into a hedge by a motor vehicle.

Godwin also modified his riding strategy to keep him away from large towns and the subsequent need to waste time in air raid shelters should the alarm sound. Raleigh wryly finished the release with the phrase:

So it appears it is going to take more than a bombastic 'house painter' to prevent him completing his task.

Autumn 1939 was fraught with danger for anyone venturing out on to Britain's roads. According to an October 1939 issue of *The Bicycle*, in the first four weeks of September, 1,130 people were killed in accidents. This was deemed to be down to two factors. The first was clearly the blackout restricting the visibility of drivers, but the second is an all-too-common theme today: drivers were not adjusting their driving habits accordingly. Car speeds remained as high as before and consequently the number of casualties saw a huge increase. Of these deaths, 148 were cyclists – a 25 per cent increase on the figures of 1938. Godwin and Bennett were out riding in one of the most dangerous periods that road cyclists had known.

By the end of September Godwin had 57,234 miles to his credit and three more months of riding ahead of him. Bennett was almost 3,000 miles behind on 54,521. The question now was not if Godwin was going to take the record, but when. He only had another 5,424 miles to ride and was still managing to average close to 200 miles per day, as was Bennett who was clearly determined to keep going until the end of the year. On Friday 13 October Godwin passed the 60,000-mile mark and must have felt a real sense of relief – he simply needed to ride 30 miles a day for the rest of the year and the record would be his.

On Monday 23 October 1939 Godwin's cyclometer showed that he had only 624 miles to ride in order to surpass the figure of Nicholson. He left Nash Mills that morning with a plan to ride just over 200 miles a day for the next three days and to take the record riding into his birth town of Stoke-on-Trent. The plan was to establish the record just outside the house of his parents. On the Wednesday morning he was within 200 miles of his goal and was then handed two telegrams, one from Raleigh and the other from *Cycling* magazine. Both implored him to return to Nash Mills with a view to completing the record in London. This was no doubt down to the extra publicity that would arise as a result of his triumphing in the capital and also to the opportunity for herding celebrities to be pictured with him. Godwin arrived in Nash Mills that evening with 15 miles remaining before the magic total of 62,658 miles was achieved. It is worth noting that he'd covered the 140 miles in close to seven hours, an average speed of some 20 miles an hour, despite having nearly 63,000 miles in his legs. Harry England was on hand to accompany Godwin to Trafalgar Square the next day, where Godwin would attend a hastily arranged press conference after cruising past the mark set by Nicholson in 1937.

At 10.15 a.m. on 26 October Godwin rode his 62,658th mile of 1939 and took the record from Nicholson at Hendon in London. Only three people were there to witness it: Charlie Davey, his manager; Harry England from *Cycling* magazine; and a photographer who captured a picture of Godwin's cyclometer, along with another of Godwin pictured with England after having his witness card signed. His cyclometer read 62,731 miles due to the 73 miles that were already on the clock when he had started. The weather that day was atrocious and Godwin is pictured in shorts, hastily doing up his jacket to fend off the sleet that had begun to fall.

It was a somewhat less auspicious occasion when compared to that of Nicholson's record-breaking moment in 1937 and Godwin still had another 15 miles to ride before he arrived at his official reception in Trafalgar Square. A small crowd of journalists and industry figures were gathered, including representatives from his sponsors Raleigh and Sturmey-Archer. He was also greeted by the first snows of the coming winter, which caused him a degree of embarrassment as he rode into Trafalgar Square and promptly crashed upon the greasy roads. One report mentions him falling on wooden blocks – sections of Trafalgar Square had previously been surfaced using wood in order to reduce the noise of horses' hooves and it may have been that some of this remained and had caught him out. But Godwin was quickly up on his feet and shaking hands with the assembled dignitaries. He advised that the early difficult weather had taught him how to crash and he'd got the hang of falling properly by now.

A whole series of photographs were taken of Godwin with the lions of Trafalgar Square as a backdrop. He was then whisked off to the Victoria Hotel for a formal presentation which featured telegrams from the heads of his sponsoring companies and numerous speeches from interested parties. Godwin himself remained ever the modest man of few words. Interviewed by *The Bicycle* magazine he had only this to say:

Feeling fit? I should think so. I've already eaten two breakfasts this morning! Yes, I eat like a horse on this job … you know I'm a vegetarian of course (have been for years). Four pints of milk a day, in addition to my meals, and then as supper a milk pudding big enough for four men.

Really the credit for this ride should go to my landlady, who has to do all the cooking for me!

When I started I lost two and a half stones in weight in the first three months. But then I began to pick up and now I weigh about four pounds more than when I started.

Sleep? Yes, I had to cut that down … in the summer I was getting about three or four hours a night.

Blackout? No it doesn't make a great deal of difference. I have got used to a small light and just plod along without worrying, a steady sixteen hours of riding every day. The main thing about this record is not to worry. I've cultivated a care-free mind and refused to let the prospect of covering thousands and thousands of miles, in all sorts of weather conditions, ever get me down.

Now I've reached Ossie's total, of course, the worst is over. I hope to reach 75,000 by December 31st and then, if possible, go on to finish out the 100,000.

When all the pomp and ceremony was over Godwin got back on his bike and rode to his lodgings in Hemel Hempstead. Even on his record day he managed to notch up 102 miles, and the day after he was back to riding over 200. Then, on Saturday 28 October 1939, Godwin took his only cycling break of the entire year. His mileage diary records the message:

Day Off. Prince of Wales.

The first thought on reading this is that Godwin was presented to royalty. However, in 1939 the title of Prince of Wales was vacant and it is therefore rather unlikely that this was the case. An alternative explanation is that Godwin met with his management and journalists at the Prince of Wales public house in Covent Garden. Having passed the record he now had real personal capital as a record breaker and it is likely that this meeting was the beginning of more formal negotiations with Raleigh concerning his contract. Up until this point he had received sponsorship and support in terms of the management provided by Charlie Davey, bicycles and components, and possibly some help towards sustenance while out on the road. Raleigh's archives do not hold a formal contract with him at this point, which indicates that the arrangement was more than likely an informal one. Godwin was still responsible for his own food and lodgings and probably relied upon savings coupled with the generosity of his friends and the cycling community.

Now he was in a position to negotiate a better ongoing deal with Raleigh Cycles. This meeting may have been the first step in formalising the arrangement, married with a gathering of cycling luminaries to formally celebrate

Godwin's triumph. Remember that his reception at Trafalgar Square had been hastily arranged and it is likely that many had missed out on shaking Godwin's hand. One thing that is certain is the fact that Godwin would not have gone to the Prince of Wales for a celebratory glass of wine or beer as he remained a staunch teetotaller. No records remain of this meeting either in the archives of Raleigh Cycles or The Pedal Club, an organisation that was born from the informal meetings of cycling journalists at the Prince of Wales. However, the fact that this remains the only day on which Godwin did not ride his bicycle in 1939 hints at the significance of the occasion.

What of Bernard Bennett during this period? As Godwin passed Nicholson's record, Bennett had a cumulative total of 58,394 miles and it must have been clear to the young rider that all hopes of catching and overtaking Godwin were now dashed. He could have retired from the race in the knowledge that he'd surpassed his own riding record by nearly 13,000 miles. He knew that Godwin was set to take the honours but was determined to see the year out and so rode on in his own personal quest to pass the mileage set by Nicholson. The week of Godwin's triumph clearly had some effect though, as Bennett's average daily figures slipped down to 116 miles per day. The newly arrived poor weather would have been a factor, but one wonders whether the youngster was finding it hard to motivate himself given the press attention focused upon his rival.

Meanwhile, over in Australia, a deathly silence reigned. Godwin had passed Nicholson's figure after 299 days of riding and, even if he only managed a century a day for the rest of the year, would add another 6,600 miles to Nicholson's total. The Australian press had briefly hinted that the British riders had benefited from pacing that was not available to Nicholson, conveniently forgetting that he had the support of a manager and team car for a large portion of his own ride. Nicholson clearly saw the magnitude of the advantage that Godwin would gain at the end of the year and quietly shelved his previously stated plans to return to the record in 1940.

Lesser riders would have reduced their mileage and ambition in November 1939 as poor weather once again battered the English countryside and the difficulties of the blackout remained. Godwin and Bennett were not lesser riders, with Godwin averaging just over 200 miles a day and Bennett 121 miles. On 27 November, Bennett got his red-letter day, riding his 62,658th mile and overtaking Nicholson's record with over a month of riding to spare. Unfortunately, he also received his call-up papers the very same day. These papers would have given him a fixed date and time for attending a medical at which his suitability for fighting would have been assessed, although they would not have given any indication as to when he would have been required to enter active service. Bennett now found himself in limbo, not knowing for sure whether he would be able to ride out the entire year. Were he to receive a formal conscription notice he would have had only three days to settle his affairs and report for active duty.

December 1939 appears to have been full of distractions for Godwin, with his mileage diary noting a number of functions that he was required to attend around the country. These included riding to the Raleigh works in Nottingham to formalise his arrangements going into 1940, and a visit to Coventry, among other functions. On 19 December 1939 Godwin received formal notification of his contract with Raleigh, in the form of a letter and a service agreement that Godwin was asked to sign.

The agreement indicated that Godwin had signed a formal contract with Ley Cycles and this appeared to remain in force until the end of 1939. The details of this contract have never been revealed, but some arrangement between Raleigh and Ley must have been entered into off the record as Raleigh/Sturmey-Archer was presented as Godwin's sponsor beyond the takeover date of 27 May 1939. Raleigh's agreement was designed to support Godwin beyond 1939 and incentivise him to gain the 100,000 mile record within 500 days. He was to be paid a salary of £5 per week and allowed incidental expenses of 20 shillings per week, to be paid up until the point that Godwin reached 100,000 miles. Godwin was also offered two bonuses: £50 if he reached the 100,000 mile mark within 160 days in 1940, and an additional £25 if this were to be done in 135 days, the latter giving an overall target of 500 days for 100,000 miles.

Were Godwin's daily average mileage to drop below 150 miles per day or were Godwin to breach the terms set by *Cycling*, which was verifying the record, then Raleigh reserved the right to cancel the agreement completely. With this agreement Godwin had achieved another apparent 'first': he was now being paid as a professional cyclist to ride miles rather than win races. His bonus scheme incentivised him to ride them as quickly as possible in order to gain the bonus figures and the 150-mile average caveat was cleverly inserted to prevent him from stringing out the ride in order to continue to draw his weekly salary. The figures may seem low in today's money, but in 1939 a salary of £5 per week was equivalent to about

£300 in 2015, and this, coupled with the bonus scheme, would have been very attractive to Godwin.

Raleigh sent the contract to Godwin via an address in Stoke-on-Trent, but it clearly did not get to him immediately as it was only returned signed to Raleigh on 4 January 1940. Godwin apologetically wrote 'So Sorry' as a footnote to his signature.

As Godwin and Bennett continued into December, plans were made for their respective finishes. Bennett was to end 1939 where he had officially begun, at the Black Horse Hotel near Birmingham. There he would climb off his bike and finish for good. A larger celebration was planned for Godwin, in keeping with the traditions of the end-of-year rides of the mile-eaters that had gone before him. Godwin was to lead a parade of clubmen around Hyde Park in London before attending a lavish reception at the Grosvenor Hotel. Adverts were placed in the cycling press by Raleigh compelling cyclists to make the trip to London in order to escort Godwin on his final miles in 1939.

Godwin's riding rate dropped significantly in December 1939 as another harsh winter took hold of the country. His daily average was down to some 175 miles per day and he even allowed himself a rest of sorts on Christmas Day, with a relatively modest 59 miles. Normal service was resumed on Boxing Day with a less modest 185 miles.

Finally Godwin's last riding day of 1939 arrived and on 31 December he entered London and rode towards Hyde Park Corner at the head of an escort of club cyclists from Rickmansworth CC. Finishing the year in Hyde Park Corner was now a cycling tradition dating from the Humbles ride of 1932.

This ride had been very carefully choreographed in order that he would ride his 75,032nd mile at the Grosvenor Hotel. The reason for this becomes apparent when looking at photographs taken of him later that day wearing a yellow woollen jumper with the embroidered phrase: 'World's Year's Mileage 75,065 Record.' Charlie Davey had calculated Godwin's finishing distance at Marble Arch and made sure that the preceding ride, along with his planned 33-mile ride home, matched the figures upon the jumper. It seems likely that a seamstress was tasked with completing this the day before and Godwin was probably under strict instructions to end the year on that figure. The pressure was on Godwin to ensure that he made the ride home without incident!

As befits Godwin's year, the weather was yet again atrocious and he more than likely welcomed the presentation of the woollen jumper. An emotive photograph shows Godwin, with Charlie Davey to his left, leading a peloton of committed cyclists. The pavements either side of the road are bedecked with snow and a frigid fog hangs in the air. Many of the cyclists in the peloton are conscripts and have arrived in their uniforms to see Godwin ride the year out.

As Godwin climbed off his bike at the Grosvenor Hotel, Marcel Planes stepped forward to shake his hand and congratulate him. Godwin was presented with a laurel wreath and whisked into a reception at the hotel. The usual dignitaries from his sponsoring companies were present, as was Sid Ferris, who was the current holder of the Land's End to John o'Groats record.

A table within the reception held an open copy of *The Golden Book of Cycling*. In 1939 this was still maintained by *Cycling* magazine and it had prepared a page in honour of Godwin ready for him to sign. The text read:

Thomas Edward Godwin

The first cyclist to average over 200 miles a day for a year, Tommy Godwin set up a new record for a year's riding between January 1 and December 31, 1939, by covering 75,065 miles.

The previous best performance was put up in Australia in 1937 by Ossie Nicholson, who rode 62,657.6 miles in the year. Godwin passed this total on October 26, 1939.

Godwin started cycling as a newsagent's delivery boy at the age of 14 in 1926 and rode his first time-trial, a 25-mile road event, the same year. Since then he has clocked inside 1 hour 2 minutes for 25 miles on no fewer than four occasions, while at the other end of the scale he has covered 236 miles in 12 hours.

In 1933 Godwin earned the seventh award in the Best All-rounder Road Riding Competition open to all amateur cyclists in the United Kingdom with an average speed of 21.255 m.p.h. His performances were: 50 miles, 2 hrs. 10 mins 12 secs; 100 miles: 4 hrs. 40 mins. 6 secs; and in 12 hours he covered 231 5/8 miles. He was then a member of Potteries C.C.

Club: Rickmansworth C.C.

Age: 27 years.

Date: December 31. 1939

As Godwin signed the book in the presence of Harry England, the editor of *Cycling*, England dryly noted that this was the 5,001st signature of Godwin's that he had seen that year. Godwin had been sending *Cycling* upwards of five postcards a day, every day, bearing his own signatures to verify the ride.

As telegrams of congratulations were read out and various toasts made Godwin was able to take a few short moments to reflect upon his achievement.

He'd smashed Nicholson's record by over 12,000 miles – essentially riding over 33 miles more than the Australian every single day for a year. He'd become the first man ever to average over 200 miles a day for a year. He'd secured an albeit temporary professional contract with one of the largest bicycle manufacturers in the country and served them well by focusing a huge amount of attention upon their flagship model, the 'Record Ace'. This bicycle went on to sell in large numbers and no doubt Godwin's achievement upon it went a long way to underwriting customer confidence. He did the same for the Sturmey-Archer hub. Godwin had also seen off a younger and more experienced rival who had come very close to taking the lead in the spring of 1939. And all of this had been done with the background of two harsh winters and a country under the direct effect of the declaration of war. Yet as always with Godwin, modesty prevailed. His recorded words that day laid much credit at the feet of his sponsors, as was his duty as a professional. He praised the reliability of his Record Ace and credited his extra Sturmey-Archer gear for his increased mileage. He then simply advised that the secret to his huge ride was 'not worrying'.

With all the celebrations complete, Godwin rode 33 miles back to his lodgings in Hemel Hempstead and thus recorded his true 75,065th mile outside his address of 5 The Chapel, Rush Mills, Hemel Hempstead, witnessed by F.G. Roome who, along with Charlie Davey, signed the last page of Godwin's 1939 diary.

Over in the Midlands, Bernard Bennett was having a lower-key ending to his year. He dismounted outside the Black Horse Hotel having completed his 65,127th mile. In his first year as a sponsored rider and at the tender age of twenty-one he'd gone almost 2,500 miles further than his Australian rival of 1937. His achievement was all the greater as, once again, he'd done this in the knowledge that another would take the honours for the year.

Bennett and Godwin swapped mutual telegrams of congratulation on that New Year's Eve. The two riders clearly had an immense degree of respect for each other and knew full well that Godwin's ultimate mileage was the result of a shared battle through the worst that the British winters could throw at them. Bennett was presented with a cheque and a cup from his sponsors, with the company clapping the loudest at the ceremony more than likely Brooks saddles, as Bennett had used the same one for over six years of riding and recorded a total mileage of 147,000 miles upon it. While Bennett had not taken the ultimate glory, he had served his sponsors well in the fight, with New Hudson gaining huge marketing capital over the two years that Bennett had been in its service.

Sadly, Bennett was unable to continue the battle on to 100,000 as he had an appointment for another fight. It is no surprise that Bennett had passed his army medical and now had an early January date for his formal conscription. Before he went to war Bennett had one last tangle with Godwin – a very amiable one. On 10 January 1940, Raleigh hosted a luncheon in Nottingham to celebrate Godwin's success and the epic battle between the two riders. Raleigh magnanimously invited Bennett and New Hudson to the event and it is believed that this is the first time that the two riders actually met. During the previous year they had come close to each other when riding in similar areas but never actually passed on the road. The managing director of Raleigh, G. Wilson, paid warm tribute to Bennett, as did Godwin, who stated that he was not a fan of public speaking and would rather ride another 20,000 miles than make a speech but went on to allude to the impact that the youngster had had upon his own mileage:

'We competed for the biggest day's ride, the biggest week and the biggest year. I should never have topped 75,000 miles but for Bennett's unceasing efforts to pass my figures.'

Raleigh presented a large silver rose bowl to Godwin and a silver cigarette case to Bennett in recognition of his efforts. H. Brueton of New Hudson presented Godwin with a cup and the words: 'We have come to this function because we can be good losers.' Brueton then went on to advise that Bennett had offered to ride unaided and without the support of New Hudson when it became clear that he had no hope of catching Godwin, but that New Hudson was having none of it:

'Although we were beaten, we were sportsmen enough to recognise that in any other year Bennett would have secured the record. It was just bad luck coming up against a superman like Godwin, and naturally, we continued to back him to the end.'

Harry England from *Cycling* magazine then took the floor and summed up the two riders: Bennett, 'always with a broad smile', and Godwin, whose outstanding characteristic was his 'big heart'. The ever-present Marcel Planes was on hand to shake his head in wonderment that the mileage figures he'd laid down in 1911 had been doubled in a single calendar year. He enthused over the healthy state of the two riders and urged the rest of the general public to ride 10 miles a day and 'seriously affect the income of the medical profession'.

This was the last recorded press interaction with Bernard Bennett, who soon afterwards left to join the army and fight for his country abroad. The details of his war record are unclear and his complete absence from any future mention initially led to the conclusion that he had perished on the field of battle. However, after many years of trying to track him down, I finally made contact with surviving family members. They remember Bennett after the war and told me that he'd had a terrible time after being taken prisoner and suffering horribly in an enemy camp. Bennett suffered a partial loss of memory as a result and returned to Britain unaware of the mark he had made on the British and international cycling scene. It took him many years to regain this memory and he eventually played a small part in cycling once again, as proprietor of a bicycle shop in the Kings Heath area of Birmingham. In his later years Bennett moved to the Dorset area, married and had two daughters.

Bennett sadly passed away on 23 March 1969, at the relatively young age of fifty-one. His death certificate records that it was a heart problem that led to his demise. This was a quiet and untimely end to a young man whose heroic endeavours over two years were almost lost to the cycling world. No trophies are awarded in his name, no markers alert visitors to the areas that he once rode and cycling history makes fleet mention of him as an 'also-ran' in the heyday high-mileage period of 1936 to 1940. Bennett deserves far more recognition than this. To date only one other rider has officially surpassed his 1939 mileage and that is Tommy Godwin. And as stated by Godwin himself, the record figure of 75,065 was as much down to Bennett's harrying as anything else.

Godwin continued riding into 1940 in his quest to take yet another record and arrive at 100,000 miles in fewer than the 587 days taken by René Menzies. If he wanted to finish within 500 days and secure the largest of the bonuses promised by Raleigh, he needed to ride an average of 200 miles per day. However, January 1940 was giving no quarter and yet again Godwin found himself fighting terrible weather, with his real problems beginning on 16 January when he recorded the onset of snow in his mileage diary. There was no let-up for the rest of the month, as snow continued to fall and Godwin only managed to ride an average of 170 miles a day. February was no better and a report in *Cycling* noted that on one particular day Godwin had managed to crash eighty-four times – five times an hour on average. A note on 3 February in his own hand stated: 'Roads in very bad condition, but raining heavily'. He only achieved 109 miles that day, low by Godwin's usual standards.

Godwin would clearly have been riding into the bad weather with his head down, hoping that the onset of spring in March would allow him to ride his required daily average. His hopes were dashed as the bad weather continued and his diary was littered with frustration, with 'Snowing hard' recorded right up until 20 March 1940. Occasional breaks in the weather allowed him to sneak in the odd 200-mile-plus day in an attempt to keep on track, but Godwin also started to note days blighted by punctures, a smashed wheel and crashes.

Godwin was now riding without either a rival to spur him on or the benefit of a team car. He was alone in the winter of 1940 with only self-motivation to keep him going. It may have been this fact that saw him seek out the companionship of other cyclists; a diary entry on 25 March 1940 showed that he'd competed in a 25-mile time trial on the Leicester Road and ridden a credible 1 hour, 8 minutes and 5 seconds – that's over 22 miles per hour, and he'd ridden 202 miles the day before. It's a reminder of Godwin's pedigree as a racing cyclist and of his craving for competition. That same day he rode an additional 158 miles on his way up to Manchester for a meeting with *Cycling*. A month later he took nearly three minutes off that 25-mile time, racing in the Addiscome CC event.

Improving weather in April 1940 saw Godwin up his daily mileage rates and bring the 500-day target right back on track. On 17 April his total stood at 95,267 with 4,733 miles to ride and twenty-seven days left to do them in. This required a daily average of 175 per day and Godwin knew that he was entirely capable of that. Charlie Davey got out the calendar and between the two of them they plotted a finale for the achievement of the magical 100,000 figure.

At the start of his attempt Godwin had alluded to a potential attack upon a Road Records Association place-to-place record. And while he had raced in at least two time trials in 1940, there had not been a high-profile public demonstration of his pure speed. It was decided that Godwin would undertake a demonstration ride along the Pilgrims' Way as a final swan-song ride prior to a his planned 100,000-mile finish at the Paddington Race Track. The 120-mile-long Pilgrims' Way is an ancient route from Winchester to Canterbury, formerly trodden by Christian pilgrims on their way to visit the shrine of Thomas á Becket in Canterbury. Davey decided that this would be an ideal route for Godwin to demonstrate that he still had racing pedigree (or as quoted by Davey, 'turn 'em round and stay the course'). Press announcements were made with a schedule that showed Godwin riding the route at an average pace of 'evens', or 20 miles per hour. This was not a record schedule, but still an extremely fast ride as the route is not flat.

Godwin set out on 1 May 1940 from Winchester and was immediately confronted by a brisk headwind. He still managed to ride at 19.5 miles per hour, increasing this to above 20 in the second hour as he climbed the Hog's Back hill. Halfway through the ride it began to rain, but Godwin was well on track for a 20-miles-per-hour finish until he was thwarted by two punctures and a railway level crossing that held him stationary for some two and a half minutes. Godwin arrived in Canterbury to stop the clock at 6 hours, 8 minutes and 43 seconds. He'd not quite achieved his goal of 'evens' but had clearly demonstrated that even after some 97,000 miles of riding he was still able to ride with the pedigree of a real racer.

Godwin's splits for his Pilgrims' Way ride were:

Place	Miles	H:M:S
Winchester Cathedral	0	
New Alresford	8.5	0:26
Alton	18.5	0:57
Farnham	27.5	1:23
Chilworth	39.5	2:01
Dorking	50	2:31
Reigate	56	2:48
Redhill	58	2:54
Nutfield	60	3:01
Godstone	63	3:10
Westerham	69.5	3:32
Riverhead	74	3:47
Wrotham Heath	83	4:13
Aylesford	90	4:30
Charing	105	5:22
Canterbury Cathedral	120	6:08:43

He was accompanied to the finish by a number of riders from the Canterbury Cycling Club who harried him for autographs at the finish while he was being interviewed by the assembled cycling press. One asked whether he would go back and attempt the ride again in order to gain the official record. Godwin answered no, but indicated that he had his eye on the 24-hour unpaced track record that had been set by Hubert Opperman. It seemed he was planning to bring another record back to England from Australian shores, although he stated that an attempt was unlikely during the war years as the blackout would prevent the track being lit through the night.

Firm plans were now put in place for Godwin's finish. He had cannily ridden at a pace that would allow him to complete his 100,000 miles on his 499th day. This would have optimised his daily salary while ensuring that he received the maximum bonus from his contract with Raleigh. Press announcements advised that Godwin would be the guest of honour at the Whit Monday track meeting at Paddington, which had been scheduled for the bank holiday on 13 May 1940. The plans were thwarted by Winston Churchill becoming prime minister after the 'Norway Debate' and the newly formed coalition government immediately cancelling the 13 May bank holiday. The race meeting was postponed for a week. Godwin, determined to finish within the 500 days, decided to carry on as planned to the Paddington track and see his cyclometer tick over into a six-digit distance.

He began the day's ride from Froxfield with 99,925 miles registering upon his cyclometer and a plan to ride to Paddington, picking up the extra 75 on the way. This was the same cyclometer that had had 73 miles on the clock when Godwin started riding in 1939, so the 100,000 mile mark was simply for show and a press reception. A 50-mile time trial was being raced in Balham that day and Godwin rode to this before arriving at Hyde Park Corner, where his cyclometer showed 99,999. With the Paddington track over a mile away, Godwin unscrewed the mechanism from his wheel and rode on to the track where he reassembled his cyclometer. At 4 p.m. in front of a number of cyclists and officials who had made the trip to see him over the line, he was pushed off by Billie Dovey to ride a ceremonial three and a half laps of the cycle track. As he finished, his cyclometer displayed a set of zeros. His Smith's cyclometer only featured five figures and Godwin had ridden it around the clock. A photo exists of the mechanism showing this and many have mistakenly thought it was taken at the start of his ride, when in fact it registered his (ceremonious) 100,000 miles. Godwin rode a further 12 miles that day, and an additional 167 the day after, thus hitting the 100,000 mile target in exactly 500 days on 14 May 1940. *The Bicycle* magazine gave a fantastic description of his appearance:

> Brown as a berry and looking the picture of health. Godwin showed no signs of the nerve strain usually associated with this record, and indeed plans to go on riding 'for a bit ... until I am called up.' Apart from his deep tan the only other outward signs of his colossal task are the superbly developed muscles of his legs. In fact, the muscle inside the right thigh is so developed that it actually causes him annoyance by chafing on the top tube!

He'd done it. In his thirteenth year as a competitive cyclist and his second as a professional rider, Godwin now owned not one, but two top placings in the world. He smashed the calendar year record and quietened any rivals who had been considering a future attempt. He'd beaten Menzies to 100,000 miles by an incredible eighty-seven days and, along the way, he'd shown that he still had the speed and pedigree of a true racing-cyclist by continuing to compete in time trials and place well. Godwin was rightly lauded at the rearranged Paddington track meeting a week later, where he rode a number of laps of honour to the sound of cheering crowds and was photographed with Billie Dovey and Marguerite Wilson – the two leading ladies of the 1940s cycling movement.

Godwin would have taken the applause and presentations with his usual modest candour. In any other year this would have been the beginning of a lucrative career as a professional cyclist, especially given the size of his sponsor Raleigh. Godwin had even considered riding in the Tour de France after completing the record – but the war had put paid to all that. Later in May Godwin received his call-up papers and was to be drafted into the RAF. He had continued to ride after the 500 days and reduced his mileage to a mere 90 miles a day for a three-week period before finally climbing off his bicycle and going to war. Godwin's first task was to take the RAF medical, which he passed with flying colours apart from a tendency to walk with his heels raised from the ground. The medic commended him upon his fitness, which Godwin told him was entirely down to cycling. The medic replied that this would only be the case if a cyclist limited themselves to 50 miles or less a day. Godwin told him of his 500 days of 200 miles and was immediately ordered to strip so the examination could be repeated with greater care!

Godwin served in the RAF as a physical training instructor and one can only imagine the lack of patience he would have had with any young conscript moaning after a short period of exercise. He wrote back to *Cycling* magazine in August 1940 advising them that he was planning to acquire home trainers for the airmen under his care and eventually get them out training on bicycles on the road.

Godwin served out the war in the RAF, during which time he met and married his wife Betty, with whom he was later to settle down with in the Stoke area and raise a family. But as soon as peacetime returned and he was demobbed, Godwin found himself itching to return to racing and the amateur time trialling scene that he'd loved so much as a younger man. But cycling can be a cruel sport and, despite the curtailment of Godwin's professional career due to the war, the National Cyclists' Union and Road Time Trials Council classed him as a professional and banned him from racing, just as they had initially done with Walter Greaves.

At times such adjudications verged on the ridiculous. The amateur rider George Fleming was almost banned from racing in the 1940s after having his photo taken at one of Claud Butler's bicycle shops. This picture was published in the press and the RTTC subsequently considered it an 'endorsement' and began proceedings to ban Fleming from amateur racing. Fleming made a series of appeals to the committee, claiming that he was unaware the photo would be used for publication. Eventually they acquiesced. Similar bannings caused no end of confusion as to what classed a rider as professional in the first place and the RTTC was continually having to revisit its definitions – in one case when a professional boxer decided to race as an amateur, as the rules mentioned professional 'athletes' not cyclists. In another case, the RTTC had to clarify to a club that it was able to accept an application from an acrobat who had been paid by a circus troupe to perform a hand-balancing act. Walter Greaves had similar problems after his ride, which the RTTC considered to be a professional year. Greaves appealed on the basis that he did not attain professional status in the time-trialling discipline, was forced to do so for his year attempt through poverty and had received no further monies since his record year. His appeal was successful.

The RTTC and NCU were not so lenient with Godwin. This may have been down to his drawing a salary from Raleigh in the 1940s on his way to the 100,000 miles, or because he had ridden with a much higher profile as a sponsored rider than Greaves. Despite a huge amount of lobbying from the cycling community and Godwin's club mates, the authorities remained resolute. Once a professional, always a professional.

Now, following his record ride, Godwin shared a similar fate to so many of the cyclists who had given up a year of their lives before him, and he faded from the spotlight. With the war meaning that neither fame nor fortune were forthcoming and the racing rug pulled from underneath him, Godwin would have been forgiven for retreating from cycling, wounded by the way in which he had been treated. However, he had cycling ingrained inside him. It was what he did and he could not simply park his enthusiasm for riding a bicycle.

Unable to race, Godwin joined the Stone Wheelers in the 1940s, a cycling club close to his roots in Stoke-on-Trent. He quickly assumed the mantle of club coach and took many young riders under his wing, guiding them to success in time trials and place-to-place records. Riders such as Godfrey Barlow, Phil Griffiths and William Humphries all lay testament to the 'tough love' Godwin meted out during races. Griffiths recalls Godwin standing by the roadside gruffly announcing that riders were 'down' on their times even when they were in fact going well. His brand of encouragement appears to have come from his ethos of always seeking improvement, rather than of congratulating a job half done.

Humphries tells of an incident during the first 50-mile time trial that he rode one summer in Shropshire. Godwin was in attendance to aid the riders from the Stone Wheelers club and handed him a drink as he raced the return leg of an out-and-back course. Humphries offered Godwin a cheery 'thanks' and rode harder to the finish, only to be met by a stern Godwin who suggested that any rider able to shout 'thanks' during a 50 was not trying hard enough and should consider sticking to shorter distance races. Apparently the drink handed up to Humphries was a Godwin 'special brew' that consisted of apple juice, peppermint and an undisclosed secret ingredient that Humphries suspected was either salt or glucose. Godwin used to ride to events weighed down by these brews and by the food that he handed up to the young racers. The club did not have the luxury of supporting cars for these races and so their club coach retreated to the mode of transport he knew best.

Photographs of Godwin in this period show that he was still riding a Raleigh Record Ace and Humphries notes that it was rumoured that Godwin received a new bicycle from Raleigh every two years, replete with a Sturmey-Archer hub like the one he had used to ride his record mileage.

The large company had clearly not forgotten their star rider, whose modesty prevented him from any kind of self-promotion after the event. Those who knew Godwin tell of a man who never talked of the record unless asked. His own daughter Barbara only found out about it at the age of fifteen, after being told by one of Godwin's friends. When she asked him if he was a famous cyclist he replied, 'who's told you that rubbish?'

Godwin had no predilection for boasting or one-upmanship. In fact, Godwin gave away almost every single trophy and prize he received from his entire career as a racer and record breaker. Barbara tells that he just did not feel he needed to have them as reminders of his successes. As soon as a visitor admired a Godwin trophy, it was theirs – including a large grandfather clock that had stood in the family home. Godwin even parted with the silver rose bowl presented to him by Raleigh in recognition of his record. He gave it to his coalman who admired it while having a cup of tea in Godwin's kitchen.

These acts speak volumes of a man who came from a generation of grafting cyclists who simply let their legs do the talking for them. After the disappointment of losing his racing career he quietly got on with the task of helping others improve theirs. This is perhaps why the year record began to fade from cycling after Godwin's tremendous 500 days. The war and Godwin's own modesty quickly eroded the memories of his tremendous achievement and so the year record began to die.

This was evidenced by Menzies' brief resurrection of the ride in 1952. *Cycling* were no longer interested in ratifying the ride and he was forced to turn to *The Bicycle* magazine instead. His was the only serious attempt since Godwin's in 1939 and his eventual success at beating his own figures in his sixties received little media attention.

Godwin continued to ride for the rest of his life as a key member of the Stone Wheelers club. He became great friends with George and Edie Hemmings, two fellow club members who had known him for many years prior to the war. George and Edie told many stories of Godwin in his later years, clearly painting him as a family man who lived for his cycling and the comradeship of wheels on the road. In George's words:

'That's something that Edie and I have known all our lives. Great friendship. It started on Pot Banks; it finished up in the pits; it carried on in the army; it was something – well Godwin and all those in the club, we were millionaires in a way and yet we're not. Nobody could've had better happiness than us, thanks to friendship.'

Thomas Edward Godwin died on 20 July 1975, cycling home from a ride with friends to Tutbury Castle. He'd set out, on a Raleigh Record Ace fitted with a Sturmey-Archer hub, with George Hemmings and Kevin Oakes on their own as the club ride had decided to head to Matlock instead. Godwin had left Hemmings and Oakes at a roundabout in the Meir, having decided against riding to another tea shop in preference for heading home alone. He collapsed at a roundabout near Hanford and, despite the valiant efforts of a dentist and nurse who were passing by, he died of a heart attack by the side of the road at the age of sixty-three. The greatest endurance rider the world had ever known quietly slipped from the earth and the annals of cycling. His death was reported in the local Staffordshire press, who also celebrated his record, but his passing appeared to go almost unnoticed nationally.

Godwin had made a huge impact upon many who knew him both within and outside the cycling community. After his death his family received a number of letters of condolence from strangers they had never met. One told of Godwin giving a young lad the deposit for his first bike on the strict condition that he told nobody where the money had come from. Others spoke of a man who quietly helped those worse off than himself without any request for recognition in return.

Today there are very few artefacts remaining to herald the incredible achievement of Tommy Godwin in 1939. A plaque has been placed outside the Fenton Manor sports centre after a long and protracted campaign by local cyclists. There is a street named after him and the Stone Wheelers present a number of trophies annually in his name. In 2014 Godwin was posthumously inducted into Stoke's sporting hall of fame and in the same year Raleigh Cycles launched the Tommy Godwin Challenge, encouraging cyclists to complete a single ride in excess of 205 miles in order to recognise his achievement.

Godwin had seemingly pushed the cycling year record beyond the reach of all others. His epic battle with Bennett had doubled the original total set by Planes in 1911. He had ridden a daily average of over 205 miles. Most cyclists would quiver at the thought of a single ride of that length, let alone 365 consecutive days of them. His statistics are enough to put any boasting cyclist – myself clearly included – back in their place and yet Godwin sought little recognition during and after his ride.

Godwin's quiet and unassuming modesty played testament to the nature of the mile-eaters. His primary motivation was doing what he loved best

– simply riding his bike – and the year record allowed him to focus upon this. Godwin set himself a target and did everything within his power to ensure that it was achieved. He accepted the nature of long-distance riding and got on with the job, regardless of the barriers that man or nature put in the way. His modesty, resilience and racing pedigree were the perfect set of ingredients with which to do this and they created a rider capable of leaving us with such an astonishing set of numbers – and maybe tell us why the record still stands today.

It took thirty-one years for another rider to come forward to take on the challenge of the year and, in striking contrast to Tommy, show us exactly the wrong approach to take.

KEN WEBB –
THE GREAT PRETENDER?

After 1940 the mileage year record began to fade from the cycling agenda and the momentum that had carried the record for so many years was lost.

There were a number of reasons for this. World War II was clearly the main culprit, with the likely contenders for the title either conscripted or prevented from riding due to other war-time restrictions. Up until 1940, the impetus behind the record had come from the British *Cycling* magazine, but the effort and manpower required to verify each attempt had clearly taken its toll. After Godwin's ride ended *Cycling* quietly abandoned the record and refused to verify any future attempts. The Century Road Clubs of America and Great Britain did not appear to be interested in promoting the contest – they were more focused upon growing and maintaining their membership of 'century' riders. They may also have been discouraged by the onerous requirements of verifying year record rides, which required the diligent checking of mileage cards on a daily basis and also the ability to carry out spot checks of riders out on the road. With *Cycling* no longer verifying any attempts, no cycling body had the resources or will to act as an adjudicator, including the Road Records Association, which stated that an attempt could never be properly verified under its rules.

Perhaps the modesty and lack of self-promotion from the record-breaking riders themselves was a factor in the record dropping from the spotlight, but it is possible that the single most compelling reason why nobody stepped forward to attempt the record was the sheer magnitude of the mileage that Godwin had ridden in 1939. Equally, a record attempt required sponsorship, which brought with it professional status and a barrier to those wanting to continue to race as amateurs after the year was up.

Prior to 1940 it was conceivable that any professional rider could have expected an approach from a sponsor or colleague suggesting that they have a go at 'the year'. This seemed to be out of the question after the war and beyond; companies need publicity to bring them results. With the lack of interest now surrounding the year, sponsors were more interested in higher-profile (and shorter) events that would prove more lucrative in a shorter space of time. The record remained largely forgotten up until 1970, eclipsed by mass-start road races such as the Tour de France and by shorter place-to-place or speed records.

Even Menzies' attempt in 1952 did little to reawaken interest, despite Godwin publicly endorsing the ride and offering advice. Menzies set out knowing that Godwin's mileage was likely way beyond his capabilities and stated from the start that his target was to beat the total of his old rival Nicholson.

It was not until a married father of two lost his job in 1971 that another attempt on the record was made. In early August 1971, Sussex rider Ken Webb announced that, having been made redundant, he was preparing to make an assault upon the year record. Webb was from Gossops Green in East Sussex and, at the age of forty-one, had lost his job at Redifon (which later became Rediffusion). Webb claimed to have previous form in endurance cycling, calculating that while commuting to work in Oxted, some 20 miles from his home, he had cycled some three times around the world, and that he had logged some 250,000 miles over a twenty-five-year career as a cyclist, with visits to forty countries along the way. In addition, Webb said that while serving in the Fleet Air Arm (the part of the Navy responsible for the operation of aircraft) in Singapore, he had ridden the Tour of Singapore several times, although no records exist to verify this claim.

Unlike Godwin, Webb was not a racing cyclist by nature. He was well-recognised on the cycling club scene in the East Sussex area and the picture printed of him alongside his announcement in the *Crawley Observer* showed him wearing a cap and jersey bearing the name of Witcomb, a frame manufacturer based at the time in Deptford in London.

Webb said that he had always planned to attempt the record in retirement but that redundancy had brought his ambitions forward and he was therefore now seeking sponsorship to undertake his ride. His plan was to begin in September 1971 and ride an elapsed year rather than the calendar year that *Cycling* had always insisted upon. This came with two advantages over the riders who had attempted the record previously. Firstly, Webb would not have to start and end in the depths of winter, as other riders had been forced to do: it takes a certain amount of time to 'ride yourself in' to a year attempt and allow the body to become accustomed to the rigours of the road. Doing this in the summer months is clearly much easier. And if a rider is behind towards the end of a year-record attempt, it is much easier to maintain commitment and make up a deficit on the long sunny days offered by summer. There was also some psychological advantage in getting the winter period over and done with in one go. The second advantage gained would be that 1972 was a leap year. Webb kept quiet about this fact, but it effectively gave him an extra day over Godwin's 1939 attempt.

His announced schedule was ambitious. The plan was to beat the record with some three and a half months to spare by averaging over 16 miles per hour from the start and cycling 250 miles per day in a fifteen-hour period. Webb began to train with a series of 200-mile rides and one of 300, but his attempt got off to a bad start before he had even turned a pedal. He'd written to hundreds of companies both locally and nationally in order to seek sponsorship for his ride. In his eyes the response had been dismal and he did little to help his case when he made an outburst in the press:

> Thirty-seven firms are interested in the ride but local industry has not been so helpful. Only one firm on the industrial estate BMB have even answered my request for sponsorship. All the others have given me the cold shoulder. I'm pretty sickened by the response.

Understandably the local firms did not take well to his criticism and no further sponsorship was forthcoming. But Webb decided to press on with his plans, in the hope that he'd attract further attention and therefore generate some real and tangible support. He'd been studying the riders before him and quoted Menzies who had set off in 1937 with exactly the same approach: 'What I'm hoping is that once I get going the firms will see that it's a good proposition.'

Webb did manage to secure an overdraft from his bank manager and attracted some sponsorship from Ernie Witcomb, owner of London-based Witcomb Cycles, who gave him two bicycles. Webb had convinced Witcomb that he was up to the task and in return had signed a contract of 'exclusivity' to promise that, were he to take the record, he would not be poached by another organisation.

Webb also made contact with Tommy Godwin, who invited Webb to ride up to Stoke and stay with the still-current record holder. Bizarrely, Webb then advised the local press that Godwin was acting as a coach for his attempt, which was not the case. Godwin had clearly shown an interest in Webb's attempt and had previously stated that he *wanted* his own record to be broken, but no family member or friend remembers Godwin offering to coach Webb. It is more likely that he was willing to offer friendly advice and encouragement. Godwin did share his mileage diaries with Webb, telling him that were he himself to make another attempt, he too would have opted for a September to September year in order to get winter over and done with in one period rather than two.

Webb started his ride on 1 September 1971, from the *Cycling* offices in London. The next day he rode to a civic reception in Crawley where he was seen off ceremoniously by his wife and two daughters, along with the Chelsea footballer Marvin Hinton. Webb rode a claimed 253 miles that day and soon reported that he was riding fourteen to fifteen hours a day, as he had originally planned, and completing most of his riding from home.

But Ken Webb's attempt on the record year started to hit the brakes in October 1971, after fewer than fifty days of riding. Up to 14 October he had claimed to have ridden 10,380 miles in forty-four days. If these figures were correct then Webb had begun his record with a daily average of 236 miles, including a 'spurt' from Tuesday 12 October to Thursday 14 October where he must have ridden at least 310 miles each day in order to have achieved the figures that were being recorded in *Cycling* magazine.

Prior to his start, *Cycling* carried a long interview with Webb, covering his plans and issues with sponsorship, but avoiding mentioning the verification of the ride. The exact details of this mileage verification were never published. In a later article, *Cycling* magazine stated that Webb 'kept in touch' with it using the same process that had been used by other year-riders. He carried a series of mileage cards and asked local people of 'repute', such as AA patrolmen, policemen or postmen, to verify that he was at the place stated and that his mileometer figure matched that claimed upon his card.

Recall that there had been a rigorous process of checking mileage figures for other rides. Prior to Webb, *Cycling* editor Harry England had ensured that rides were being completed through three checks: spot checks on the road to ratify average speeds against those claimed, a cyclometer check at the offices of *Cycling* every two weeks and, finally, follow-up calls or letters to mileage-card signatories to ensure that they existed at the addresses claimed and had actually signed the cards. What was not clear was exactly who was checking Webb's cards. There is no doubt that they were being posted to *Cycling*, as future articles discussed their receipt and the rides documented. However, it was not apparent whether *Cycling* was actively checking the figures and the signatures.

On 15 October Webb did not ride at all as he was forced into searching for employment to keep his ride going. He stated to the press that he was unable to ride for six days and recorded almost no mileage for this period. *Cycling* reported that he climbed back on to his bike on Wednesday 20 October 1971, after a visit to the job centre to claim for unemployment benefit. Webb stated that he was back on his bike by 21 October and then ended the month as follows:

	Miles	Average Speed (mph)
Monday 25 October 1971	264	15
Tuesday 26 October 1971	264	15
Wednesday 27 October 1971	305	17
Thursday 28 October 1971	309	17
Friday 29 October 1971	301	17
Saturday 30 October 1971	347	14
Sunday 31 October 1971	310	17

If Ken's claims are to be believed, he rode 2,100 miles over this seven-day period. This striking feat was apparently accomplished despite the fact that there are only an average of eleven hours' daylight in October. Even more impressively, Webb had stated that most days involved around eighteen hours of riding, apart from the 347-mile ride where he rode for the full twenty-four hours. This means that he was riding at an average of around 17 miles per hour for over six hours, in the dark, unaccompanied and unaided, and that the 310 miles ridden on the final Sunday was with effectively no recovery from his 24-hour Saturday effort. Webb was claiming that he could ride over 300 miles a day for five days, in the winter months, and only sixty days into his record attempt – barely time to have settled in to the routine of a year ride and for the legs to become accustomed to repeated use. The next week Webb claimed 15,568 miles within sixty-eight days, meaning a second week running with a huge average – 278 miles per day. To put this into further context, when added to his claimed mileages from the days before, the figures would have given Webb sixth place in the 2014 Race Across America – one of the toughest endurance races in the world, in which participants cycle 3,000 miles non-stop across the USA. At those rates, he would have finished that race in close to ten and a half days. Impressive stuff for a rider with no verified racing and endurance pedigree.

This was quietly reported in *Cycling* on 6 November 1971, which begs the question why the magazine was now reporting upon a week's mileage that had never been recorded before, even in major races with profess-ional support?

There were two periods in October 1971 that showed Webb cycled 300 miles or more on three consecutive days. These days were of a similar distance to Godwin's best but, unlike Godwin's, were apparently ridden unpaced – and Godwin was a rider with a background of racing in 12- and 24-hour time trials. Webb had no racing pedigree at all. Yet these mileages appeared to go unchallenged by *Cycling*.

Webb made some strange claims a month later that again went un-challenged. In an article entitled 'More Support for Ken Webb', *Cycling* reported that Webb had made a visit to the doctor that week, who was apparently amazed at Webb's physical condition. And so he rightly should have been – Webb declared that his resting heart rate, recorded at twenty-three to twenty-four, had been a little raised during the visit and that it was usually down at around eighteen to twenty. An elite athlete would expect to see a figure down in the low thirties. A rate of eighteen to twenty is unheard of. These claims, if true, meant that Webb had not only recently smashed the record for the most miles ridden in a week, but had a resting heartbeat that was lower than the lowest figure ever recorded – which Guinness World Records puts at twenty-six. (Recorded in a chap named Daniel Green, who took the title from Martin Brady in 2014 with a resting rate of twenty-seven, who in turn took it from five-time Tour de France winner Miguel Indurain, whose resting rate was twenty-eight.) Again, it seems odd that these figures were not challenged in any way in the maga-zine and that they were simply relayed from Webb's mouth to the page.

In the second week of November 1971, Webb's funds had begun to drop perilously low. He stated that the turning point came when one of his daughters offered him her wage packet, unopened, in order to help support the family. Webb now secured a full-time job, working 36.5 hours a week at a local electronics company. He started on 10 November. This apparently severely curtailed his ability to ride during the week. He told the press that he was managing only 100–130 miles a day when at work and having to make up the rest at weekends. To make matters worse, he'd fallen out with his sponsor Witcomb Cycles and advised publicly that it had 'closed the door' upon him as of 12 November. The reason behind this was not clear, but it was likely down to a lack of confidence in him gaining the record with his current need to work, as well as with the fact that Webb was constantly bemoaning the lack of support he was receiving in the press rather than promoting the virtues of his ride and his equipment.

Webb attempted to ride as far as he could within the confines of employment by taking a detour on his way to work to lengthen his commute (30 miles), sometimes riding in his lunch break (20 miles), and then riding home 'the long way' before an evening meal and another ride through the night (80 miles). At weekends he was apparently going without sleep in order to attempt to make up the lost mileage and, on several occasions, claimed to have ridden continuously for 24-hour periods.

Later that month Webb managed to secure a new sponsor in Byrite Tyres Ltd., a Crawley company who had read of his plight in the local press. They had agreed to help him to the tune of £10 per month, as did another lone supporter, who sent *Cycling* magazine a cheque for £1 along with a note stating that: 'It's not much but I hope it helps him on another mile or two.'

The period between 27 November 1971 and 17 December 1971 threw up the greatest anomaly in Webb's mileage figures. The exact details of his rides are not recorded anywhere as *Cycling* magazine have not retained his cards and they do not appear to be held within any of the cycling archives or museums. However we do know, through figures he gave to the press, that Webb had totalled 18,340 miles by 27 November and 22,785 by 17 December. This meant that he rode 4,445 miles over twenty days – an average of 222.25 miles a day, which would seem entirely reasonable were Webb not working. But for fifteen of those twenty days Webb was in full-time employment and had stated that he could only ride a maximum of 130 miles, Monday to Thursday. This gives him twelve days riding at 130 miles.

12 working days x 130 miles = 1,560 miles

This leaves 2,885 miles to be covered in eight days – 360 miles per day.

Webb could clearly not have ridden 360 miles on a Friday as he had to work at least part of the day. If we allow him an extra 70 miles after work every Friday (on top of his usual 130), that gives:

Monday–Thursday: 1,560 miles
Fridays: 3 x 200 = 600 miles
Total: 2,160 miles

He now has to cover 2,285 miles across five weekend days: 457 miles a day, which, at an average of over 19 miles per hour in 24 hours, is clearly impossible.

The numbers are hard to explain unless Webb had provided incorrect figures or had somehow found a way to increase his mileage during the working week.

Weekend mileages closer to 300 miles would be more achievable. If he were doing that he would have had to ride:

Weekend days: 5 x 300 miles a day = 1,500 miles
Fridays: 3 x 200 = 600 miles

This gives him 2,100 miles and an additional 2,345 miles to ride in 12 working days, or 195.4 miles per day.

These seem equally impossible. On weekdays he would have had eight hours at work, four hours to sleep and one hour 'misc.', leaving eleven hours to ride 195.4 miles at a minimum of 17 miles per hour. On Fridays, he would have had to finish in the very early hours of the morning before riding for forty-two out of the forty-eight hours available over the weekend to gain his 600-mile figure. To achieve these figures at his stated average speed he must have been surviving on four hours of sleep a night during the week and less than three at weekends – for a twenty-day period. Equally, he was managing to find signatures at his various destinations all through the night.

This period of Webb's ride remains unexplained, especially given that his publicised figures actually drop over the Christmas period when he took a holiday from work and should have been able to ride without distraction. A more reasonable set of figures were posted leading up to Christmas, with a figure of 231 recorded on Christmas Day and 266 on Boxing Day.

Webb continued riding into 1972 despite a collision with a motor car that saw him briefly out of action. He had been on his way to ride the North Bucks reliability trial. Webb's January figures showed a riding average close to 190 miles per day and, in February, he stated that he was now behind target to catch Godwin but confident that he could make up the miles as the weather improved. Ernie Witcomb, his sponsor, was now back on the scene and had apparently engaged an advertising company to help Webb seek full-time sponsorship. Webb reported that he was riding through terrible conditions, including sub-zero temperatures that froze the roads and his drivetrain forcing him to ride 'fixed' for long periods. This did not seem to affect his riding averages at all though and he claimed a ride of 248 miles on the day this had happened, completing the miles over four shifts of five hours in a twenty-hour period. He clearly impressed his local cycling club, the Crawley Wheelers, as they honoured him with life membership in February 1972.

March 1972 saw Webb hospitalised with an ear infection which required an operation. The doctors advised him that he'd be kept in overnight, but Webb – like many injured year-riders before him – apparently ignored their advice and was riding to Brighton three hours after having the procedure.

In a meeting with *Cycling* he took yet another opportunity to bemoan his lack of sponsorship: 'No one even bothers to answer my letters any more, and considering the publicity awarded those connected with me through all the newspaper coverage I've had, I reckon I've had a raw deal.' Webb told *Cycling* that he'd ridden 214 miles in approximately twelve hours (approximately 18 miles per hour) prior to their meeting and was now over 200 miles ahead of his planned schedule. He went on to compete in the East Surrey 22.5-mile time trial, recording a time of 1 hour and 5 minutes as part of a 322-mile ride in twenty-four hours.

During March, Webb managed to average 235 miles a day while working. This may have included holiday time as well, but by 19 March 1972, after 201 days of riding, he had a total of 42,128 miles, giving him a daily average over the ride of some 210 miles per day. Things improved even more during April as Webb upped his daily average to 243 and gained an apparent 3,487 miles on Godwin's previous record. Given his working status, suspicions now began to be raised. If Webb was surviving on four hours' sleep he was riding an average of nearly 19 miles an hour, including stops.

These suspicions were confirmed when Webb made a springtime visit to stay with Tommy Godwin in Stoke-on-Trent over a weekend. Godwin had remained silent upon the subject of Webb's ride and was happy to host the aspirant as part of his year. Godwin's friends and clubmates George and Edie Hemmings got wind of the visit via Godwin's wife Betty and made an excuse to visit Godwin at the same time. Godwin's close friends and fellow cyclists Phil Griffiths and Frank Edge came along as well, to meet Webb and take their own view of the high-mileage rider. As they entered Godwin's house they noted that Webb's bike and gloves appeared almost spotless, which appeared odd as the weather had not been good that day.

Apparently Griffiths asked Webb where he had ridden from and Webb replied that he'd left Leicester and ridden all the way across to Stoke, some 70 miles in less than three hours. Griffiths calculated that this was an average speed of 25 miles per hour. At the time Griffiths was the reigning Best British All-Rounder for 1971 and advised Webb that he himself could not cover the distance at that speed and asked how Webb had managed it. Things became awkward and Webb decided to leave. Godwin had remained silent throughout the confrontation and simply signed Webb's mileage card, but his wife Betty was quietly fuming. She followed Webb from the house in a car driven by Frank Edge to ascertain his direction of travel. Webb had claimed to be riding to Manchester. Instead he rode to the train station.

Suspicions in the Stoke-on-Trent community had been roused when Webb initially introduced himself to Godwin the previous year. Many commented that he was always immaculately turned out in white clothing despite claims of huge rides. Now these suspicions were heightened by the apparent lies concerning his average speeds and riding plans. Godwin's closest cycling friends, the Hemmings family, began to keep tabs on Webb's claims, while Godwin stoically refused to enter the debate.

Webb was now riding a new bicycle and had clearly severed all ties with his former sponsor Witcomb after he managed to damage a bike they had provided beyond repair. He was briefly unseated by a squirrel mid-June during a 309-mile ride one Sunday but continued to ride and work at an average approaching some 217 miles per day. Webb reported that a medical examination had shown him to be 'run down', probably due to a lack of hot meals causing a vitamin deficiency. He also stated that his job meant he was having to curtail his mileage ambitions to 78,000 miles for the year and would only push the record past Godwin's mark by just short of 3,000 miles.

Through June and July Webb did not feature much in the local or national press while he continued to increase his daily mileage. By the end of July *Cycling* noted Webb's total as 71,578 miles and Webb told the press that he was due to beat the record set by Godwin on 7 or 8 August 1972, with some twenty days left until the end of his year to further increase his mileage.

On Wednesday 9 August 1972, Webb claimed to have taken the record. The next day he rode on to a civic reception in Crawley with a total of 75,365 miles. Webb noted that breaking the record was an anti-climax: 'I sank £500 life savings into it and have got nothing out.' The reception was poorly attended, with only a few members of the general public gathering to see him over the line, along with the professional boxer Alan Minter and a representative from Crawley Council. Webb continued to rail publicly against the lack of support he had received throughout the ride and even stated that he'd be back in a year's time with better sponsorship to do it all again.

Cycling magazine was notably absent from the reception. It interviewed Webb later that month where he stated that he'd been fastidious in the verification of his ride, ensuring that over 20,000 mileage cards were signed by 9,000 individuals over the year and using thirteen mileometers throughout the ride. He did not explain why so many units were required when he only had one or two bicycles at his disposal. The magazine chose not to comment on the questions that were being asked about Webb's riding and full-time job. It took Stone Wheelers' club secretary, Neil Hemmings, to bring the issue of verification to the general public with a letter sent to the *Crawley Observer* and to Ken Webb himself, questioning how the mileage was possible and how it had been verified. Webb simply countered that Hemming's challenge was sour grapes: 'Possibly Stone Wheelers are upset because I did not visit them more often. Early on in my attempt I went there at Mr Hemming's invitation to dinner and to do a television interview.'

But it wasn't only Hemmings whose eyebrows were raised. Jenny Noad was a well-known racing cyclist resident in the East Sussex area at the time. She was training for a series of attempts on Road Records Association tricycle records when Webb invited her to spend a day riding in the area. Previously a *Cycling* magazine reporter had ridden with Webb and documented his own experience, stating that he had huge respect for Webb's ability, but also noting that he dropped Webb on most hills. They had ridden together for fourteen hours over 157 miles – an average speed of 11 miles per hour, way off the 14 to 15 required in order to ratify Webb's claimed mileages while at work. During the ride, Webb mentioned that often his card mileages did not tally with the distances between the points of signature. He put this down to taking 'detours' along the way.

Noad had a similar experience when riding with Webb. They had covered 88 miles in seven and a quarter hours – approximately 12 miles per hour.

During the ride Webb displayed inconsistencies in his own mileage-verification process. At one point he wrote a declared distance of 50 miles while Noad's cyclometer only read 43, and this continued throughout the ride, with Webb dismissing the discrepancy between mileometer and distance as 'odd'. At one point it stopped recording mileage completely and when Noad pointed this out Webb stopped to adjust it, yet still had his mileage card signed further up the road supposedly verifying the mileage stated on the faulty cyclometer. Noad noted that when Webb got his cards signed in a post office he would leave his bicycle outside, so the signatory was only attesting to his arrival at a point in time, not verifying his mileometer reading. Noad wrote to Hemmings independently outlining her concerns. It appeared that Webb was clearly over-estimating the distances he recorded upon his cards and paying scant regard to the figures present upon his mileometer. During her ride she had made a clear note of her own mileages and worked out that Webb's figures were some 10 to 20 per cent higher than hers. The impact of this over the year would be huge, reducing his daily totals by some 20 to 40 miles, potentially reducing his total mileage to a figure in the range of 66,000 to 73,300.

Jenny Noad was tragically killed in a hit and run accident five years later, having set a large number of women's records including distance records at 10, 25, 30 and 100 miles under the auspices of the RTTC and RRA.

Webb did little to respond to his critics other than refer them back to his mileage cards. In a letter back to Neil Hemmings he simply stated that Tommy Godwin himself had signed one of them and that he had signatures from all over the country. Webb stated that he would discuss the matter with *Cycling* and ask it to respond. *Cycling* appears to have remained silent, and in fact the magazine appears not to have been drawn into the debate at all and at no point offered any validation of Webb's mileage. This is understandable as I do not believe it had ever offered to act as an underwriting body to Webb's mileage. It appears that Webb had assumed the submission of cards to *Cycling* would be enough to satisfy the public appetite for proof, as had happened in the earlier part of the century.

The rides of Godwin, Bennett, Menzies, Greaves, Nicholson, Humbles, Planes and Dovey had all been carefully scrutinised and verified in an age when the cycling public was hugely familiar with the year mileage competition and its requirements, and when *Cycling* publicly 'owned' the record. This was now not the case; the magazine was simply a by-stander reporting the progress of a lone cyclist and relaying his claims.

Webb continued to ride on until the 'year' was out, and yet more discrepancies appeared in his own account of the ride. Webb claimed to local Hampshire press that he had competed in a 215-mile race around the area, finishing in fourteen hours with the leading group. What he did not realise was that another individual had written to *Cycling* separately to congratulate Webb on his record – and this individual had ridden with Webb during the same event, which was not a race, but was a reliability trial. And there had only been six entrants, all of whom finished together, in one group, in seventeen hours, not the fourteen claimed.

Sections of the cycling public were now starting to turn against Webb and his continual beef about 'lack of support'. One Crawley resident wrote to the local paper berating Webb for his constant moaning about his lack of money:

It appears that Ken Webb has achieved a life-long ambition, provided for his family and indulged in his hobby at a cost of about £500. He should consider himself fortunate and not continue to gripe because he has no fortune for his pains.

Perhaps, had Webb attracted more sponsorship, his ride would have been different. The early riders lucky enough to have the backing of large companies found the teams behind them keen to ensure that the mileages of their riders stood up to scrutiny, as any issues would have had a huge effect upon their brands' depiction within the public eye.

On 31 August 1972 Webb recorded his mileage as 80,647 miles. He then went on to ride to the 100,000-mile marker within 445 days, claiming to have achieved this fifty-five days quicker than Godwin had managed in 1940. Press interest had faded by now and there was little coverage of the remainder of his ride with only a few brief articles covering his taking of the second record.

The Hemmings, however, were still keeping a close eye on Webb's claims and the issue of verification surfaced once more when Webb managed to get his record printed in the 1972 to 1973 issue of the Guinness Book of Records. Tommy Godwin now finally broke his silence and publicly questioned Webb's ability to complete the stated mileage while working:

'What he says is just ridiculous. I cannot believe it is humanly possible to achieve what he says, and work, eat and sleep as well. I reckon that when he has done all those things he is left with seven hours a day. It just isn't on. I am not saying this because of sour grapes. I would love to see my record go, because I have held it long enough, but these claims are making a laughing stock of the cycling world.'

The Hemmings wrote to the Guinness Book of Records asking why Webb's record had been recorded and under what method of official verification. This was referred on to the book's cycling expert Graham Snowdon, who subsequently referred it on to *Cycling*, asking whether it was prepared to authenticate Webb's record. *Cycling* acknowledged the letter and, finally, its assistant editor Sidney Saltmarsh spoke on the matter, stating:

'It was true that Mr Webb used a system of checking cards and that he had sent them to *Cycling* office, but at no time did we undertake to act as arbiters in the matter. Mr Webb has also sent us the sealed cyclometers showing mileages. We have not examined all of them because we have not got the time. If the Stone Wheelers want to check them, they can do so. We have accepted Mr Webb at face value and he has always struck us as sincere.'

As a result the Guinness Book of Records editor Norris McWhirter took the decision to remove Webb's record from the book and re-instate Godwin as the official holder. Webb's ride had been verified by nobody but himself.

This had no apparent effect on Webb, who continued to maintain his claim for a number of years after 1972, but equally continued to over-exaggerate his own figures. At an Aberdeen Wheelers' club dinner in November 1972 he stated that he'd recorded a lifetime mileage of 638,000 miles. Three and a half years later he was in the *Crawley and District Observer*, once again announcing his one millionth recorded mile. If his claims are right he'd covered 362,000 miles in this period, or an average of 103,000 per year. Had he really smashed his own record three times on the trot? It's likely that Webb was simply yet again a victim of his own exaggeration. He appears to have continually exaggerated his own rides both publicly and privately and yet never managed to demonstrate the speed and stamina that would make his claims unequivocal.

Later attempts on the year record would cast further doubts on Webb's ride. To ride the distances he did, in the times he claimed, would have required him to ride at a pace faster than that of Kurt Searvogel – a hugely successful ultra-endurance racer who is making an attempt on the year record at the time of writing. Webb never once publicly demonstrated his ability to ride at such a pace.

I put Webb's figures of five consecutive days of 300 miles plus to Searvogel, who immediately responded that these numbers would make him one of the greatest Race Across America competitors there has ever been. Chris Hopkinson, another record-breaking ultra-endurance cyclist, felt the same. Hopkinson added that it had taken him years of conditioning and training to be able to subject himself to multiple days of riding in excess of 270 miles. He felt that, in his own experience, and that of riders under his charge, the ability to put out back-to-back triple centuries with only a few months of conditioning was open to question.

Searvogel went on to say that, having ridden six months of his own attempt, he would find Godwin's 300-mile days difficult to comprehend without the knowledge that Godwin was a racing-cyclist of some pedigree who had received support and pacing. Note that Godwin himself was unable to replicate these figures once pacing was removed. Webb had no racing pedigree and no support.

There are other issues with Webb's ride that remain unsolved. His average speed requirements through the night were relatively high, in excess of 15 miles per hour, yet he was never pictured with a large set of lights attached to his bicycle and did not appear to ride with a dynamo hub or attachment. How did he manage to maintain his speeds through the dark? Previous riders had ridden fast through the day and backed off as night-time approached, Webb would have had little choice but to maintain this when he was in full-time work, especially when he was claiming to ride 80 to 150 miles in the dark.

To this day the question as to whether Webb broke Godwin's record remains. His misguided approach to the verification of his riding mileage rules against him. The history of the year mileage record shows that the record is not complete until an official body will stand with the rider and underwrite their mileage as 'proven'. *Cycling* magazine was never prepared to take this stance, and the Guinness Book of Records tacitly agreed in its unwillingness to accept his record claim.

The only man who knows the truth is Ken Webb. I made an attempt to contact him in 2011, but, sadly, he had been taken terminally ill. Webb died in his nineties on 25 November 2013 as the last real challenger to Godwin's record since Menzies' failed attempt in 1952. He took with him the facts of his 1971–1972 ride and left behind a whole raft of questions and issues that will never be resolved. There is no question that Webb rode a significant mileage over that period, with many cyclists paying testament to seeing him out on the road and his own club appearing happy that he did enough to take the record. However, it is the hours when he rode alone that raise the most doubts and, unfortunately, these formed the majority of his ride. Questions should be asked of any man with a relatively low cycling profile who is suddenly able to ride over 1,500 miles unsupported in five days. Greater scrutiny at an early stage in his year would have gone a long way to ironing out potential problems, particularly during the ten months in which he was in full-time employment. These lessons have now been learnt and it is likely that any future challenger will take more care, knowing what happened to Ken Webb.

Ultimately, one must draw the unfortunate conclusion that there are too many flaws in Webb's record year for it to have full credence. As such his record has never been fully accepted within the cycling world.

THE YEAR RECORD REAWAKENED

I n 2012 I was at my kitchen table while Steve Abraham sat opposite me with a cup of tea cradled in his hands. Outside a constant drizzle slid down the windows and Abraham's bike dripped in my hallway. He had ridden 75 miles from his house in Milton Keynes to meet me and to find out more about the cycling year record. As he sipped his tea we began to discuss what it would take to get a modern attempt off the ground and how he could go about it. I found it hard to suppress my enthusiasm for Steve's plans – due, if nothing else, to the mileage and the rain he had ridden through in order to come and meet me.

Over the years I've had a number of approaches from individuals who'd heard about Tommy Godwin and were considering their own attempts upon the record. Almost without exception they did not understand just what it takes to ride an average of over 205 miles every single day. Most of these approaches came from keen cyclists rather than committed ones. I'd ask them what they had done on the bike that indicated they may have a chance. A few had ridden Land's End to John o'Groats, one had undertaken a two-week tour of France and there was the guy who had hardly done anything at all but 'knew he had the character to see a full year through'. I did my best to dissuade these aspirants from setting out by asking them whether they were prepared to eschew family birthdays, holidays, work, social lives and a large portion of their sleep in order to gain the record. Most weren't. One reduced his mileage aspirations and started, but lasted no more than a few weeks.

Abraham was somewhat different to these faux Godwins. He was well known within the Audax community, a group of riders who know better than anyone else what continuous high-mileage riding entails. Audax riders regularly ride through the night in their quest to gain brevets – certificates awarded for the completion of rides. Audax riders measure themselves against completion of distance alone in a 'reasonable' time, and some of their events are Herculean in their nature; the annual climax of the Audax calendar is the Paris-Brest-Paris event – 745 miles of riding with many cyclists setting themselves a target of completion within eighty hours. Abraham had ridden this countless times and had accumulated tens of thousands of miles over the years by riding in events whose mileages started at a base level of 120 miles. Each completed event on the Audax calendar scores points, and Abraham had taken the UK points record in 2007 with 23,834 miles, mainly ridden at weekends and in holiday periods. He knew what it meant to suffer over long distances out on the road and often set out from his house with a sleeping bag in his rear carrier, kipping in doorways or bus shelters prior to and after events. At last I had a rider sitting in front of me who had the potential mettle to take on the year record and give it the respect it deserved.

Abraham's main issue was support. He knew that an attempt would take real commitment and require him to leave full-time employment and dedicate a single year to cycling. Unlike Ken Webb, Abraham was adamant that this was not a task that could be attempted part-time. He had enough miles under his belt to appreciate just what an average of 200-plus miles per day meant. He had savings, but not a year's worth of resources to allow him to leave his job. We discussed sponsorship; my thoughts were that equipment would be feasible but financial support might be harder to find given Webb's controversial attempt and the fact that the record had somewhat faded from the cycling world.

Abraham left my house later that day and rode the 75 miles back to Milton Keynes. I was worried that I'd dissuaded him from having a go, but my fears were unfounded and, two years later, Abraham contacted me again, having made a firm decision to make an attempt in 2015.

Abraham had carefully analysed the requirements of a modern-day attempt and knew that he'd need to stitch together a plan to make his attempt work. Firstly, he'd need an element of financial support to cover his household bills and commitment throughout the year. His savings and endowments would cover this for a period and, like Menzies, he was prepared to risk riding without any firm cash promises in the hope that publicity would bring rewards from cash sponsors or crowdfunding. Next, he'd require help with his logistics, the mainstay of which would be 'hosts' who could feed him and provide a bed for the night as he travelled around the country. Godwin, Greaves and Planes had all received similar support from the cycling community and Abraham hoped that present-day riders would get behind his challenge and do the same. Abraham would also need equipment, clothing and mechanical services to keep him riding throughout the year. History had shown that crashes and mechanical issues were almost inevitable and he knew that he'd need to be prepared with backup bicycles ready to use at a moment's notice, along with a myriad of spares – there's never a bike shop open when you really need one.

Abraham had also identified one of the biggest issues surrounding a modern attempt – the record had been dead for many years, no official body existed to sanction it and the stark lesson of Ken Webb was there to be learnt. If you were going to ride your bike for a year in order to gain the record you needed to unequivocally prove to a potentially cynical cycling public that you really had travelled these miles. The only body in the UK who could have taken on the task was the Road Records Association, but its requirement for witnesses and pre-published riding schedules meant that it was logistically out of the question for either itself or a rider attempting the record. It would be nigh on impossible to anticipate and publish a schedule that could be rigorously adhered to for a whole year.

Abraham had been in discussion with another well-known ultra-endurance racer, Chris Hopkinson, and had helped support him over a successful round-Ireland race which Hopkinson finished in sixth place. Hopkinson sits on the board of the American-based Ultra-Marathon Cycling Association and suggested to Abraham that an approach in that direction might be warranted as its ruleset sanctions other high-mileage challenges, such as 24-hour and 500-mile leaderboard challenges. Abraham began discussions in the third quarter of 2014 and quickly found that the UMCA was supportive of an attempt. I became involved in these discussions in order to provide a historical context and, over a period of a month, we worked together to draft a set of rules for a UMCA-sanctioned year-record attempt.

The UMCA was also aware of another rider who had his eye set on the year-record prize: Kurt Searvogel. Searvogel has a huge pedigree in ultra-endurance racing, with a career spanning many years. In 2014 he and a partner set a record for the over-fifties pairs category in the legendary Race Across America, covering 3,020 miles in 6 days, 10 hours and 8 minutes. Now, Searvogel joined Abraham in becoming central to the year-attempt discussions and a large amount of debate was had concerning the verification of mileages, given the modern technology that we now had access to. This needed to be balanced in a manner such that rides could still be verified if there were technical issues. Almost all tracking mechanisms rely upon the Global Positioning System (GPS) network – what would riders do were this to fail, or if they strayed into areas where GPS signal is poor, such as built-up city areas or deep valleys? The UMCA decided upon a process of using technology backed up by signed mileage cards – mixing the old and the new. Ultimately the onus would be upon the rider to prove that they had undertaken the ride, and a ruleset was drawn up with recommendations for how this could be achieved rather than mandating a fixed technical solution. The agreed rules broadly reflect the spirit of the record as left by Tommy Godwin in 1939.

There is one exception which I argued against – the UMCA decided that their record could be attained over any consecutive period of 365 days. This differs from the record as defined by *Cycling* magazine in 1911 which had deemed it a year record, with a year defined as a calendar year. This had, after all, been rigorously enforced in the case of Walter Greaves who was forced to start late due to the unavailability of his customised machine.

The key rules the UMCA decided upon are as follows:

Record attempts are recognised in a series of age and gender categories, therefore there can be multiple record holders at any point in time.

Riders may use any bike type, or combination of bike types, except for faired recumbents. There will not be separate record categories based on bike type. [This means standard frame bikes and recumbents will be on equal basis for this record.]

Advance notice of routes will not be required. Riders will be required to have an active live-tracking device in operation for all mileage to be credited for the attempt. In addition, riders will have a trip-recording device (such as a Garmin) that will record the route taken, speed, elevation/gradient and at least one of heart rate or power. Riders will be responsible for carrying backup batteries to power whatever device is decided upon. The devices used will be subject to the approval of the records chairman. Ride data will be posted daily within twenty-four hours of the completion of the ride.

Tracking devices shall be tested at least two weeks prior to the start of the attempt to ensure that the records chairman will be able to access the data.

The records chairman shall be given access to the information from the live-tracking device and the uploaded data.

The rider is encouraged to provide photos or brief video clips from the daily rides.

It is recommended that the rider carry a witness book so that independent witnesses can sign to verify the rider's progress. Carrying a witness book is not mandatory, but failure to do so will jeopardise mileage ridden if electronic devices fail. The witness book would potentially log date and time, location, name, signature, contact info for the witness and coordinates.

If either, or both, the tracker or GPS data fails, the distance credited will be the shortest distance via cycleable road between the locations documented in the witness book.

In the case of communication failure where either or both the live tracker or the trip recorder data is unavailable, the rider shall send an explanation (email or text message preferred) as soon as possible to the records chairman. The mileage involved shall be considered to be provisional until the records chairman can decide on the validity of the explanation.

Riders will be responsible for carrying backup batteries to power the required lighting. If the lights go out during night conditions, the rider cannot continue. No mileage may accrue when riding without lights in night conditions. Be aware that 'night conditions' can occur during the day, such as in heavy fog.

If the bike or rider must be transported, the tracking devices must be turned off during transport.

Daily mileages shall be recorded to the nearest tenth or rounded down to the nearest mile.

Helmet use is mandatory.

Definition of year: an attempt may start on any day of the year and will run for 365 consecutive days.

There is no prohibition on drafting during this record attempt. (This is a mileage record, not a speed record.)

Follow vehicle: a follow vehicle will be allowed, but not required.

For a rules violation, the records chairman may impose a mileage reduction penalty of ten miles for each infraction.

The rider may proceed without the live tracker while competing in a sanctioned cycling event that is chip-timed. The ride recording device must still be used.

The age of the rider for this record attempt shall be the highest age attained by the rider during the 365 days of riding.

Alcohol may not be consumed at any time between the start and finish of all miles ridden that will be logged for that day. If alcohol is consumed after the riding for that day has been completed, a rider must allow sufficient time to elapse to ensure that alcohol has cleared the rider's system before starting their next ride.

All mileage must be ridden outdoors. Mileage on an outdoor track is allowed.

Under these rules a rider is able to start and run concurrent attempts. For example, they could begin on 1 January, ride for ten days and lower mileages and then register a new attempt as their mileage increased. The only proviso is that they must ride a consecutive period of 365 from the registration of that new attempt. The UMCA named its challenge the Highest Annual Mileage Record or HAMR for short. The rules were ratified by their board and made official after ratification by the UMCA board of directors in November 2014. Immediately afterwards, three riders registered their intentions to begin attempts in 2015.

Steve Abraham was to start on 1 January 2015 in Milton Keynes, Great Britain. Kurt Searvogel planned to begin ten days later, basing himself initially in Florida in the United States of America. William Pruett also registered an attempt to start 4 January 2015 from Burleson Texas, USA. Pruett remains a registered HAMR competitor but it appears that his registration was not a serious attempt to take on the record as he had only accumulated 2,281 miles by 7 August 2015 – I am personally 1,338 miles ahead of him as of this date and I am definitely not making a record attempt!

Australian Miles Smith also joined the battle on 11 April 2015, riding roads in the Melbourne area that Ossie Nicholson may well have ground out his miles upon eighty years previously. Smith was forced to abandon his attempt on 23 May after the diagnosis of lung problems, but his time off the bike was short and he remounted on 18 June to begin a second attempt at the record.

The stage was now set for a resurrection of the cycling year record, and the decision of the UMCA to act as a verifying body unlocked a major logistical problem that a rider attempting independent verification would face. The UMCA not only provides a process, it provides adjudication and is prepared to officially recognise mileages that have been ridden within the boundaries of its recommendations.

Abraham and Searvogel began to plan their years in earnest. Abraham turned to the Audax community that knew him so well and tentatively asked for support. The response was overwhelming and in a very short period of time he'd managed to recruit a team of helpers prepared to aid him in the managing of his ride throughout the year. A website was quickly built and used as a recruiting point for hosts to help him manage his logistics as he travelled from his base in Milton Keynes. A volunteer route-planner quickly stepped forward to construct mileage-friendly routes and adapt these to Abraham's needs as weather or other factors intervened. Abraham then appealed to the wider cycling community via the 'Yet Another Cycling Forum' website and other social media to tentatively ask for support. The response was again overwhelming and within a matter of weeks Abraham had crowdfunded enough financial support to see him on his way through the early months of the record. The response showed a new interest in the record and equally the standing that Abraham held within the cycling community that knew him.

A small team was formed to manage Abraham's attempt – Chris Hopkinson as team leader with Lesley Sung, Idai Makaya, Michael Walsh, Ian Hennessey, Andrew Morris, Phil Whitehurst, Roger Cortis and myself all playing various roles in order to bring Steve's attempt to fruition. Idai began to approach various equipment sponsors within the cycling industry and quickly managed to secure all of the necessary cycling paraphernalia and support required. Raleigh provided a nice historical touch by agreeing to equip Abraham with three bicycles from their current range. The task was by no means as hard as I had originally anticipated and further underlined the difference between the approaches taken by Abraham and Webb. Abraham had the track record and had also published a set of detailed schedules underwriting his attempt. He'd also kick-started a verification process that had led to an officially sanctioning body and as such gave confidence to equipment sponsors that their names were not going to be associated with a half-baked attempt.

As he neared his planned start date Abraham had assembled almost every piece of the jigsaw required to make a serious attempt. He'd resigned from his position as a warehouse worker and committed himself to the year. He'd assembled a volunteer team to provide the necessary support and help him gain the resources required to sustain a year riding 200-plus miles a day. He had endeared himself to a wider cycling public which was starting to become aware of the year record and to fully appreciate the commitment and endurance that any attempt would require, and he had begun to generate column inches in local and national press, most of which had no idea that such a record existed and were clearly impressed by the mileages being planned. His announcement spread like wildfire through social media, with cycling followers clearly excited by the fact that not only was Abraham to take on the record but that he had serious competition as well. This was a generation that had not seen or heard of a year-record rider and these new attempts made a welcome change from the various doping scandals that had continued to tarnish other areas of the sport. Abraham had sparked a renewed interest in this, the biggest of cycling records.

Searvogel's approach was lower key. He simply packed a camper van with two bicycles – a standard road machine and a recumbent – and headed off to Florida with his assistant Alicia Snyder, who would aid him out on the road. Searvogel had no plans to set up a network of hosts and helpers and appeared to be planning to use his own resources to finance the year and support himself. A few weeks into his attempt he made the public announcement that he was separating from his wife, although this was never linked directly to his record attempt.

I met up with Abraham a few weeks before he was due to begin his attempt. His flat in Milton Keynes was in disarray, strewn with bicycles, components and cycling paraphernalia as he sought desperately to get some order into his life before committing himself to the road. He was busy preparing one of his three Raleigh 'Sojourn' touring machines for the start and also fighting with the technology that would be required to underwrite his attempt. All of us involved knew that this would be the most publicly scrutinised set of rides since 1940. The use of trackers and GPS traces uploaded to public websites would mean that every single inch of Abraham's ride would be checked to ensure that it was actually him on the bike and that there were no anomalies.

Abraham planned to ride with not one, but two GPS units to reduce the chance of total failure, and was having to familiarise himself with the process of uploading his rides from these units to the cycling website Strava, which had been chosen by the UMCA as the preferred logging mechanism. Abraham also sought to minimise any other issues out on the road through his choices of equipment and by carrying a rack bag full of food and spares. He would not have a roving support crew so needed to make sure he always had access to nutrition. He chose tubeless tyres to minimise the impact of punctures, running a latex solution within the tyre to seal small holes where an inner tube would deflate. Disc brakes were added to reduce the wear upon the wheels' rims, and tri-bars fitted to lower Abraham's position and allow him to cut through the air with greater ease. Finally, Abraham fitted a Brooks saddle – an element that had been common to many of the mile-eaters before him.

Abraham showed no apprehension at our meeting, quite the opposite – he displayed a quiet nonchalance to the task he was about to undertake. The huge stack of brevet cards (recording cards similar to the mileage cards issued by *Cycling*) in his front room was clear testament to the fact that he knew what to expect from long days out on the road. He'd not undertaken any specific training as his body was well adapted to endurance riding.

He knew what to eat and how to set his pacing such that he'd not over-exert himself – planning to ride at a steady pace, usually lower than 17 miles per hour across any full riding day. He clearly felt that the mileages claimed by Ken Webb were achievable and had devised two riding schedules: one aimed at 82,835 miles and the other at 87,129. In both schedules his intention was to ramp up his mileages from a steady start of 170 miles a day to a peak of 288 in the summer months.

Searvogel had also developed a schedule, slightly less ambitious, but with a detailed daily projection that took him to a mileage of 78,544.89 miles after 365 days. His plan was to ride faster than Abraham, starting with ten hours a day in the early weeks and increasing his riding time window as the year went on. Searvogel planned to start at 17 miles per hour and ramp this up to an average speed of 20 miles per hour or more. He also stated that he would ride long distances for six of the seven days each week, with the seventh limited to a single century as a recovery day.

So, as 1 January 2015 began to approach, there was a renewed interest from the cycling world in the year mileage record. Three men had come forward to attempt to beat Godwin's mileage under the watchful eye of the UMCA. Two of these three had backgrounds that indicated their intentions were serious. A new transatlantic battle was shortly to be waged between Abraham the Audax legend and Searvogel the highly decorated ultra-endurance cyclist.

It was Abraham who took the first shot, leaving his flat in Milton Keynes one minute after midnight on 1 January 2015. Abraham's official start was be at a time trial organised by his cycling club, the North Bucks CC, on New Year's Day, but he was keen to get in some early miles and rode nearly 104 miles to the start of the race. He recorded a modest time of 33 minutes and 27 seconds for the 10 miles and then carried on to end his first day's riding on 222.6 miles, a distance he recorded in sixteen hours of riding at a moving speed of approximately 14 miles per hour. The weather that day was best described as 'typically British', with blustery winds and rain. Abraham continued to ride to his schedule through the remainder of the month, finishing January with a total 5,743.6 miles, putting him ahead of Tommy Godwin who had only ridden 4,773 in the same period.

Searvogel began on 10 January 2015 and had the advantage of knowing Abraham's figures for the prior nine days. His first ride set the tone for the rest of the month as he rode 230.7 miles in 11 hours and 26 minutes of riding, at an average speed of 20.2 miles per hour – a remarkable start even though the route chosen had been pan-flat roads on the east coast of Florida in good weather. Like Abraham, Searvogel rode a strong January, completing 4,512.2 miles despite his ten-day-late start.

February would be the first month where the two riders could be properly compared. Abraham continued to ride to his schedule with 5,359.8 miles, but was eclipsed by Searvogel who, still riding in the Florida area, notched up 5,678.6. Both riders were some 1,000 miles ahead of Godwin's 4,415 for the second month of the year, but their respective performances are difficult to compare at this stage of the record – recall that Godwin suffered severely bad weather from January to March in 1939 and increased his mileages by a huge factor as he went into April and May and good weather returned. Of the 2015 contenders, it was Abraham who was having the worst of the weather, with icy conditions in February leading eventually to a crash when one of his hosts, who was accompanying him on a ride, lost his wheel on ice and brought Abraham down with him. Abraham was relatively unscathed and managed to remount and ride on, unlike his host who was subsequently found to have broken his hip. This early crash was a reminder of just how fragile a year-record attempt can be – one simple mishap on the road can end all the hard work and thousands of miles of riding already put in.

By the end of March 2015 the two riders had established their own rhythms. Abraham kept his heart rate low and rode at a steady pace that rarely exceeded 16 miles per hour. His monthly total of 5,784.6 showed an average of 186.6 miles per day, which he gained by leaving his flat some-where close to 5 a.m. and returning some fifteen to seventeen hours later. His overall total was now 16,888 miles, compared to Godwin's 14,726 over the same period. It was a decent lead, but how would Abraham cope in the next quarter when Godwin had really raised his game? Searvogel had upped his pace further and ended March with an additional 6,383.4 miles to his credit, ridden at a total moving average of 18.75 miles per hour. His daily average of 205.9 miles over the month had marginally exceeded that required to beat Godwin's 365-day pace, but it had not all been plain sailing for the USA-based rider, who had been fighting poor weather conditions and issues with his bike. Searvogel had also had to suffer at the hand of online naysayers who had dismissed his achievements against those of Abraham by citing the flat roads and better weather in America as incomparable to conditions in the UK. Searvogel countered these accusations with a simple offer to any rider who felt his days in the saddle were easy – 'Come ride with me.' To date nobody has taken him up on this.

In the first quarter of 2015 Abraham had ridden roads relatively close to his base in Milton Keynes. There had been occasional ventures north to York and west into Wiltshire but in the main he'd limited most of his riding to roads within a 100-mile radius of his flat. On 28 March Abraham rode from his flat to be hosted for the night at the house of a cyclist in Exeter. This was a long ride of over 200 miles into a continuous headwind that saw Steve finish in the early hours of the next day. Determined to get up early and ride back east to take advantage of the tailwind, he was on the road at 6.16 a.m. the next morning. He had managed the 27.6 miles to Wellington by 8.10 a.m. when he was hit from behind by a moped rider and knocked from his bike, breaking two bones in his left ankle. A rapid diagnosis led to a need to operate and Abraham was forced into an overnight stay in hospital. The news spread quickly by social media and a legion of cyclists held their breath to see if Abraham would be in any fit state to continue his attempt. Unable to ride for seventeen days, it looked as if his year-record ambitions were over, kicked out from under him by an accident for which he was entirely without blame.

Behind the scenes, furious discussions began to take place. The UMCA had clarified that the record attempt would continue to be valid were Abraham to ride upon a recumbent trike. A company called Inspired Cycle Engineering was contacted as it had previously adapted recumbent trikes for disabled riders. It advised that one of its machines could be modified to allow Abraham to pedal with one leg while resting the other on a stand. Inspired Cycle Engineering quickly met with Abraham to make measurements and soon delivered an adapted trike to his flat for his first fitting. The UMCA rules also allow miles ridden upon a track to count towards the record, as long as that track is outdoors. Milton Keynes Bowl is replete with its own outdoor track and discussions with its supervising body paved the way for Abraham to use it on a daily basis. A route was devised to get Abraham from his house to the Bowl by cycle paths, avoiding traffic. His trike was even fitted with a set of holders for him to store his crutches while he pedalled with one leg.

There was much discussion as to whether it was wise for Abraham to return to riding so soon after an ankle operation. However, the decision came from Abraham himself in the name of damage limitation. He'd given up his job and his savings to take on the record and saw nothing but frustration in being stuck inside and recovering in a sedentary manner. Abraham felt he had nothing to lose by riding as many miles as he could with one leg while resting the other. There was an element of risk, but he was prepared to take this as he could potentially ride some 100 miles a day around the bowl and marginally slow his increasing deficit to Godwin.

His first outing on the trike on 16 April 2015 saw him achieve 54.7 miles, all at a very steady speed close to 10 miles per hour. His trike riding continued until 8 May 2015 when he was finally able to mount a two-wheeled bike and ride 114.5 miles to Needham Market. The next day he rode a 185.9-mile Audax ride.

As I write this on 16 June 2015, I look at Steve Abraham's tracker and note that he is still out on the road. Yesterday he managed 206.8 miles as a result of slowly ramping up his daily distances in order to properly rehabilitate his ankle. Abraham has never allowed himself to give up on his record attempt and still persists despite a set of statistics that tell him that, with 25,880.2 miles in the bag, he has another 49,184.80 to go and 199 days to do them in. That's an average of 247.16 miles per day; daunting figures for any cyclist on a single ride. Over a continuous period of 199 days they seem impossible, but Abraham remains unbowed. He knows the history of this record and he also knows that no rider ever took it without cycling through some form of adversity. And so he pedals on.

And what of Kurt Searvogel? He too has fought adversity, but nowhere near as profound as that of Abraham's seventeen-day absence. Despite the growth of an abscess, a bad case of food poisoning and a number of crashes, Searvogel has shown that he can maintain his speed and distance. As of 15 June 2015, after 157 days of riding, Searvogel has a total of 32,339.9 miles – an average of 205.98 a day and currently almost equal to the daily average required to beat Godwin's record. Searvogel continues to ride without the support of a major sponsor or any other outside influence. It's just him, his bikes, a camper van and Alicia. Look at Searvogel's mileage again – it's within a few thousand miles of Marcel Planes' 1911 benchmark and Searvogel will likely pass that mark in half of the time taken, which shows us just how far cycling has come since the beginning of the last century.

Today's riders are the most scrutinised ever to take on the year challenge. Every metre of their riding is uploaded to internet sites via trackers and GPS devices; their heartbeat data is publicly available, allowing detailed scrutiny of their power output and pacing. The public can follow them in real time, making it nigh on impossible to cheat, but also, in Abraham's case, allowing many riders to take a few hours out from work to cheer him on as he passes by their localities. While this technology is there to prevent indiscretions, it also provides us with a huge amount of data that we can use to analyse the physical performance of a year-record rider. Regardless of the outcomes of Abraham and Searvogel's years they will have provided cycling with a year's worth of data that has never been seen before.

One thing we do know from their last six months is that riding daily averages equivalent to those ridden by Godwin in 1939 is incredibly demanding. They either have to be done at high speed, as per Searvogel, or over long hours and with little sleep, as is Abraham's strategy.

Even though the two riders have not completed their years at the time of writing, they deserve their places in the history of the record. They have been integral to resurrecting widespread public interest in the year. Abraham and Searvogel epitomise the year-record riders that have gone before them. They've both self-started their attempts rather than wait for a lucrative sponsorship deal to enable them to get going. They've both ridden through adversity while keeping a watchful eye on a competitor riding on a different continent under differing conditions. What is more, neither is riding for any tangible reward. Neither has the promise of a professional contract at the end. Neither has any guaranteed monetary incentive to complete their year. Both men are testing themselves against the year record, in the words of George Mallory, 'Because it is there.' This is the single greatest defining characteristic of a true year-record rider.

A question now hanging in the air is that of the nature of the year mileage record. Can Searvogel or Abraham *truly* beat Godwin's record, given that seventy-five years have passed since Tommy's ride and much has changed in that time?

The first issue must be the definition of 'a year'. Godwin and his predecessors all set out to ride the largest number of miles in a single *calendar* year. *Cycling* magazine was insistent upon this in 1911 and Greaves and others were penalised for starting late. When Menzies and Webb set out to complete '365-day' years, neither was sanctioned by the original rules.

Therefore, in order to beat Godwin's record, one must ride a single calendar year. Abraham set out to do this from the outset, while Searvogel started late and has ten days of no riding to make up for if he is going to stake a proper claim.

Another consideration is the technology and equipment available to the modern riders. Lighter bicycles, technical clothing, streamlined positioning and all manner of supplements, creams and other substances help to make long days out on the road a little more bearable. Of course, riders have always made best use of the latest technology available. Godwin rode state-of-the-art four-speed hub gearing and his Raleigh 'Record Ace' compares well to lightweight, modern, steel-framed touring machines. Greaves took advantage of bleeding-edge Cyclo gearing systems and Dovey rode the latest-model bicycle adapted specifically for women.

The greatest marginal gains to the modern riders are undoubtedly to be found in tracking and verification technology. Godwin and the riders before him had nothing like what is available now. Each one had to find a signatory at every major turn in the road, no matter what the weather conditions or time of day. Without these signatures they ran the risk of having their mileages rounded down by *Cycling* to the lowest distance between the last two verified points. And gaining these signatures costs time – the rider has to stop, talk to a pedestrian, explain their mission and sometimes convince the passer-by that they really are not mad, but undertaking a valid challenge. Repeat this five to ten times a day and thirty minutes to an hour of riding time could be lost, and then a post office had to be found and stamps purchased to see the cards off on their way to *Cycling*.

Then there are the conditions under which Godwin and Bennett rode. The two riders suffered a terrible winter at the start of their rides and, for the final four months, were handicapped by the demands of a country at war. We must hope that this situation never arises again, but it should always be recognised that the two men had their riding curtailed by the blackout and must have suffered mentally – imagine waking up each morning and nervously checking the doorstep for a piece of paper summoning you to battle.

But perhaps we should never let conditions be a comparison between attempts. How can we expect a rider to recreate the circumstances of those who have gone before? The record has always been about the miles and not where, when or how they are ridden. Remember that Godwin should also be compared to *his* predecessors. He did not ride his year with one arm, so did he beat Greaves' record? And Greaves, like Nicholson, had gears for his entire year and Humbles rode many of his months fixed, so did Greaves beat Humbles? But Humbles had the support of a sponsor, while Planes rode unaided for the entirety of his year, so who was the victor in that battle?

The fact is that each record year is unique and stands in its own right. Perhaps none can ever be truly broken. The mileages can certainly be surpassed but the riding experiences are difficult to replicate. Maybe we should look at the cycling year record in a different manner. It is not a record to be beaten or one to have a current holder. It's a benchmark set by a rider at a certain point in time and it should rightfully bear that rider's name. That benchmark is established by surpassing the mileage of the previous incumbent while recognising that the conditions of their attempt can never be truly replicated. And even if a previous record is not surpassed, any serious attempt is undoubtedly a challenge of the highest order for the rider, and equally deserving of its place in the history of the year – provided it is ridden in the spirit of the mile-eaters and seen through to its conclusion. We should sit back in awe and stare at a page of 'records' named after those who set them.

Having set out on this journey to uncover the stories of these mileage-eaters a view has formed in my own mind. Alongside Godwin's mark, the rides of Planes, Humbles, Nicholson, Greaves, Bennett, Menzies and Dovey all stand, concurrently, as records in their own right. I will always find it hard to include Webb for the simple reason that too many questions remain unanswered about his year, but, when Abraham and Searvogel finish, their names will surely be added to that list, regardless of whether the magical figure of 75,065 miles has been exceeded.

The cycling year record is more than a single number. It is a journey through time, with each attempt made in its own set of conditions, conditions that can never be normalised to level the entire playing field. It has a beauty in this aspect that makes it comparable to mountaineering: we all recognise the achievements of those who have scaled the highest peaks, but the speed or difficulty of their climbs are of little consequence to we who would not even make the trek to Base Camp. This is how we should recognise the year-record riders: they are our cycling mountaineers, laying siege to a task that requires levels of endurance and dedication that we cannot comprehend, each of them trying to push the distance ever further in the name of conquest, and nothing more. Their individual records should stand in perpetuity, with the latest owned by all of them in recognition of the parts they have played in raising the record mileage to where it stands at the present day.

RIDER
STATISTICS

Marcel Planes

Nationality :—British
Born :—6 August 1890
Place of birth :—London, UK
Died :—10 August 1960

Age at start of ride :—20
Marital status at start of ride :—Single
Sponsor :—None
Base for ride :—Soho, London, UK

Date record passed :—11 December 1911[†]
Location record passed :—N/A

Bike
Make :—Mead
Model :—Coventry Flyer Modèle Superbe

Planes was clearly enamoured with his
Mead 'Coventry Flyer Modèle Superbe'
as it had seen six years and 50,000 miles
of service prior to his 1911 record attempt.
The bicycle had a single 74-inch gear and
an Eadie Coaster braking system. During
his record attempt he broke the bottom
bracket spindle, replaced the chain and
front wheel bearings and wore out seven
tyres. Planes' bicycle would have cost
approximately £2 15s. in 1911 and
would have weighed around 45 pounds
(20.5 kilograms).

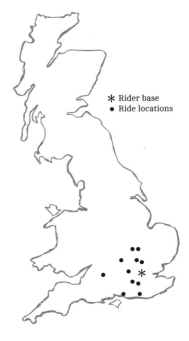

✳ Rider base
● Ride locations

(† Record for number of centuries
ridden. Planes was the first to
establish a year-record mileage.)

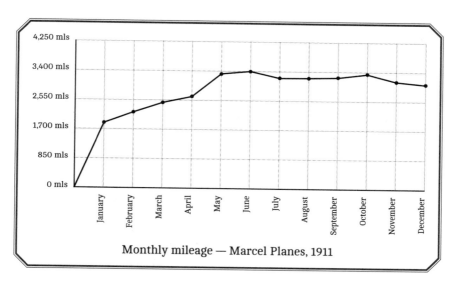

Monthly mileage — Marcel Planes, 1911

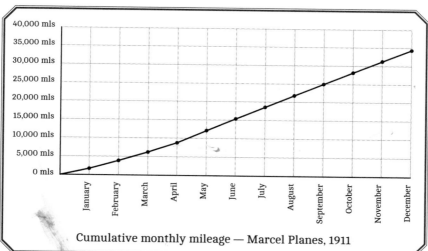

Cumulative monthly mileage — Marcel Planes, 1911

	Day	Week*	Month
Shortest	36 miles (7 Dec 1911)	0 miles (first week Jan)	1,743.4 miles (Jan)
Longest	200 miles** (4 Jun)	865 miles (w/e 2 Oct)	3,384.2 miles (Jun)
Average	94.2 miles	660.9 miles	2,863.8 miles

(*Note all shortest/longest weeks are over seven days, starting on the first day they rode in the year. w/e = week ending.)
(**First double century.)

Arthur Humbles

Nationality :—British
Born :—1910
Place of birth :—Hackney, London, UK
Died :—1980

Age at start of ride :—21
Marital status at start of ride :—Single
Sponsor :—Hercules Cycles and Dunlop
Base for ride :—Islington, London, UK

Date record passed :—
11 December 1932
Location record passed :—
Hyde Park, London, UK

Bike
Make :—Hercules
Model :—Empire Club Racer

Humbles rode a Hercules 'Empire Club
Racer' which was a fairly standard club
touring bicycle of the time. The bike
came with Dunlop sports tyres, Dunlop
Endrick rims, Dunlop saddle model H.30,
handlebars with Marsh level grips and
special racing narrow barrel hubs.
This model cost £5 15s. 6d. in 1932 and
weighed somewhere between 20 and
30 pounds. The bicycle was initially
fitted with a rear hub holding 18- and
20-tooth sprockets – the rider would
change the gear by loosening the chain
and moving it manually. Humbles
eventually replaced this with a three-
speed Sturmey-Archer hub almost
halfway through his record year.

∗ Rider base
● Ride locations

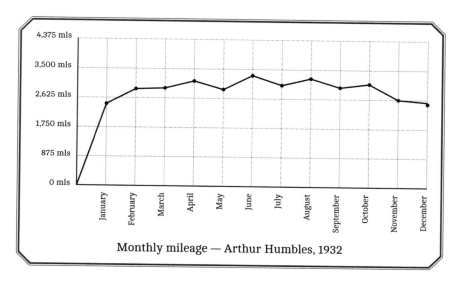

Monthly mileage — Arthur Humbles, 1932

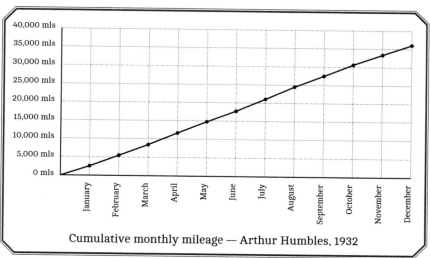

Cumulative monthly mileage — Arthur Humbles, 1932

	Day	Week*	Month
Shortest	35 miles (date unknown)	0 miles (first week Jan)	2,518 miles (Jan)
Longest	172 miles (date unknown)	805 miles (w/e 8 Jun)	3,409 miles (Jun)
Average	98.4 miles	692.4 miles	3,000.6 miles
(*Note all shortest/longest weeks are over seven days, starting on the first day they rode in the year. w/e = week ending.)			

Ossie Nicholson

Nationality :—Australian
Born :—15 July 1908
Place of birth :—New Norfolk,
Tasmania
Died :—9 November 1965

Age at start of ride :—24
Marital status at start
of ride :—Separated
Sponsor :—Bruce Small Pty
Base for ride :—Melbourne, Australia

Date record passed :—
30 October 1933
Location record passed :—
Elizabeth Street, Melbourne, Australia

Bike
Make :—Malvern Star
Model :—Unknown

Nicholson rode a Malvern
Star bicycle equipped
with a Cyclo TriVelox
(three-speed) derailleur
system, Dunlop tyres and
an apparently all-British
set of components.
At the time this model
cost £6 10s. 1d. and
weighed around
29 pounds.

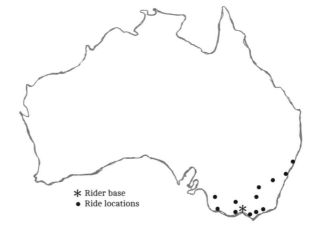

* Rider base
• Ride locations

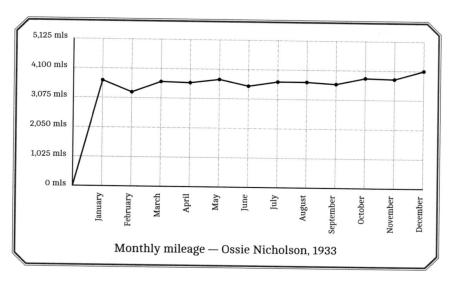

Monthly mileage — Ossie Nicholson, 1933

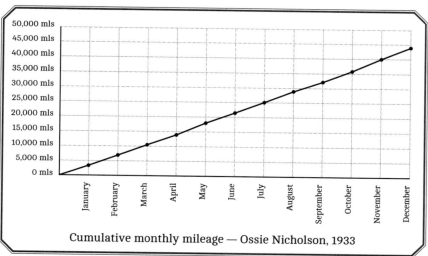

Cumulative monthly mileage — Ossie Nicholson, 1933

	Day	Week*	Month
Shortest	92.8 miles (mid Jan)	709.1 miles (w/e 9 Dec)	3,251 miles (Feb)
Longest	250 miles (7 Dec)	1,093.75 miles (w/e 23 Dec)	4,069.75 miles (Dec)
Average	120.5 miles	846.1 miles	3,666.4 miles
(*Note all shortest/longest weeks are over seven days, starting on the first day they rode in the year. w/e = week ending.)			

Author note. Nearly all of Nicholson's 1933 figures are averages.

Walter Greaves

Nationality :—British
Born :—30 March 1907
Place of birth :—Bradford, UK
Died :—9 November 1987

Age at start of ride :—28
Marital status at start of ride :—Single
Sponsor :—Coventry Bicycles Ltd.
Base for ride :—Bradford, UK

Date record passed :—
13 December 1936
Location record passed :—
Hyde Park, London, UK

Bike
Make :—Three Spires
Model :—King of Clubs

Greaves rode a custom-modified Three
Spires bicycle with a three-speed TriVelox
derailleur gear. He had a twist-grip gear
changer fitted to the bike (taken from
a motorcycle) and a mechanism that
coupled both front and rear Resilion
brakes together so that he could operate
them via a single lever. Greaves rode
using an unsprung Middlemores saddle,
but commented that he found this
remarkably comfortable throughout
the year as it kept its shape extraordinarily
well. The standard-spec 'King of Clubs'
cost £5 10s. in 1936.

✱ Rider base
● Ride locations

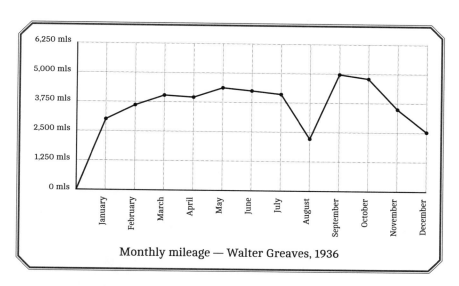

Monthly mileage — Walter Greaves, 1936

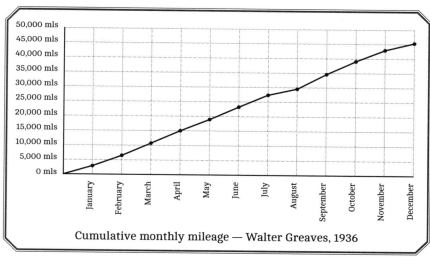

Cumulative monthly mileage — Walter Greaves, 1936

	Day	Week*	Month
Shortest	40 miles** (20 Jan)	0 miles (w/e 17 Aug)	2,210 miles (Aug)
Longest	222 miles** (early Oct)	1,279 miles (w/e 4 Oct)	4,968.4 miles (Sep)
Average	124 miles	872.8 miles	3,782 miles
(*Note all shortest/longest weeks are over seven days, starting on the first day they rode in the year. w/e = week ending.)			
(**By 14 October 1936.)			

Bernard Bennett

Nationality :—British
Born :—4 February 1918
Place of birth :—Birmingham, UK
Died :—23 March 1969

Age at start of ride :—18
Marital status at start of ride :—Single
Sponsor :—None
Base for ride :—Birmingham, UK

Date record passed :—N/A
Location record passed :—N/A

Bike
Make :—Unknown
Model :—Unknown

As Bennett was riding as an amateur
no exact record of his 1937 bicycle
was ever printed in the press as this
would have been deemed 'sponsorship'.
It is most likely that he rode a 23-pound
New Hudson 'Featherlight Club', which
he modified with the addition of a
derailleur gear.

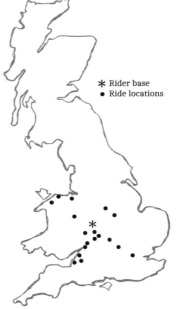

✳ Rider base
● Ride locations

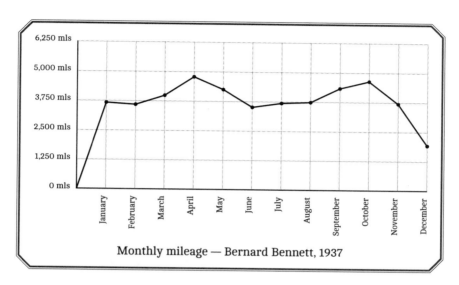

Monthly mileage — Bernard Bennett, 1937

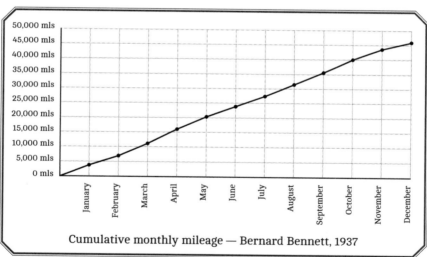

Cumulative monthly mileage — Bernard Bennett, 1937

	Day	Week*	Month
Shortest	26 miles (25 Jun)	160.75 miles (w/e 22 Dec)	1,931.65 miles (Dec)
Longest	226 miles (29 Apr)	1,204.5 miles (w/e 3 Oct)	4,786 miles (Apr)
Average	125.5 miles	880.8 miles	3,816.8 miles
(*Note all shortest/longest weeks are over seven days, starting on the first day they rode in the year. w/e = week ending.)			

René Menzies

Nationality :—French
Born :—1889
Place of birth :—Caen, France
Died :—January 1959

Age at start of ride :—48
Marital status at start of ride :—Married
Sponsor :—Rudge Whitworth
Base for ride :—Cricklewood,
London, UK

Date record passed :—
29 September 1937
Location record passed :—
Alexandra Palace, London

Bike
Make :—Rudge Whitworth
Model :—Aero Special No. 75

Menzies began his record attempt aboard
a Weaver (of Leyton) bicycle equipped
with a Smith's cyclometer, but he
later switched to a Rudge-Whitworth
'Aero Special' with a Cyclo three-speed
derailleur, Constrictor tyres, Conloy
rims and Boa pedals. The bicycle
weighed approximately 25 pounds
and would have cost £8 11s. in 1937.

✳ Rider base
● Ride locations

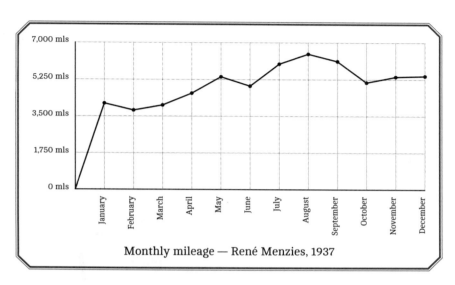

Monthly mileage — René Menzies, 1937

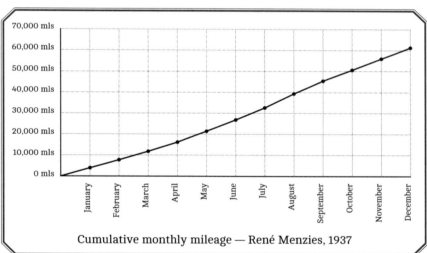

Cumulative monthly mileage — René Menzies, 1937

	Day	Week*	Month
Shortest	53 miles (19 Feb)	790 miles (w/e 4 Feb)	3,838 miles (Feb)
Longest	250 miles (31 Mar)	1,565 miles (w/e 2 Sep)	6,459 miles (Aug)
Average	168.7 miles	1,183.9 miles	5,380.1 miles
(*Note all shortest/longest weeks are over seven days, starting on the first day they rode in the year. w/e = week ending.)			

Ossie Nicholson

Nationality :—Australian
Born :—15 July 1908
Place of birth :—New Norfolk,
Tasmania
Died :—9 November 1965

Age at start of ride :—27
Marital status at start
of ride :—Separated
Sponsor :—Bruce Small Pty
Base for ride :—Melbourne, Australia

Date record passed :—
29 September 1937
Location record passed :—
Melbourne Showground, Australia

Bike
Make :—Malvern Star
Model :—Unknown

For his 1937 record attempt,
Nicholson again rode a
Malvern Star bicycle.
This 29-pound bike was
equipped with a Cyclo
TriVelox derailleur system
and a Brooks Comfort saddle.
It would have cost £7 19s. 6d.
in 1937.

✳ Rider base
● Ride location

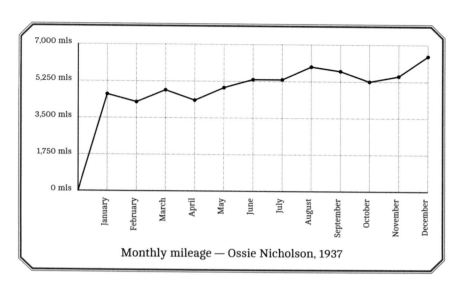

Monthly mileage — Ossie Nicholson, 1937

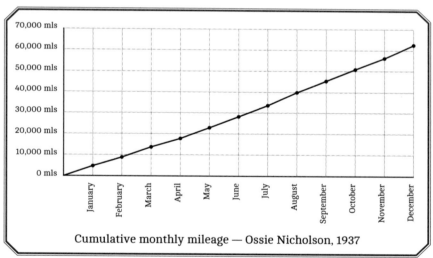

Cumulative monthly mileage — Ossie Nicholson, 1937

	Day	Week*	Month
Shortest	84 miles (Feb)	648 miles (w/e 8 Apr)	4,279.6 miles (Feb)
Longest	261.2 miles (12 Aug)	1,655.8 miles (w/e 16 Dec)	6,481 miles (Dec)
Average	171.7 miles	1,204.9 miles	5,221.4 miles
(*Note all shortest/longest weeks are over seven days, starting on the first day they rode in the year. w/e = week ending.)			

Author note. Nearly all of Nicholson's 1933 figures are averages.

Billie Dovey

Nationality :—British
Born :—13 April 1914
Place of birth :—Camden, London, UK
Died :—12 May 2014

Age at start of ride :—23
Marital status at start of ride :—Married
Sponsor :—Rudge Whitworth and
Cadbury
Base for ride :—Mill Hill, London, UK

Date record passed :—N/A
Location record passed :—N/A

Bike
Make :—Rudge Whitworth
Model :—Unknown

Billie rode a Rudge Whitworth ladies
model with a saddle made by Brooks
that was apparently a miniature replica
of their ladies' B16. The bike featured
three-speed (60-66-74) Cyclo gears,
Dunlop Silver Sprite tyres and a
Bayliss-Wiley freewheel hub unit.

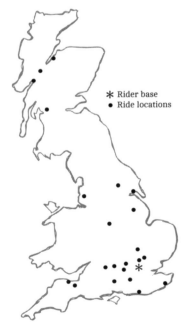

∗ Rider base
● Ride locations

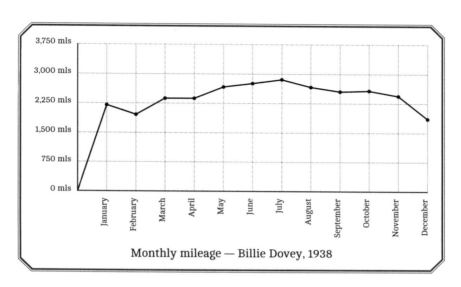

Monthly mileage — Billie Dovey, 1938

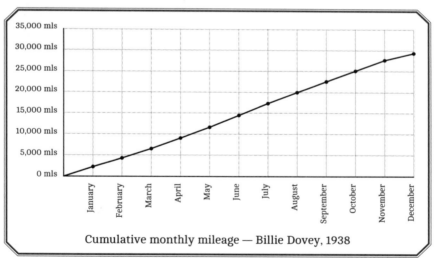

Cumulative monthly mileage — Billie Dovey, 1938

	Day	Week*	Month
Shortest	13 miles (15 Feb)	302.3 miles (w/e 30 Jan)	1,880.3 miles (Dec)
Longest	189 miles (mid July)	739 miles (w/e 22 Jul)	2,880.5 miles (Jul)
Average	81.1 miles	569.3 miles	2,467 miles

(*Note all shortest/longest weeks are over seven days, starting on the first day they rode in the year. w/e = week ending.)

Bernard Bennett

Nationality :—British
Born :—4 February 1918
Place of birth :—Birmingham, UK
Died :—23 March 1969

Age at start of ride :—20
Marital status at start of ride :—Single
Sponsor :—New Hudson
Base for ride :—Birmingham, UK

Date record passed :—N/A
Location record passed :—N/A

Bike
Make :—New Hudson
Model :—Featherlight Club

Bennett rode a New Hudson 'Featherlight Club' built with Reynolds 531 steel tubing. Weighing in at around 23 pounds it came equipped with a Cyclo Oppy derailleur gear, Dunlop high pressure 27in. x 1.5in. tyres, Brooks B17N saddle, Miller lamp, Bayliss-Wiley Unit rear hub, Webb pedals and a Smith's cyclometer. It cost £9 16s. at the time.

✳ Rider base
● Ride locations

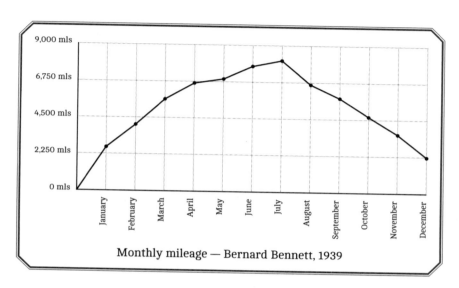

Monthly mileage — Bernard Bennett, 1939

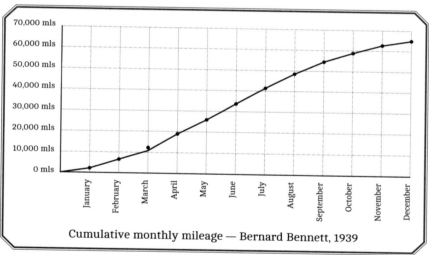

Cumulative monthly mileage — Bernard Bennett, 1939

	Day	Week*	Month
Shortest	22 miles (27 Jan)	268 miles (w/e 28 Jan)	2,254 miles (Dec)
Longest	314 miles (14 Jun)	2,095 miles (w/e 17 Jun)	8,143 miles (Jul)
Average	178.4 miles	1,252.4 miles	5,427.3 miles
(*Note all shortest/longest weeks are over seven days, starting on the first day they rode in the year. w/e = week ending.)			

Tommy Godwin

Nationality :—British
Born :—5 June 1912
Place of birth :—Stoke-on-Trent, UK
Died :—20 July 1975

Age at start of ride :—26
Marital status at start of ride :—Single
Sponsor :—Raleigh
Base for ride :—Hemel Hempstead, UK

Date record passed :—26 October 1939
Location record passed :—Hendon,
London, UK

Bike
Make :—Raleigh
Model :—Record Ace

Godwin began his record attempt on a
Ley 'TG Special' custom-built frame made
from Reynolds 531 steel tubing. The bike
was fitted with a Baylis-Wiley bottom
bracket, Williams chainwheel and cranks,
high pressure 27-inch Dunlop tyres,
a Brooks saddle, a Solite front hub and
a Sturmey Archer three-speed hub gear
– later replaced with a four-speed model.
   In May 1939 Godwin switched to
a Raleigh 'Record Ace'. This steel-frame
bike again featured a four-speed Sturmey-
Archer hub gear (57, 74, 86, 97 inches),
as well as a Brooks B17 Flyer saddle and
Dunlop Sprite tyres. It weighed around
28 pounds and would have set you back
£11 0s. 3d. in 1939.

✳ Rider base
● Ride locations

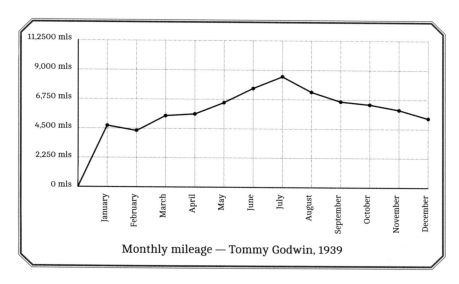

Monthly mileage — Tommy Godwin, 1939

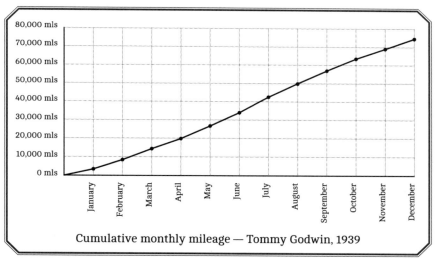

Cumulative monthly mileage — Tommy Godwin, 1939

	Day	Week*	Month
Shortest	59 miles (25 Dec)	1,017 miles (w/e 28 Jan)	4,415 miles (Feb)
Longest	361 miles (21 Jun)	2,084 miles (w/e 22 Jul)	8,583 miles (Jul)
Average	205.7 miles	1,443.6 miles	6,255.4 miles
(*Note all shortest/longest weeks are over seven days, starting on the first day they rode in the year. w/e = week ending.)			

SOURCES AND
ACKNOWLEDGEMENTS

In writing this book I've had the pleasure of meeting and talking to many people over a ten-year period. So many have contributed to this book in some way or another and if I have missed a name off the list it is down to my fading memory rather than a lack of appreciation.

I must give special thanks to a number of individuals who have gone that extra mile to help me unlock the stories of these riders. Firstly, Barbara Ford, Tommy Godwin's daughter, who started my journey in 2005, providing me with so many detailed insights into Tommy's life but also using her genealogy expertise to trace the families of other riders. This book would not have happened without you Barbara, especially your ninja people-search skills. Also I am hugely grateful to Neil Hemmings for the information he provided from his family archives, the loan of Tommy's mileage diaries and for helping me dig further into the Ken Webb story. Huge thanks to Joe Greaves for being so helpful with information and photos concerning his father Walter and for pointing me at the hill from which he gathered his herbs. I'm also indebted to the Planes family, particularly Martin Planes, for sharing the information they had concerning Marcel. It was a real pleasure to meet Jacky Vickers, Jeff Vickers and Pauline Ruff who spoke so fondly of Marcel. I must thank Billie Fleming posthumously for the wonderful few hours I spent with her discussing her record year. I'll never forget this remarkable lady who was so matter-of-fact about her incredible achievement.

I also thank the following individuals who have played their part in helping me find the information necessary to write this book.

Freda Davies, Paul Whatley, Feargal McKay, Roger Bugg, Andrew Ritchie, Rich Kazimir, Gus Johnson, Les Bowerman, Doug Petty, Stuart Collins, Robert Davis, Andrew Harrington, Peter Samwells, Anne Hunt, Brian Rourke, Phil and Peter Hambley, Godfrey Barlow (author of *Unsurpassed – The Story of Tommy Godwin*), Brian Griffiths, Hugh Gladstone, Dave Smith, Ken Vipond, Dan Joyce, Neil Leighton, William Humphreys, Paul Swinnerton, Neil England, Kurt Searvogel, Peter Rose, Roger St Pierre,

Lillian Brentnall, Joanne Collett, Andrew Millard, Jo Wood, Diana Freeman, Keith Robins, Gordon Higginson, Jack Thurston, Steven Abraham, Drew Clarke, the *oneyeartimetrial.org.uk* crew: Idai Makaya, Ian Hennessey, Lesley Sung, Mike Wallis, Phil Whitehurst, Lionel Joseph, Andrew Morris and Chris Hopkinson. Bill Potts must also feature within this list as it was he who told me about Tommy Godwin in the first place.

The following institutions have proved invaluable to my research with their catalogues of cycling magazines and historic papers: the Nottingham Raleigh Archive, the National Cycling Museum, the Coventry History Centre and the National Cycling Archive at Warwick. *Cycling Weekly* magazine have helped me along the way by publishing two of my articles and introducing me to Billie Fleming.

As always the staff at Vertebrate Publishing have been a pleasure to work with, in particular Tom Fenton who edited this book. My thanks also to Jon Barton, John Coefield, Nathan Ryder and Jane Beagley. And to Simon Scarsbrook for his fantastic cover illustration.

But the largest 'thank you' must go to my wife, Helen Barter, who spent nearly three months of her life digging into the cycling archives and cataloguing her finds in order to help me assemble this story. Without her hard work and thorough research this book would never have been written.

The information used to write this book has been gathered from a hugely diverse set of sources. The cycling press of the time provided the mainstay of the commentary concerning the riders' records, in particular *Cycling* magazine, *The Bicycle* magazine and *The Cyclist*. Press archives have also proved invaluable, including those on the National Library of Australia website (*www.nla.gov.au*). The Century Road Club of America website (*www.centuryroadclub.com*) was also very useful when researching the early American riders. But the real insights have come from the families of the riders themselves. I've made every effort to verify the facts stated within this book but in some cases this has been difficult when they have only come from a single source and subsequently cannot be cross-checked. If you have any information that you think may add to the story or believe any of the text within to be incorrect please don't hesitate to get in touch. I'd love to hear from you.

Dave Barter @*citizenfishy*
   dave@phased.co.uk

Errata and further information:
   www.cyclingyearrecord.co.uk

INDEX